THE PHILOSOPHY OF TEACHING

THE PHILOSOPHY OF TEACHING

John Passmore

Harvard University Press
Cambridge, Massachusetts
1980

Library of Congress Cataloging in Publication Data

Passmore, John Arthur.
  The philosophy of teaching.

  Includes bibliographical references and index.
  1. Education – Philosophy.   2. Teaching.
I. Title.
LB1025.2.P375   1980   371.1'02   80-11476
ISBN 0-674-66565-1

Printed in Great Britain

Contents

'Of all the practical arts, that of education seems the most cumbrous in its method, and to be productive of the smallest results with the most lavish expenditure of means. Hence the subject of education is one which is always luring on the innovator and the theorist. Every one, as he grows up, becomes aware of time lost, and effort misapplied, in his own case. It is not unnatural to desire to save our children from a like waste of power.'

Mark Pattison, *Milton* (1879), p. 45.

Preface

I have had this book by me for a long time, setting it aside, more than once, to embark on other tasks. Its roots lie many years back, in my own training as a secondary school teacher and in work I did on learning and discussing for the Army Education Service, parts of which were published in the post-war years by the Melbourne University Press. Then, later still, I was asked by the Australian Vice-Chancellors Committee to act as chairman of what turned out to be an entirely abortive committee on University Teaching. In 1965, Melbourne University invited me to give the Fink Lectures on 'Analytical Philosophies of Education'. The first chapter is a reworking of those lectures. In 1967, I presented early drafts of what, if I remember correctly, are now chapters 3-7 at a seminar of the London Institute of Education under the auspices of Professor Richard Peters. In 1970 I led a similar set of seminars, covering, I think, the material in Chapters 2, 8, 9, 11 and 12. The tenth chapter grew out of my book on *The Perfectibility of Man* (London and New York 1970); earlier versions of it have already appeared in various places. The last chapter is based on a lecture delivered to the British Society for the Philosophy of Education. I have never before published a book which is largely made up of lectures delivered at various places and times. But every chapter has been rewritten, sometimes very extensively, to occupy its present place.

Why did I not publish earlier? To be frank, I have never been satisfied either by what I have written or by almost anything I have read about teaching. The chance of writing even a reasonably good book on any branch of the philosophy of education is statistically very low indeed. This is no accident. It is terribly difficult to write in a manner which is neither philosophy for philosophy's sake, with an occasional example from teaching, nor just a series of commonplace banalities. It is this latter judgment that I most fear from critics of what I have now written. This is especially so as I have no single thesis to sustain, whereas the best books on schooling, the ones most worth reading, the classics in the field, are nearly all of them fanatical, offering us educational salvation through following a single recipe. I say that regretfully, as one whose own book is, precisely, directed against fanaticism, the fanaticism of unfettered free development, the fanaticism of regimentation. Why should the fanatics have all the best tunes? Just in virtue of the momentum, the drive, the conviction, which fanaticism carries with it and which it is hard, or impossible, to achieve in a book which tries to find a middle path.

There is another problem. Over the time during which I was composing this book, the character of my principal opponents has changed. I was at first arguing against the 'radical reformers', with their hostility to information, habits, the efficient exercise of capacities. Now the greater danger, as I see it, is once more coming from the apostles of utility, the bureaucrats, the regularisers. I cannot hope, in the light of this fact, quite to have sustained a single tone.

Why publish at all? A serious question, to which I am not sure that I know the answer. I hope it is not merely to get rid of what has for so long reproachfully eyed me from my desk, as an unfinished task. There is room, I have finally managed to persuade myself, for a book which at once welcomes the imagination, the critical spirit, enthusiasm, but insists all the same on the need for information, for training, for habituation. Dull, perhaps, like all attempts to find a middle way, but the correct view, often enough, is not very exciting; the best way of being exciting is to go wildly wrong, with massive oversimplifications.

I should like to express my thanks to the Institute of Education in London, which has twice given me hospitality as a Visiting Scholar; to All Souls College, Oxford, for a Visiting Fellowship which made it possible for me, in exceptionally congenial surroundings, to bring the book into its final shape; to my own Australian National University for the continuous provision of its remarkable facilities; to my wife, also trained as a teacher, for her very considerable help and support at every stage in the composition of the book; to my daughter, Diana, for her comments from the standpoint of a practising teacher; to Miss Isabel Sheaffe who has had to cope with the task of typing a long series of revisions; to Ms Lyn Walker for assistance at many points. And last, but not least, to my old friend Professor Richard Peters for his constant encouragement, even although the paths I have taken do not lead in the same direction as those he has himself explored.

More formal acknowledgments are due to a number of publishers, for permission to reprint paragraphs from earlier versions of chapters: to the Melbourne University Press in respect to 'Analytical philosophies of education' (*Melbourne Studies in Education*, 1965); to

Routledge & Kegan Paul Ltd. and the Humanities Press, New Jersey, in respect to 'Teaching to be critical' (R.S. Peters (ed.), *The Concept of Education*, 1967); to the editors of *Quadrant* in respect to 'Caring about and carefulness in education' (January-February 1975); to the Workers' Educational Association of New South Wales for 'Sex education' (Owen Harries (ed.), *Liberty and Politics*, 1976); to the University of London Press and Hodder and Stoughton for 'A note on care' (W.R. Niblett (ed.), *The Sciences, the Humanities and the Technological Threat*, 1975).

Canberra, 1979   J.P.

PART I

Programmatic

Chapter One
Towards a Philosophy of Teaching[1]

If a man were to call himself an economist and then it were to be discovered that he had never heard of marginal utility, was wholly ignorant of the work of Keynes, had no knowledge of economic theory and had acquired no skill as an economic analyst, he would at once be denounced as an imposter. In contrast, a journalist can write a book called *The Philosopher's Note-Book*, a series of aphoristic reflections on the minor joys and the minor calamities of everyday life, without anybody challenging his right to call himself a philosopher, even if he has never heard of an infinite regress, has not so much as a nodding acquaintance with the work of Plato, Hume or Wittgenstein, is entirely ignorant of logic and displays no powers of philosophical analysis. For although philosophy has so far established its right to be regarded as a systematic discipline as to be taught in universities as such, with its own professional journals and professional organisations, it has never wholly lost that older, popular, meaning which permits anyone to call himself a philosopher who engages in general reflections about human life and human affairs.

The popular use survives in a great many books which bear the title 'philosophy of education'. So, to take a case, W.H. Kilpatrick explicitly identifies philosophy with a 'point of view' or 'an outlook on life'[2] and philosophy of education, therefore, with having a point of view about education, or an outlook on the kind of life which is lived in our schools. To make such remarks as 'the schools ought to teach children how to behave' is automatically to qualify, on this criterion, as a philosopher of education, just as to qualify as having a 'philosophy of life' it is only necessary to give vent to such aphorisms as that 'a man has to look after himself'.

Not surprisingly then, some philosophers of education have asked themselves whether what they are engaged in is a branch of philosophy or a quite independent subject[3] – a question nobody would ask about, for example, the philosophy of science. For whereas the philosophy of science has always been intimately linked with the general problems of philosophy and has required of its practitioners the ordinary philosophical skills, much of what has passed as the philosophy of education has had not the slightest connexion with what was simultaneously going on in university departments of philosophy; it required no philosophical training and deployed no philosophical skills.

To make the situation still more confusing, even when those who are quite certainly expert philosophers have written about education, what they have had to say has often not been at all philosophical, in the professional sense of that word. Bertrand Russell is a striking example. In the preface to *On Education* he made it clear that he was writing as a parent to parents, not as a philosopher to philosophers. Whereas in *Our Knowledge of the External World* he had argued that the philosopher should avoid large untested generalisations and should remember that advocacy is no part of his task, his *On Education* abounds in large generalisations and is through-and-through advocacy. It is in no sense an application of Russell's general philosophical views to the special field of education. One could not possibly guess, reading *On Education*, that Russell was at that time committed to the philosophy of logical atomism. No doubt, there is what we might call an 'attitudinal' connexion – Russell himself once called it a 'psychological' connexion – between Russell's educational writings and his philosophical writings: the same spirit of criticism, the same faith in enlightenment, is exhibited in both works. But that is the most we can say. And Russell is not unique in thus dissociating his views on education from his professional philosophising. To take only one other case, the logical positivist Herbert Feigl has emphatically asserted that there is no formal connexion between his empiricism and his defence of a liberal education.[5]

But are they right? Other philosophers have argued that such a dissociation is a form of self-deception, that to accept a particular metaphysics, a particular ontology, is at once to be, in principle, educationally committed. So R.C. Lodge attempted to persuade us that 'there are only three typical directions between which philosophers choose; and consequently, there are only three main types of educational philosophy' – realist, idealist and pragmatist.[6] If a proclamation issued by the Philosophy of Education Society was less parsimonious, meticulously distinguishing, for example, a wide variety of realisms, its basic assumption is the same: that to each 'philosophical school' there necessarily corresponds a philosophy of education.[7]

Lodge sets out, in his fuller discussion, to present 'all three views, leaving it to the students to decide for themselves which they prefer and find most helpful'. Those of us who believe that philosophy is a serious attempt to solve problems will naturally resent any such suggestion that to study the philosophy of education is to be in the position of someone deciding in an intellectual department store what philosophical suit fits him best, or what philosophical cut appeals to his taste. If it is thus understood, the philosophy of education cannot but bring philosophy into disrepute. One remembers Nietzsche:

> Imagine a young head, without much experience of life, being stuffed with fifty systems ... and fifty criticisms of them, all jumbled up together – what an overgrown wilderness it will come to be! What a mockery of a philosophical education! It is, in fact, avowedly an education, not for philosophy but for an examination in philosophy.[8]

There is, fortunately, a fundamental objection to Lodge's procedure: most of the philosophical propositions which, on his view, serve as a 'foundation' for a philosophy of education have in fact no relevance whatsoever to the solution of educational problems, whether theoretical problems, technical problems or problems of policy – problems, that is, in understanding what happens, in determining how most efficiently to bring something about, or in determining what we ought to try to bring about.[9] That is why they can be presented to the educator as philosophies between which he can take his pick; it will not in fact matter which he chooses. Except insofar as he acquires from a particular philosopher a new vocabulary in which to formulate his educational programmes, the educator can go on saying and doing exactly what he said and did before he decided to become, let us say, an idealist rather than a realist.

To illustrate this point let us look at an essay by another American philosopher, John Wild, entitled 'Education and human society: a realistic view'.[10] Wild begins by attempting to define what he calls 'realistic philosophies'. He ascribes to them the following doctrines: 'The universe is made up of real, substantial entities, existing in themselves and ordered to one another by extra-mental relations. These entities and relations really exist whether they are known or not. To be is not the same as to be known ... These real entities and relations can be known in part by the human mind as they are in themselves ... To know something is to become *relationally* identified with an existent entity as it is.'[11]

In what possible way could educational conclusions be drawn from such premises? Wild goes on to make a considerable number of educational pronouncements — that 'the child, of course, should be interested in what he is learning', that 'the school is not the whole community but a vital institution within it', that 'the tendency of many teachers to treat young children as little Ph.Ds has had a debilitating effect on our culture'.[12] If anyone were to reject these dicta would he be compelled to reject Wild's ontological theses? Obviously not. And on the other side, a Berkeleian idealist, although he would directly contradict Wild's philosophical realism, might well sympathise with his educational pronouncements. In other words, in order to agree with what Wild tells us about education it is neither necessary nor sufficient first to adopt his ontology. It looks, then, as if it is a matter of indifference to the educationist which of these traditional philosophical positions he accepts. 'Where will be the difference', as Wittgenstein asks in his *Zettel*, 'between what the idealist-educated children say and the realist ones? Won't the difference only be one of a battle-cry?'[13]

Lodge, however, denies this. He tells us, for example, that 'the realist would educate the individual to become an unresisting piece of matter, permeable to physical law and opening himself entirely to its almighty influence'.[14] If this be so, then certainly it is a matter of great importance whether an educator accepts or does not accept a realist philosophy of education. But Wild is a realist and does not propose to educate children in this way; I have never met a realist who did. Indeed, what would it be like to do so? Even if, as Lodge seems to do, we identify realism with materialism, why should the materialist educate the child to become an unresisting piece of matter? The child is already, according to the materialist, a piece of matter, so there is no question of educating him to become one. And as for unresisting, why should the educator, merely because he is a materialist, try to make the child unresisting?

An authoritarian will do so, at least he will try to make the child unresisting to 'established authority'. But although in the Soviet Union authoritarianism is associated with materialism, there is no logical connection between the two; indeed some traditional Roman Catholic schools are quite as authoritarian as Communist schools and share a great many educational practices with them. When we look more closely at Lodge's 'realist', 'idealist' and 'pragmatist', indeed, we see that they are simply names he has given to certain types of educational policy. It is not at all the case that in order to put forward those policies one must, if one is to be consistent, adopt the philosophical tenets to which these names usually refer. A Liberal Catholic like Maritain can write with approval of the educational ideals of John Dewey, even though their metaphysical theories lie poles apart. In short, the conclusions which traditional philosophers of education sought to sustain flow neither from epistemological, nor ontological, nor metaphysical premises. That is exactly why Feigl and Russell divorced their educational from their philosophical writings. There is no possible passage from logical atomism to Russell's radical educational innovations, from logical empiricism to Feigl's defence of liberal education.

Those philosophers of education who are commonly, if not very illuminatingly, grouped together as 'analytic' – the names of Hardie, Scheffler, Peters, O'Connor immediately spring to mind, but there are many others – do not dispute this conclusion. They still believe, nevertheless, that it is possible to undertake strictly philosophical work in education, that the professional philosopher *qua* professional philosopher has a task to perform in relation to educational theory which is peculiarly his, neither mere preaching nor amateurish psychology and sociology, even though it does not consist in deducing educational policies from ontological premises. What task, then? In general terms, to clarify, to remove confusion by the use of analytic methods. This is the approach suggested by C.D. Hardie's *Truth and Fallacy in Educational Theory*, in which 'analytic' philosophy of education first got under way, although Hardie does not commit himself to the extreme Wittgensteinian doctrine that 'philosophy is not a body of doctrine but an activity', that it 'does not result in "philosophical propositions" but rather in the clarification of propositions'.[15]

Hardie's book reminds us, rather, of G.E. Moore's *Principia Ethica*, and especially of those chapters in which Moore criticises the ethical theories of his predecessors. 'It appears to me,' Moore wrote in his preface, 'that in Ethics, as in all other philosophical studies, the difficulties and disagreements, of which its history is full, are mainly due to a very simple cause: namely the attempt to answer questions, without first discovering precisely *what* question it is which you desire to answer.'[16] In a similar spirit, but in a manner influenced by subsequent philosophical discussions – he refers particularly to Broad and to Wittgenstein – Hardie set out to discover exactly why educational theorists disagree and what they are disagreeing about. 'If two educational theorists disagree,' he writes, 'I think it should be made clear whether the disagreement is factual or verbal or due to some emotional conflict. If this is to be done it is necessary always to state each theory in the clearest possible way so that no ambiguity may be allowed to flourish undiscovered.'[17]

So, it would seem, the educational philosopher's concern, unlike, say, the educational psychologist's concern, is not directly with the processes of education but rather with what theorists have already said about such processes. His task is to formulate as clearly as possible the points at issue in particular controversies between educational theorists and then to try to determine which of them are controversies about facts, which of them are about words, and which of them are but thin disguises for emotional – or, we might add, political and social – conflicts. His problems, that is, are set for him by the unclear nature of educational theories; his method consists in clarifying them; he has solved his problem once he has discovered what kind of theory they are.

There is, however, something more than a little unsatisfactory in this conception of the philosopher as an odd-job gardener, who enters an educational field taken over by weeds, unthrifty plants and straggly trees and leaves it neat and tidy by applying to it such processes as pruning, weeding and edge-cutting. It is impossible for a mere labourer to determine which plants are worth cultivating, what trees are worth pruning, and what edges are worth making precise. Only the man who is used to growing things can make decisions on that kind of point.

To drop the metaphor, it is very largely in the process of trying to develop a theory, encountering obstacles in testing it, meeting with misunderstandings when we try to communicate it, that we discover the points at which it needs to be clarified, the distinctions which need to be made, the ambiguities which have to be removed, the expressions which ought to be more precisely formulated. To insist upon clarity at the outset, a clarity independent of the needs of a particular enquiry, is, in the pejorative sense of that word, the essence of 'scholasticism'. This is the great temptation of analytic philosophy – to collapse into the making of pointless distinctions, the construction of unnecessary definitions, becoming in the process as dreary, as little related to any fundamental problems, as the pseudo-philosophy it replaces.

Let us look, however, at what Hardie actually does as compared with what he says he is doing. He chooses for discussion three doctrines about education which are, he thinks, typical; that children ought to be educated according to Nature (Spencer); that the object of education is to produce good characters by means of instruction (Herbart); that education should proceed by practical instruction in the affairs of life (Dewey). These doctrines, thus formulated, have the form of prescriptions, even of slogans, rather than of theories. But Hardie's procedure is first to restate them in the form of theories and then critically to examine them in that theoretical form. He is not content, even though this is what he has led us to expect, to determine their logical status; he asks himself whether the theories accurately describe the processes of education.

The final effect is that *Truth and Fallacy in Educational Theory* commingles what are clearly philosophical considerations with considerations deriving from psychology and sociology. Take Hardie's treatment of the slogan 'A child's education should be such that it is free to develop according to the laws of its own nature'. Hardie first of all looks at this slogan in terms of a general theory about theories, derived from the philosophy of science, namely, that 'to describe the changes which take place in any system we need to know ... first of all the initial state of the system and secondly, we need to know the natural laws involved'.[18] Applying this general principle to the educational dictum that a child's education should be such that it is free to develop according to the laws of its own nature, he converts it into a theory to the following effect: 'The initial state of the child and the laws which govern the interaction between that state and the environment are analogous to the seed of a plant and the laws which govern the interaction between that seed and the environment'. Then comes his criticism: the laws of learning discovered by psychologists, he argues, make it apparent that the process of learning is not in fact analogous to the growth of a seed.

The commingling of psychological and philosophical considerations in Hardie's book derives from the fact that he had his eye from the beginning on the need for establishing 'educational science' – i.e. a systematic attempt, using the ordinary procedures of science, to discover under what circumstances, and with what consequences, one person succeeds in teaching another* – and makes

---

* In using the phrase 'educational science', I do not want to beg the question whether the inquiries I here have in mind form a 'single science'. Obviously, some of them are psychological in character, e.g. studies of the way in which the personality of the teacher can affect the child's capacity to learn; some of them are sociological, e.g. studies of the way in which teaching affects the social mobility of pupils; some of them are economic, e.g. studies of the ways in which teaching can affect economic growth. It might be less misleading but it would certainly be more cumbrous to speak of 'scientific investigations into education' rather than of 'educational science'. Certainly, there is no 'educational science' in the least comparable with physics or even with economics, and no possibility, therefore, of constructing a philosophy of education which would be at all like the philosophy of physics. (This point has been especially emphasised by Max Black in 'A note on "Philosophy of Education"', in the *Harvard Educational Review*, 26 (spring 1956), pp. 154-5). On the other hand, only the most inveterate opponents of the social sciences would deny that there can, in principle, be fruitful empirical investigations of a scientific character into education. And it is convenient to use the words 'educational science' for this network of investigations.

use of philosophy, in the professional sense of the word only as a help in determining exactly what previous theorists have embryonically contributed to such a science. His procedure is a testimony, however unwitting, to the very limited role of a philosophy of teaching. The concern of the philosopher of teaching, it would seem, is with theories of teaching, not with teaching itself. And even then, the philosopher can do nothing to show, without moving out of his own sphere into psychology or sociology, that these theories are true or false; the most he can do is to clarify them.

Perhaps we can go further than this in reducing the importance of the philosophy of education. Why should the philosopher participate even at this preliminary stage? The clarification of educational concepts, theories, expressions, is best left, one might well suppose, to those who are immersed in the task of trying to develop educational science, not by philosophers called in as specialist advisers. For after all, it is biologists who have clarified the idea of inheritance and the idea of reproduction; it is chemists who have clarified the idea of air and the idea of acidity; it is botanists who have clarified the idea of a flower and the idea of a leaf. And in each case without the help of philosophers. Should it not be left to educational scientists, as one of their theoretical tasks, to clarify the central concepts of teaching?

Before we come too rapidly to this conclusion, with its consequence that clarificatory philosophy has as little to contribute to the theory of teaching as it has to chemical theory, we need to look again at Hardie's procedure. On the face of it, there is something rather odd about taking such an obviously prescriptive dictum as 'children ought to be educated in accordance with Nature' and transforming it into a theory which can be overthrown by psychological or sociological evidence. Hardie himself later came to feel that he had been far too charitable in thus interpreting the writings of traditional educational philosophers. What they put forward, according to his later view, were not theories at all but, at best, loose analogies. No deductions could be made from them, deductions capable of testing their truth. It was a mistake, therefore, to suppose that they could be overthrown by, for example, a reference to the laws of learning.[19]

We might put the matter thus: Hardie had been anxious to develop sound educational theories 'on the model of one of the natural sciences'. He went to traditional educational philosophers in the hope of finding such theories in their writings. But although some of the positions he criticises are, so to speak, possible ingredients in educational science, they are certainly not equivalent to what

Spencer or Froebel or Pestalozzi was actually saying. For Spencer, Froebel and Pestalozzi were not trying to develop educational theories 'on the model of the natural sciences'; they were laying down educational policies, although no doubt they called them 'educational theories'. And much the same is true of Wild, of Maritain, even of Dewey.

What he should have done, it might therefore be argued, is, first, to demonstrate that the so-called theories were not theories at all and, secondly, to clarify what in detail they amount to, what point they have, as slogans, metaphors, analogies, policy-statements. This takes time and care, the sort of time and care Scheffler devotes to such a task in *The Language of Education*. Hardie, on this view, underestimated the potentialities of analytic techniques; his hasty conversion of slogans into supposedly equivalent theories leapt over precisely the points at which careful analysis is called for.

On this interpretation of the philosopher's task, it will still be true that his concern is with what other people have had to say about teaching rather than directly with teaching itself. The difference is that his task will be not so much to clarify their theories as to expose them as pseudo-theories. And then, once they are exposed as such, to bring out their importance as slogans, metaphors, analogies, how they help us, in such capacities, in our thinking about teaching.

Once more, however, such an interpretation of his responsibilities at once ascribes a humble task to the philosopher and leaves us wondering why even this task should fall to him. No doubt, the philosopher has had considerable practice in distinguishing theories from pseudo-theories – that is part of his everyday business. In fields like education where metaphors, slogans, loose analogies, policies, are so often dressed up as theories he can properly exercise his talents and his training by unmasking them. But once he attempts to go beyond that point, to consider just how any particular metaphor or analogy or slogan actually operates in educational controversies, he is, on the face of it, embarking upon a task which only those who are deeply involved in such controversies can fruitfully undertake, just as only those who are deeply involved with dramatic poetry can tell us how Shakespeare used metaphor, even if such a person may have something very general to learn from, let us say, Max Black's theory of metaphor. We still do not seem to have hit upon any point at which the philosopher *qua* philosopher can contribute directly to our understanding of teaching, as distinct from offering a modest guidance in the clarification of other people's theories about teaching.

But let us take yet a third look at Hardie's *Truth and Fallacy*. The theoretical assertions to which he reduces educational dicta, we then observe, are not always propositions in psychology or sociology and the considerations to which he appeals in criticising them are not always the results of research in these fields. For example, he offers as another possible interpretation of 'a child ought to be educated in accordance with Nature' (a doctrine he ascribes to Pestalozzi) the following: 'Sense-impression of Nature is the only true foundation of human instruction, because it is the only true foundation of human knowledge.'[20]Nothing has been more characteristic of philosophy, from Plato on, than the attempt to determine the relation between sense-impressions and human knowledge.

This is not, what at first sight it might seem to be, a psychological problem, as becomes clearer if we set it out thus: 'When we claim to know, for example, that war broke out in 1914 or that $2 + 2 = 4$, is having this knowledge logically equivalent to our having had certain sensory experiences?' Hardie himself contests the view that 'the sense-impressions of nature' are the only true foundations of human knowledge by turning to, first, Russell's distinction between knowledge-by-acquaintance and knowledge-by-description in order to argue that knowledge by description, not immediately based on sense-impressions, can still be fruitful, and, secondly, to Wittgenstein's *Tractatus* in order to argue that a proposition of mathematics, although knowledge, 'does not express a thought',[21] and is certainly not based on sense-impressions. If such familiar philosophical theses as 'all knowledge is founded on sense-impressions' play an important part in controversies about the nature of instruction, then it looks as if philosophical arguments are, after all, directly relevant to pedagogical issues. To reject the view that all knowledge is based on sense-impressions is to deny that, insofar as it aims at the imparting of knowledge, teaching must proceed by giving children sense-impressions. And this is a conclusion of very considerable pedagogical consequence.

The direct importance of philosophy emerges in a rather different way from Hardie's later essay, 'The philosophy of education in a new key'. Traditionally, he says, it has been supposed that philosophy gives us knowledge about the way things are. Philosophy was therefore divided into metaphysics which was to give us knowledge about God, freedom and immortality, epistemology which was to give us knowledge about the mind and its objects, and ethics which was to give us knowledge about right and wrong. But to think of philosophy thus, so Hardie argues, is a mistake. Philosophy has knowledge to offer, to be sure, but knowledge concerning ways of thinking and talking about the world, not knowledge concerning the world itself – that should be left to science. The proper division of philosophy is into such branches as the philosophy of language, the philosophy of science, the philosophy of mathematics.

Each of these, he continues, is of direct relevance – as traditional metaphysics, epistemology and moral theory are not – both to the criticism of established educational theories, by bringing out their linguistic, formal, and mathematical defects,[22] and to the daily work of the teacher. Every 'philosophy-of' aids the teacher to see more clearly what he is doing when he teaches the subject that 'philosophy-of' is about. So, for example, the philosopher of science, by giving students a better grasp of the connection between science and commonsense, can help to prevent the teaching of science from becoming a kind of magic, pursued by members of a secret cult. The philosopher of history, similarly, can make it plain just how history teaching must differ, in its criteria of success, from the teaching of the social sciences.[23]

From Hardie's writings, then, we have managed to extract two ways in which philosophy bears directly upon controversies about the processes of teaching, as distinct from controversies about the formal structure of educational theories. The theory of knowledge and 'philosophies-of' are both in this position. No doubt, Feigl and Russell were right enough; we cannot directly deduce either from the theory of knowledge or from 'philosophies-of' the desirability of the sort of educational policies which they were concerned to expound and defend. But we can reasonably hope, with the aid of philosophical arguments, to see more clearly in what successful teaching will consist.

We have still not exhausted the ways in which philosophical investigation can directly bear upon the processes of teaching. Consider, for example, the volume of essays and extracts brought together by Israel Scheffler as *Philosophy and Education*.[24] The first interesting point about these essays and extracts is that very few of them were designed as contributions to the philosophy of education; the anthology includes a chapter from R.M. Hare's *The Language of Morals*, two chapters from Gilbert Ryle's *The Concept of Mind*, along with philosophical essays on such topics as 'Reason and rule in arithmetic and algebra'. Yet the second interesting thing is that whether or not they were designed as contributions to the philosophy of education, they are intimately concerned with the processes of teaching, not merely with the logical structure of theories about education. For the views which they put forward – about rules and rationality, about 'knowing how' and 'knowing that', about the nature of a moral education – are all of them directly related to the daily work of the classroom. Consider, as another instance, the question which Wittgenstein discussed in *Philosophical Investigations*: 'What is it to understand?', 'How are we to judge whether a person has understood what we have told him?' A teacher clearly needs to know when he can rightly be satisfied that his students have understood what he has tried to teach them. When they can reproduce it in examinations? When they can apply it to new situations? When they modify their conduct in the light of what they have learnt? How does understanding a foreign language differ, if at all, from understanding a work of art, understanding a scientific theory, understanding history, understanding people? One can scarcely dismiss such questions as these on the ground that they have no bearing on any actual pedagogical problems.

It might be replied, no doubt, that it is a psychological enquiry – a matter for scientific investigation – to determine when a child understands. It is certainly, in the long run, a matter for experimental investigation whether a particular method of teaching is better than another at improving, let us say, the child's understanding of mathematics. The philosophy of teaching cannot tell the teacher what teaching procedures to adopt any more than the philosophy of science can tell the scientist what research procedures to adopt. All it can do is to throw light on the question by the use of what criteria a teacher is to judge when a mode of teaching, as when as a scientist is to judge that a mode of research, is successful. It cannot settle the question how a teacher is to interest his pupils in mathematics, or how much practice they will need if they are to get a firm grasp of what they are doing, any more than either it or psychology can settle the policy issue whether mathematics, and if so to what level, should be a compulsory subject, how much of the school curriculum should be devoted to it, or whether, even, an attempt should be made to get children to understand mathematics as distinct from learning a set of tricks. But granted that children are to be taught to understand mathematics, it compels the teacher to face the question how he is to judge whether this project is successful or unsuccessful. Or if his object is to teach them mathematical tricks, whether *that* objective has been realised.

It is notorious that educational psychology, for all the time and energy that has been devoted to it, has contributed disappointingly little to the solution of educational problems. There are no doubt many possible explanations of this barrenness. One explanation is offered by Wittgenstein: 'For in psychology there are experimental methods and *conceptual confusion* ... The existence of the experimental methods makes us think we have the means of solving the problems which trouble us; though problems and methods pass one another by.'[25] Only by trying to make the concepts clearer can we hope to avoid this confusion; only thus can we hope to arrive at a situation in which problems and methods mesh.

But what of the two objections I raised previously, that analysis unrelated to problems is empty, and that when it is related to problems it is best undertaken by those who are working at those problems? On the first point, there are a great many genuine controversies about teaching which call for close conceptual analysis. There has been too little, not too much, discussion of such questions as the circumstances in which we can properly say of a child, for example, that he has been 'well trained'; that he has learnt to 'appreciate' literature; that he acquired the ability to 'think for himself'; that a particular form of teaching will develop his understanding or his imagination.

On the second point, in discussing such concepts as these we are not moving outside philosophy; the philosopher is the person to analyse them just because *they are themselves philosophical concepts*. He has an authority in relation to them which he does not have in relation to 'flower', or 'acid', or 'inheritance'. (I do not, of course, mean to suggest either that what he says must be 'taken on authority' or that there is likely to be a single philosophical view on the points at issue.) That explains why an anthology on the philosophy of education can contain essays and chapters from books which were designed not as contributions to the philosophy of education but as contributions to ethics or epistemology.

Ryle has argued, indeed, that the philosophy of education constitutes a large segment of what has traditionally been called 'epistemology' or 'the theory of knowledge'. In part, he says, traditional epistemology was metaphysics in disguise. As such, it has no special relation to teaching. But much of the time traditional epistemologists, when they wrongly thought of themselves as being psychologists, were actually engaged in 'a branch of philosophical theory concerned with the concepts of learning, teaching, and examining'. This branch of theory, he suggests, 'might be called "the philosophy of learning", "the methodology of education", or, more grandly, "the grammar of pedagogy".'[26] So, even if no conclusions of interest to the teacher follow from such principles as John Wild's 'to know something is to become *relationally* identified with an existent entity as it is' – a typical example of metaphysics disguised as epistemology – the situation is very different in the case of epistemologists who are talking about learning, teaching, examining. They are directly contributing to the philosophy of teaching.

And something similar is true of those moral philosophers who are interested in the philosophy of action, in 'moral' or 'philosophical' psychology. Sometimes their real concern is metaphysical; what they are trying to do is to show that human beings form no part of the natural world. Then what they have to say does not bear upon teaching. But the first three books of Aristotle's *Ethics* have long been read as, in part, a contribution to the theory of teaching; Wittgenstein's *Philosophical Investigations* can certainly be read in that way. One begins to see why, if certainly in exaggeration, John Dewey once wrote that 'philosophy may even be defined *as the general theory of education*'.[27]

There are many other ways in which philosophy bears upon education as a whole, as distinct from problems about teaching. Very obviously, for example, the theory of justice has consequences for decisions about educational selection. But I have chosen to discuss only the philosophy of teaching, a segment, and only a segment, of the philosophy of education.

The philosophy of teaching is that part of the philosophy of education which concerns itself, not with the formal structure of educational theory, not with those problems in social, political and moral philosophy which arise out of the character of the school as an institution and its relation to society, but primarily at least, with teaching and learning – with problems which arise in *any* attempt to teach systematically in *any* social system which places *any* value whatsoever on the transmission, by way of formal teaching, of knowledge, capacities, attitudes. This inquiry is properly describable as philosophical, or so I have suggested, insofar as it takes as its point of departure concepts which are of central concern to one or the other branches of philosophy – concepts like observation, experience, understanding, imagination, appreciation, capacities, criticism, rules, habits. Its methods, too, are philosophical, not experimental. Most philosophers, from Heraclitus to Wittgenstein, have contributed to the philosophy of teaching, even if not under that name. Mine has been the more modest task of trying to bring it into shape as a subject.

By its very nature, in looking to universal principles, the philosophy of teaching is abstract, as philosophy is always abstract. Although I have tried always to keep in mind the concrete teaching-situation, I am only too conscious of the fact that from the point of view of a teacher struggling with a class of children for whom everything he cares about is a bad joke or a bureaucracy whose main objective is to keep him in his place, much of what I have to say will sound impossibly academic, in the bad sense of that word. On many of the controversies now being fought out in our schools, about the selection of students, about grading, about the government of schools, about politicisation, about the relation between schooling and employment, I shall be saying absolutely nothing. Not because I believe that the philosopher has no professional concern with such questions – I have, indeed, written a little about them elsewhere[28] – but because they do not fall within my present, very limited, province.

In concentrating upon the abstract and the universal I shall, of course, subject myself, in the present social mood, to the accusation of retreating from the actual, displaying in the process a typical admixture of callousness and reactionary hypocrisy. I have defended science against such charges in *Science and Its Critics*;[29] I shall leave it to my readers to apply that defence to the case of the philosophy of teaching. But in the end, my defence must rest on what follows: if what I there say, where its intent is universal, has no application except in the schools of a capitalist society, I have failed.

NOTES

[1] The argument in this chapter in part derives from, and can in part be supplemented by, two articles of mine in *Melbourne Studies in Education* (1965), pp. 41-79 on analytical philosophies of education and my 'Philosophy of education in a new key', in *Contemporary Philosophy: A Survey* (Florence 1971), pp. 60-7.

[2] W.H. Kilpatrick, *Philosophy of Education* (New York 1951), p. 3.

[3] See, for example, Elizabeth S. Maccia, 'The separation of philosophy from theory of education', in *Studies in Philosophy and Education*, vol.2 (spring 1962), pp. 158-69.

[4] 'Reply to Criticisms' in P.A. Schilpp (ed.), *The Philosophy of Bertrand Russell*, (Evanston 1946), p. 727.

[5] Compare Herbert Feigl, 'Aims of education for our age of science' in *Modern Philosophies and Education*, Fifty-Fourth Yearbook of the National Society for the Study of Education, Part 1 (Chicago 1955), p. 304.

[6] R.C. Lodge, *Philosophy of Education* (New York, revised ed. 1947), p. viii.

[7] *Educational Theory* 4 (January, 1954), pp. 1-3.

[8] Friedrich Nietzsche, *Thoughts Out of Season*, III, p. 8.

[9] For a little more about 'problems' see my 'Can the social sciences be value-free?' in H. Feigl and M. Brodbeck (eds), *Readings in the Philosophy of Science* (New York 1953), pp. 674-6.

[10] Published in *Modern Philosophies and Education*, the Fifty-fourth Year Book of the National Society for the Study of Education (Chicago 1955), pp. 17-56.

[11] ibid, pp. 17-18.

[12] ibid, pp. 31, 33, 36.

[13] Ludwig Wittgenstein, *Zettel*, trans. G.E.M. Anscombe (Oxford 1967), 414, 74e.

[14] *Philosophy of Education*, p. 78.

[15] *Tractatus*, 4.112.

[16] G.E. Moore, *Principia Ethica*, reprint edition (Cambridge 1948), p. vii.

[17] C.D. Hardie, *Truth and Fallacy in Educational Theory* (Cambridge 1942), p. ix.

[18] ibid., p. 2.

[19] Compare C.D. Hardie, 'Philosophy of education in a new key', *Educational Theory*, 10 (1960), pp. 255-61.

[20] Hardie, *Truth and Fallacy*, p. 5.

[21] *Tractatus*. 6. 21.

[22] See, for example, D.J. O'Connor, *An Introduction to the Philosophy of Education* (London 1957).

[23] See also I.N. Scheffler, 'Philosophies-of and the curriculum', in J.F. Doyle (ed.), *Educational Judgments* (London 1973), pp. 209-18.

[24] I.N. Scheffler, *Philosophy and Education* (Boston 1958).

[25] Ludwig Wittgenstein, *Philosophical Investigations*, 3rd ed., trans. G.E.M. Anscombe (Oxford 1968), 232e.

[26] Gilbert Ryle, *The Concept of Mind* (London 1949), p. 318.

[27] John Dewey, *Democracy and Education* (New York 1916), p. 383.

[28] See, for example, 'Civil justice and its rivals' in E. Kamenka and Alice Tay-Soon (eds), *Justice* (London 1979) pp. 2-49.

[29] John Passmore, *Science and Its Critics* (New Brunswick and London 1978).

Chapter Two

The Concept of Teaching

It might seem natural, even mandatory, to begin with a definition. 'What is teaching? Teaching is ...' A good many philosophers, especially of the analytic persuasion, have set out to construct such a definition, with the praiseworthy objective of clarifying educational discussion. Let us look at a particularly favourable specimen of the sort of definition that has emerged. 'Teaching,' writes Israel Scheffler, 'may be characterised as an activity aimed at the achievement of learning, and practiced in such manner as to respect the student's intellectual integrity and capacity for independent judgment.'[1] Questions crowd in upon us. Is it true that teaching must be aimed at the achievement of learning? Cannot a human being teach unconsciously, by his example? ('He taught me, although he certainly did not mean to do so, that authorities were never to be trusted.') On the other side, is it enough, if an activity is to count as teaching, for it to be *aimed* at the achievement of learning? Wouldn't it be odd to claim that we have taught someone to swim even although, after all our efforts, he still cannot swim? Since we commonly condemn certain styles of teaching as 'authoritarian' how can it be true that to teach is, *by definition*, to 'respect the student's intellectual integrity'?

These sound like real problems; a seminar, I am sure, could have a most animated time discussing them. But however lively, the discussion would be fruitless. (This vital distinction between a *lively* and a *fruitful* discussion is too often ignored by enthusiasts for tutorial methods.) The word 'teaching', like most other words in regular daily use, does not have sharply defined limits. A teacher can quite properly complain: 'I have been teaching that class mathematics for six months yet they have still not learnt a thing.' So it looks as if Scheffler is right: to teach is to 'aim at the achievement of learning' but not necessarily to achieve it. Yet, with equal propriety, a pupil in such a class can describe the same situation thus: 'That teacher did not teach me anything.' And this presumes that if the pupil did not achieve learning, the teacher was not teaching, but only *trying* to teach. 'Teaching,' it would seem, sometimes means 'aiming at achieving learning' and sometimes means 'actually achieving learning', is sometimes an attempt-word and sometimes a success-word. No doubt, as we have already suggested, it would be more than a little odd for a teacher to say 'I taught him to swim, but he still can't swim'. And yet there is no impropriety in the sardonic comment: 'He taught me swimming, so naturally I can't swim.' As this example suggests, the force of 'teaching' can vary with the syntax which surrounds it: 'taught' in 'he taught me to *swim*' does not behave in the same way as 'taught' in 'he taught me *swimming*'. 'Teaching,' in fact, is a deeply-rooted word, with a long history; it has a multitude of idiomatic applications; these cannot be summed up in a definition which will give us the 'essence' or the 'real meaning' of teaching. Any such definition will immediately conjure up counter-examples.

Very well, it might be replied, certainly there are no 'essences' or 'real meanings', but to talk sensibly and clearly about teaching we *need* a precise definition. Provided only that such a definition is consistent with some of the central ways of using the word 'teaching', it does not matter that there are variant idioms or expressions to which it does not apply. If the definition, inevitably, will be to some extent stipulative rather than descriptive in its relationship to ordinary language, that is characteristic of all theoretically useful definitions and does not reduce their usefulness.

The view that in order to be clear about what we are doing in any serious intellectual investigation we need to begin from precise definitions has a long history; it goes back to Plato. Definitions play a considerable rôle in Euclid's geometry, for so long regarded as the supreme example of what inquiry ought to be. It was a common eighteenth-century view that social inquiry was not as successful as physical inquiry only because it made use of obscure and ill-defined terms. And that attitude of mind has persisted into our own century. Consider this example from Crossman's *Plato Today*: 'If we do not know precisely the meanings of the words we use, we cannot discuss anything profitably. Most of the futile arguments on which we all waste time are largely due to the fact that we each have our own vague meanings for the words we use and assume that our opponents are using them in the same senses. If we defined our terms to start with, we could have far more profitable discussions.'[2] This we might call, with a reference to Plato's dialogues, the 'Socratic' fallacy, the fallacy which consists in supposing that we cannot sensibly employ terms which we cannot define. 'When I give the description "The ground was quite covered with plants" – do you want to say,' asked

Wittgenstein, properly disputing this, 'I don't know what I am talking about until I can give a definition of a plant.'³ There is, indeed, no better way of starting what Crossman calls 'futile arguments' than by looking for the 'true definition' of open-textured words.

I do not want to suggest that there is *never* any point in offering a definition, or at the very least a general description of the way in which we intend to use a word. We may sometimes need to remove ambiguities. In the Wittgenstein example, it will not matter should somebody wrongly suppose that Wittgenstein is talking about industrial plants rather than about flowering plants. But in the sentence 'I should like to see the whole of Australia covered with plants', the ambiguity could be important and elucidation necessary – although all we need say, if it becomes apparent that we are being misunderstood, is: 'I am using the word "plant" in its botanical sense.' That is far from being a definition.

Confusion certainly *might* arise out of the fact that we all of us sometimes use the word 'teaching' in such a way that any attempt to get someone to learn something counts as teaching and sometimes in such a way that only those who are *successful* in getting someone to learn can properly be described as teaching. But I do not know of any important pedagogical confusion which *in fact* has this ambiguity as its source. Ordinarily, either the context makes it clear what is meant or the ambiguity is of no consequence; nothing rests on it. Most of the time 'teaching' will mean, for our purposes, 'trying to teach'. For we are interested in what teachers are trying to do and what counts as success. We want to be free to use the phrase 'successful teaching' which would be pleonastic if teaching was *identified* with successful teaching. If circumstances do arise in which the ambiguity turned out to be important, we can easily enough clarify the situation by substituting, according to which is appropriate, 'trying to teach' or 'succeeding in teaching' for 'teaching'. On the other hand, to attempt to stick to a rigid definition, to remember *never* to write, for example, 'he does not teach his class anything' but always 'he does not succeed in teaching his class anything' would be to cut across the grain of usage so sharply that we should almost certainly succumb to habit at one point or another.

There is an interesting contrast at this point between 'teaching' and 'education'. For 'education' *does* create troublesome ambiguities. It is sometimes used to mean upbringing in general. That is what John Locke's *Some Thoughts Concerning Education* is about; it is what Hume has in mind when he condemns 'education' as the source of our confused and irrational beliefs. But sometimes it means, more narrowly, 'schooling', as when it is said that '15 per cent of the National Income is devoted to education'. And sometimes it means, more narrowly still, that sort of schooling which issues in what we call 'an educated person'. In very many instances, the context will make it clear what is meant. When John Wain remarks, for example, that 'there is no such thing as education in the Soviet Union' he must, very obviously, have the last sense of 'education' in mind; to reply to him with a barrage of statistics would be patently absurd. But it is less obvious that to deny that education has any 'aims' is not to deny that a particular style of upbringing or school system can have aims. What it means, rather, is that we do not try to turn out educated people 'as a means to a further end'. At such points, confusion has arisen and continues to arise. A systematic book on the philosophy of education would need, in fact, to distinguish between education$_1$ (upbringing), education$_2$ (schooling), education$_3$ (producing educated men) – to say nothing of education$_4$, the *study* of these processes. I shall myself use the word 'education' but little. When I do use it, I shall try to make perfectly clear in which of these senses I am using it.

I suggested that it is a mistake to go in search of a formal definition of teaching. There is, however, a familiar logical point to be made about teaching: it is a triadic relation. For all X, if X teaches, there must exist somebody who, and something that, is taught by X. (This is true whether 'teaching' means 'tries to teach' or 'succeeds in teaching'.) A slightly less familiar point, perhaps, is that teaching is a *covert* triadic relation as opposed to an *overt* triadic relation, such as 'gives'.

Except in very special idiomatic uses, or where the missing constituents of the relationship are obvious from the context, we cannot understand the expression 'he gives'; it is not a statement. Neither, with the same proviso, do we understand 'he gives books' or 'he gives to his uncle'. There is no statement short of 'he gives books to his uncle'. So the triadic character of 'giving' is *overt*. In contrast, 'he teaches', 'he teaches arithmetic', 'he teaches backward children' are all of them intelligible statements, just as they stand. If we still say that teaching is a triadic relation or that, in the language of Sir John Adams, it 'carries two accusatives' – in spite of the fact that 'teaches' can be used as an intransitive verb and in 'he teaches arithmetic' and 'he teaches backward children' it has only one accusative – this is because we recognise that if anyone teaches there *must be* something he teaches and someone he teaches it to, even when these are not mentioned. In other words, if we cared to inquire, as all the same we do not always need to inquire, there must be some answer to the question 'Whom and what does he teach?'. That is why I described teaching as a *covert* triadic relation; its triadic nature is not at once apparent in the grammar of our language.

The main importance of the fact that 'teaching' is a covert as distinct from an overt triadic relationship is that we can easily overlook its triadic nature, whereas it is almost impossible to overlook the triadic nature of 'gives' or, to take a concept closer to 'teaches', of 'tells'. The fact that 'he teaches' can function as a complete statement encourages the belief that 'teaching' is the name of a specific skill, at which a person is 'good' or 'bad' irrespective of what he is teaching or to whom he is teaching it, just as swimming is the name of a skill and a person is good or bad at swimming wherever and whenever he swims. The belief that to be able to teach is to be able to teach anything is still with us, to the delight of educational administrators in systems in which a shortage of chemistry teachers is calmly met by transferring a biologist or a teacher of French to that task. But it is sufficiently obvious that a person can be good at teaching philosophy to graduate students yet bad at teaching football to six-year-olds; that to be a good teacher he must not only *know* something about what he is teaching but *care* about both it and the pupils he is teaching it to. Whether a teacher has a 'certificate' to mark the fact that he has acquired certain skills is much less important than that he knows what he is talking about and cares about his pupils learning what he hopes to teach them.

'Teaching', in fact, is rather like that other triadic relation 'curing': to say that a person is good at curing adults of neurotic disorders is not at all to suggest that he will be equally good at curing the neuroses of children – he may be one of those people who dislike children – let alone that he will be equally good at curing adults of influenza. The test of whether he is good at curing, too, will not be whether he displays in a polished form the currently fashionable techniques – although, admittedly, some of his fellow-doctors may fall into the trap of judging him in these terms – but whether his patients get better. The test of a good teacher, similarly, is not whether he writes clearly on the board, or keeps good discipline, or knows how to work the latest visual aid, but whether his pupils learn what he tries to teach them. To emphasise, always, that to teach is to teach something to somebody is one way of bringing home such facts as these.

Another way of failing to do justice to the triadic character of teaching is to describe it as 'child-centred'. The slogan 'we teach children, not subjects' is no doubt useful as a weapon against those who forget that teaching is teaching *somebody* and place all their emphasis on the traditional structure of what is taught. Especially but not uniquely in such well-articulated subjects as mathematics, the teacher can easily succumb to the temptation of supposing that if his lessons are academically well-organised, orderly, thorough, nothing more can reasonably be expected of him, that if, under these circumstances, his pupils do not learn this can only be because they are stupid. (The 'pearls-before-swine' syndrome.) All teaching is pupil-centred in the sense that its object is not merely to expound a subject but to help somebody to learn something; it fails as teaching, whatever its logical virtues as exposition, if it does not have this effect. But at the same time the teacher is trying to teach pupils *something* and it is by no means unimportant what that something is: whether, as in Fagin's case, it is how to pick pockets or, as in Socrates' case, how to think critically. He has to teach *both* pupils *and* 'subjects'. Merely to interest the child, merely to respect him as a person, to care for him, to love him – none of these dyadic relations, whatever their importance, is equivalent to teaching him, although some of them may be necessary conditions of doing so. The great problem for the teacher, as the triadic structure of teaching brings out, is to reconcile respect for the child and respect for what is being taught. But fortunately these two are by no means irreconcilable. To present a class with, let us say, a feeble imitation of science, under the pretence of teaching science but on the real ground that it will keep the class amused, is to respect neither science nor pupil.

Returning to the formula '*X* teaches something to somebody', let us ask what in this formula can be substituted for the *X*, the 'something' and the 'somebody'. We normally suppose that *X* here stands for some individual person – in American books on education a woman, in English books, as in this book, a man. But it is worth noting that in everyday speech it is often replaced not by the name of a person but by such words as 'nature' or 'experience' or 'the environment'. 'Nature,' we say, 'teaches the birds to build their nests.' Nature, too, 'teaches lovers what to do'. 'Experience', similarly, 'has taught him to trust nobody.' At a more professional level, Maria Montessori lays it down that 'in our schools the environment itself teaches the children'.[4]

It is tempting to dismiss such utterances as 'metaphorical', irrelevant to any serious study of teaching. But their prevalence has a certain significance. They unconsciously bear witness to the importance of teaching in human life, an importance which is so great that we sometimes exaggerate it. When we see somebody performing a complex task, we tend automatically to presume that someone has taught him to do it; if we cannot find a human teacher we substitute 'nature'. We do this even when there is not even any evidence, as in the case of the birds or the lovers, that the behaviour in question has been learned. When it clearly *has* been learned, we are still more likely to look for a teacher, in the form of 'experience' or 'nature' or 'the environment'.

This tendency must be resisted: for it is a very important fact that there can be learning where no one teaches. Since, as well, our present concern is only with that sort of learning which does flow from teaching, we can properly defy idiom and admit as a substitute for X in 'X teaches something to somebody' only names of persons or such definite descriptions – like 'the headmaster' – as can, in principle, be replaced by personal names. By the very nature of the case, it is only to such a teacher that I can address myself.

What proper names, however, can be substituted? To answer that question, we have first to draw attention to a certain ambiguity. 'Teach' can be used to refer either to an occupation or to a particular act. If 'teaching' is being used in its occupational sense, as in 'X teaches science to senior students', X can only be replaced by names of members of the teaching profession. But in 'X is teaching somebody to do something' it is at least a highly plausible view that the result of substituting the name of any person whatsoever, excluding only babies, idiots, etc., for 'X' would be, with reference to a particular something and a particular somebody, to make a *true* statement, i.e. that there is not a single human being who has never taught anything to anybody. In this sense, 'anybody can teach' is a true statement, little though professional teachers may like to admit that fact. Not only can anybody try to teach, but anybody can succeed in teaching, something to somebody. Adults teach children, children teach children, in the most primitive and the most complex of societies. That all human beings teach is in many ways the most important fact about them: the fact in virtue of which, unlike other members of the animal kingdom, they are able to transmit acquired characteristics. If they were to give up teaching, content to love, they would lose their distinctiveness. But the antithesis is a false one; the loving parent will certainly teach, as one expression of love. The helplessness of the newborn child ensures as much. (The hostility to any sort of instruction one sometimes finds among 'radical' educational reformers is, like so much radicalism, reactionary in the extreme and anti-human to boot.) When Professor Oakeshott writes that 'initiation into the *geistige Welt* of human achievement is owed to the Sage, the teacher ... it is the Sage, the teacher, who is the agent of civilisation'[5] he is, I am submitting, exaggerating the rôle of the Sage-teacher. We are initiated into civilisation by an enormous number of people, initiated into what is good as well as into what is bad in our 'spiritual world'. The Sage is important because he initiates *changes* in our 'spiritual world', not because he alone can initiate us into civilisation: our parents, our friends, the books we read, do most of that.

The situation is completely different, however, as soon as one thinks of teaching as an occupation or specifies in certain particular ways the 'something' and the 'somebody' in 'he teaches something to somebody'. It is by no means true that everybody could be by occupation a teacher – his capacity to teach, his knowledge, his patience, may be too limited to make that possible – or that everybody can teach dyslectic children to read, or can teach quantum physics or advanced mathematics. That is precisely why we now have a class of professional teachers who are subjected to special training or encouraged to acquire a special degree of knowledge about particular subjects. The traditional Greek view that teaching was everybody's task, and therefore nobody's particular task, broke down once the Greeks developed subjects like mathematics to a point at which it was no longer true that everybody could teach them.

We must, then, very carefully distinguish the two propositions 'everybody can teach something to somebody' and 'everybody can teach anything to anybody'. We have schools, and make attendance at them compulsory, because the second proposition is false; we exaggerate the virtues and the necessity of schooling, because we fail to recognise the truth of the first proposition. Experiencing in his own youth the impact of the eighteenth-century German anti-schooling movement – he was himself mainly taught by his father – Goethe was moved to dismiss it as a 'pedagogical *dilettantism*'. 'The pedantry and heaviness of the masters appointed in the public schools,' he wrote, 'had probably given rise to this evil. Something better was sought for, but *it was forgotten how defective all instruction must be which is not given by persons who are teachers by profession.*'[6] Goethe understood clearly enough what was a principal source of the anti-schooling movement in his, as in our own time.[7] But he was led in reaction to enunciate too strong a principle, which came, however, to be taken as gospel, especially in Germany and the United States.

Even within the school, and anxious to avoid the exploitation of children in the old monitorial system, we do not ordinarily make anything like enough use of the fact that children can be better than teachers at teaching some things to some children. Children often understand the difficulties other children are experiencing better than their teacher can; children are often much more ready to ask questions of their fellow-children than of their teachers. Our schools have emphasised competition and worried about 'copying' to a degree which wastes the teaching capacity of children both in the same class and from higher classes. And this is to say nothing of the fact that children can learn by teaching.

The truth which gives force to Illich's support for 'de-schooling' is that many children learn more effectively out of school than in it, from their peers or their elders than from teachers. But the fact remains that outside the schoolroom they might never meet with what they particularly need to learn or anybody capable of teaching it to them. To abolish schools might make little difference to very bright children, if they have access to books and helpful parents. But it would certainly make a great difference to children who do not possess these advantages. There is much to be said for decentralising teaching and for bringing into the teaching process those who do not wish to devote their lives to teaching but still have a particular contribution to make. (The tendency of the last century has been precisely the reverse – to close the schools to all but trained teachers, to centralise teaching in schools.) But schools and trained teachers are none the less necessary.

The falsity of the proposition that anybody can teach anything to anybody is what justifies teacher-training. Recognising this, we might still be attracted by the view that it is quite unnecessary to train teachers, except by teaching them *what* they are going to teach. The attempt to set up courses on teaching methods, one must certainly admit, leads as often as not to the collecting together of mere trivialities at the level of 'always adjust your teaching to the level of the children you are teaching'. These trivialities can acquire force in practice-teaching: there is sometimes a real point in telling a particular teacher-in-training that he is forgetting how little the children know, or that he is going too fast. Many University teachers, indeed, are incompetent because nobody has ever told them that they are inaudible, or that what they write on the board is invisible, or that they take too much for granted. But it is not surprising that teachers are often completely contemptuous of the intellectual content of the teacher-training they have had – even when they are prepared to admit the value of practice-teaching. Things that can usefully be said to people, in a particularised form, in criticism of their skill may be quite empty when they are written down as very general principles.[8]

It does not follow, however, although the idea has its attractions, that except as practice-teaching, the training of teachers ought to be abolished, that for the rest, teachers should simply be selected out of those who have been well-educated, with no further ado. Indeed, teacher-training should perhaps be extended to the training of University teachers. For one thing, before anybody begins to teach a subject he ought to be encouraged *to think about it in a particular way*, to ask himself what is the point of teaching it at all, by what criteria he is to judge his success in teaching it, what part it plays in the general education of a child, what pupils can get out of it who are not going to take it as their career. These are not questions which are at all likely to be raised in the course of a University education. (Admittedly, they are often not adequately discussed in teacher-training courses either.) Secondly, teaching particularly difficult subjects or handicapped persons is an expert capacity and can be learnt in the manner of any other expert capacity. This is true, at least, of some sorts of handicap. Others call upon a tolerance, a capacity for sympathetic understanding, a willingness to respond to tentative gestures, which are not forms of expertise. But even to become clear about such distinctions is to have made a certain progress as a teacher. There are, too, special 'problems in method' – problems in teaching children to read, or in teaching foreign languages – where the teacher needs to be clear about, and to have some way of deciding between, alternative procedures. It is nevertheless salutary for anyone who is engaged in training teachers always to remember that everybody teaches and that some untrained people teach extremely well. That may discourage attempts to make a mystique out of teaching, to build up a set of knacks into 'principles of education', perhaps with the help of a language especially designed to make the trivial sound profound.

If the teacher-trainer remembers the triadic character of teaching, this will help him, in particular, to avoid the temptation – so widespread in the last part of the nineteenth century when teachers of education were commonly known as 'masters of method' – to suppose that there must be some single method, *the* method of teaching, which is applicable in the teaching of any subject to any pupil. There may, of course, be such a method, just as there may be some nostrum which will cure anybody of any disease. I have done nothing to *demonstrate* that there is not. But considering the diversity of what is taught and the diversity of those who are taught, it is, to put the matter mildly, highly unlikely that there is a single method. To judge from history, the attempt to formulate such a method leads either to a mechanical, artificial approach to teaching, as in the so-called 'Herbartian lesson plan', or the vacuity of teachers' manuals.

Reacting against the view that there is a single method of teaching, universally applicable, we may be led to conclude that the teacher has no other rôle than to provide his students with the conditions in which they can learn. But to take this view is to underplay the rôle of the teacher. When he demonstrates to a class how to do something, for example, he is doing a great deal more than, in a fashionable phrase, 'facilitating learning'. A parent 'facilitates learning' when he provides a quiet room for a child to work in, or arranges for him access to a library; a teacher goes far beyond this. The educational theorist J.E. Adamson once wrote that 'the whole business [of learning] is between the individual and his worlds, and the teacher is outside it, external to it ... Within that mysterious synthetic activity through which the individual is at once appropriating and contributing to his environment, forming and being formed by it ... the teacher has neither place nor part.'[9] What Adamson is saying is partly true, leaving aside the neo-Kantian vocabulary in which he expresses it. It is true that the pupil has to do the learning. It is true, too, that what he learns about, or learns to do, is 'in the world'; it is not his object to learn about the activities or the intentions of the teacher. But the fact remains that although what the child learns about is independent of the teacher, he learns it *through* the teacher. The child learns Newton's laws of motion through the statements of the teacher; he learns French *as* the language spoken by his teacher, even though what he learns – unless he is badly taught – is not simply to utter the sentences his teacher has uttered. In the end, the teacher drops out of the process of learning; the child does not learn his teacher's French but French.* But that does not make the teacher the less essential. To emphasise that anybody can teach and that 'teaching' is not the name of a peculiar method is by no means to reduce the teacher to a merely passive rôle.

To turn now to the 'something' and the 'somebody' in '*X* teaches something to somebody'. First for the 'somebody'. Can everybody be taught? It is a purely empirical question, of course, whether and how much particular individuals can learn. The truth of the matter, with the obvious provisos, would seem to be that everybody can learn in the same sense that everybody can teach – from which it does not follow that everybody can learn everything. All I can say on this point is that teachers have a moral duty not to abandon hope – to be constantly in search of changes in procedures which will have the effect that they can teach those children they now find unteachable, can initiate them into worthwhile activities into which they cannot yet see ways of initiating them. There is a danger that teachers will simply give up, confronted with the problems of mass schooling, and

---

* With an eye on such facts the teacher is sometimes called a catalyst; the comparison is an inexact one, but what is meant is true.

pretend to be teaching when they are simply acting as custodians. (They may tell us that what they are doing is 'developing the child's personality'.)

A somewhat more general point arises if we ask whether what is to be substituted for 'somebody' in '*X* teaches something to somebody' is the name of a person or of a class. In many of the classics of education – Locke's *Some Thoughts Concerning Education* and Rousseau's *Emile* – it is presumed that 'somebody' must stand for an individual child, taught in isolation from his fellows. Indeed, we might be tempted to argue somewhat as follows: only individuals can learn, hence teaching can only be the teaching of individuals. Admitting that there are many things that can be done to a class as well as to an individual pupil – both an individual pupil and a class can, for example, be detained after normal hours – it might still be argued that a class cannot be *taught*, that when it is said that 'Jones teaches mathematics to that class' this is only an abbreviation for 'Jones teaches mathematics to Smith, Brown, Robinson, etc.'. And such practical conclusions are sometimes drawn from this argument as that the Oxford tutorial system must be the best way of teaching, that small classes must be better than large classes, that the ideal University would be a teacher and pupil sitting at opposite ends of a log.

But it would certainly be wrong to suppose that the 'real' teaching relationship is between a teacher and each individual member of the class, if this is taken to mean that when a teacher addresses himself to a member of that class he is only teaching that particular child. (From which it would follow that a member of a class of thirty inevitably wastes most of his time, since the teacher is often addressing someone else; the smaller the class the more teaching for each pupil, etc.) That is the importance of Dewey's emphasis on the classroom as a social institution; both what the teacher can teach and how well he can teach it are influenced by the structure of the class, the types of children it contains, the way it is selected and organised, its place in the school. To teach a child by himself is very different from, and not necessarily superior to, teaching him in a class. If teaching were identical with 'talking at', class-teaching would inevitably be inferior. But even in an authoritarian class, the pupil can learn from the questions his fellow-pupils ask and from his teacher's reaction to them. Where discussion is encouraged, this is even more obviously so. And if the class is broken up into sub-groups for collaborative work he has even more to gain. In such a group, he can learn how to explain himself, to communicate, to understand, to criticise and to receive criticism – *can* learn, to be sure, not *will* learn, for such learning is not automatic, as is sometimes supposed. It will be perhaps best to say that what X teaches is *somebody-in-a-class*, treating the case where X is the sole person taught as a limiting case.

The question how that class is best constituted if the teaching is to be most effective, e.g. whether children can best be taught in a small or a large class, in a class of intellectual equals or in a diversified class, is an empirical one. It need only be observed, once more, that there might well be no answer to it in its general form. Some children may learn better in small classes, some in bigger classes; some with their intellectual equals, some in diversified classes; some subjects may be best taught in a certain type of class, others in a different type of class. Considering the great diversity of what can be taught and of the pupils to whom it is taught, this is, at least, what we should *expect* to find.

What of the 'something' in 'human beings teach something to somebody-in-a-class'? So far, very conventionally, I have written as if the 'something' were ordinarily a subject. But the idea of a 'subject' is obscure. Of course, we can define a subject in entirely practical terms, which are by no means obscure; we can say that a subject is whatever has a period allocated to it in the school week. Then it is obvious that, for example, physical training, religious instruction, English, French, mathematics, physics, history, geography are all 'subjects', and so can be typewriting, cooking, driving, or anything else to which a teacher cares to devote an hour of school time. But there is another, narrower, sense of subject, analysed, for example, by Hirst in his essay 'The logical and psychological aspects of teaching a subject', where he describes a subject as something that has a 'logical grammar' and is governed by 'logical principles in terms of which the explanation and theories distinctive of the subject are validated'.[10] On this showing, very many, perhaps most, of what appear as 'subjects' in a school timetable will not be subjects at all. Skills, like cooking or typewriting, do not, on the face of it, have a 'logical grammar' or 'logical principles of validation'. No doubt we proverbially say that 'the proof of the pudding is in the eating', but what is used to 'validate' cookery is certainly not a logical principle, not even in that very generous sense of the word 'logical' characteristic of Hirst-style British philosophy. English and French, as distinct from English and French grammar, do not seem to be 'Hirstian subjects' either. (One reason why the teaching of English and French *grammar* has often been substituted, so oddly, for the teaching of children to write English and French is that it looks to be more intellectually respectable, making of English and French something more like a 'subject' in Hirst's sense of the word.) Hirst himself mentions three subjects: mathematics, physics and history.[11] But I should question whether even learning history involves 'learning the use of a network of related concepts', let alone whether there are any methods of explanation peculiar to history or any logically special way of 'validating propositions' about 'the economic effects of the [corn] laws, the famine in Ireland, the political policy of Peel and so on'. With an occasional exception in ancient and medieval history, the concepts of history are the concepts of everyday life, the methods of explanation are everyday methods, and logically speaking – although they may involve peculiar technical problems – so are the methods of validation.[12] We are left in fact with mathematics and physics out of Hirst's list; we might wish to add other sciences.

This being so, it is sufficiently obvious that if we limit the concept of a subject in this somewhat special way, it is only rarely that when someone is teaching he is teaching a 'subject'. For that reason, we might be attracted by the suggestion that we should replace the schema '*X* teaches something to somebody' by the schema '*X* teaches somebody to φ' where 'to' no longer acts as a preposition but as the sign of an infinitive. This has the further advantage that it raises the question exactly what the teacher is actually hoping to achieve when he sets out to teach a subject. So we might say of someone that 'he teaches children to understand the nature of science' or that 'he teaches children to be scientists' or 'he teaches children to think critically about the impact of science on society', rather than, much less revealingly, 'he teaches science'.

In reaction against the rigid formal teaching of artificially-formalised 'subjects', this way of thinking came to the fore in the second quarter of the present century, in the writings of, for example, John Dewey and T.P. Nunn. But although it is true that in teaching subjects the teachers are always teaching pupils to do this or that, and although it is important to ask, in relation to any subject, exactly *what* they are teaching their pupils to do, it would be quite wrong to suppose that all they can do when they teach is to teach a student to do something. They are commonly teaching him, among other things, *facts*. And even if learning these facts sometimes helps the student to do various things, this need not be the case; their interest and importance as *facts*, e.g. the fact that the world is in motion, may be quite independent of the value of anything they help the pupil to do.

Hirst is right, too, in emphasising that subjects can have formal structures, which the child has to learn to accommodate himself to and to appreciate. The emphasis on activities can easily lead to a somewhat scatterbrained approach to learning, as Dewey himself came to realise. The view that what is taught, always, is how to do something is as untenable as the view that what is taught, always, is a formally structured subject. The range of what can be substituted for 'something' in '*X* teaches something' is, indeed, too great to be summed up in any single word less vague than 'something'. A person is teaching when he is imparting facts, cultivating habits, instructing in skills, developing capacities or awakening interests, teaching someone to swim or to appreciate classical music, how a moon-rocket works, or that, and why, the planets move around the sun. So let us leave our 'something' stand; it will, indeed, be my constant theme that we should not try to replace it by an expression with a more limited range of application. To sum up, then, I shall be talking about the sorts of things somebody – most commonly a professional teacher – can teach to somebody-in-a-class. 'Sorts of things' in the most general sense.

NOTES

[1] Israel Scheffler *Reason and Teaching* (London 1973), p. 67.

[2] R.H. Crossman, *Plato Today* (London 1937), pp. 71f. This passage is cited by Karl Popper in *The Open Society and Its Enemies*, 4th ed. (New York 1962), vol. 2, pp. 16-17 as part of his critique of 'essentialism'. See also his notes in vol. 2, pp. 293-4. But I cannot entirely agree with what Popper says on this theme, as will be apparent from my observations: verbal clarifications are, I think, a *little* more important than he allows.

[3] Ludwig Wittgenstein, *Philosophical Investigations*, 1, 70.

[4] Maria Montessori, *The Child in the Family*, trans. N.R. Cirillo (New York 1970), p. 138.

[5] Michael Oakeshott, 'Learning and teaching', in R.S. Peters (ed.), *The Concept of Education* (London 1967), p. 159.

[6] J.W. von Goethe, *Dichtung und Warheit*, trans. John Oxenford as *The Autobiography of Johann Wolfgang von Goethe* (London 1971, repr. 1974) p. 27 (my italics).

[7] See, for example, Everett Reimer, *School is Dead* (Hamondsworth 1971), or Paul Goodman, *Growing up Absurd* (London 1970).

[8] Compare James D. Koerner, *The Miseducation of American Teachers* (Boston 1963).

[9] J.E. Adamson, *The Individual and the Environment* (London 1921), p. 27.

[10] P.H. Hirst, 'The logical and psychological aspects of teaching a subject', in *The Concept of Education*, p. 59.

[11] A rather different, broader, view is sketched in his 'Liberal education and the nature of knowledge', included in R.S. Peters, *The Philosophy of Education* (Oxford 1973), pp. 87-110.

[12] Compare John Passmore, 'Explanation in everyday life, in science, and in history', reprinted in G.H. Nadel [ed.], *Studies in the Philosophy of History* (New York 1965), from *History and Theory*, II, 2, pp. 105-23.

PART II

The Grammar of Pedagogy

Chapter Three
Developing Capacities

In the course of his life, whether as a result of experience, of imitation or of deliberate teaching, every human being acquires a number of capacities for action. Abnormal cases apart, he will learn to walk, to run, to speak, to feed and clothe himself; in literate societies he will learn to read, to write, to add; particular individuals will learn to drive a car, to play the piano, to repair diesel engines, to titrate, to dissect. Some of these capacities he normally acquires before he enters school; others he may acquire through a system of apprenticeship, may teach himself or be taught by a friend. But many of them are learnt in schools.

It is a tempting view, indeed, that teaching simply consists in helping pupils to acquire such capacities and that learning consists in acquiring them. So Max Black has suggested that 'all education aims, in the first instance, at "know-how".'[1] And certainly such other objectives as the development of tastes, the inculcation of habits, the arousing of interests, the imparting of information, all rest on capacities. To form the habit of quoting accurately, one must first learn how to copy a sentence; to develop a taste for poetry one must first learn how to understand a language; an interest in mathematics grows out of a capacity to solve mathematical problems; to acquire information one must be capable of listening, reading, observing.

This is an important fact. To keep it firmly in mind helps to dispel any suggestion that to train the child in order to develop his capacities is improper, that – since, inevitably, the teacher largely decides in what the pupil is to be trained – it treats the pupil as a mere instrument of the school or, beyond the school, of industry or some other social force. For whatever else teachers are trying to do, however idealistic or however radical their aims, whether they hope to encourage their pupils to appreciate literature or to understand the world around them, to change society or to express themselves more adequately, they will have to develop the child's capacities through a measure of training. To learn how to do anything at all is to submit to a degree of discipline.

Take the case of self-expression. This is sometimes envisaged as an outpouring of internal resources, in relation to which the teacher has the rôle, only, of a sympathetic listener. But pupils who cannot effectively communicate or effectively act cannot express themselves; they cannot make it plain to others who and what they are. Self-expression entails a control over language or some other form of expression, a control which rests on discipline. If young men and women, convinced that they are expressing themselves, sometimes write or talk so vaguely, so obscurely, with so confined a vocabulary, so limited a control over their means of expression, that nothing comes through to us when we listen to them except that some sort of internal rumbling is going on, a kind of spiritual flatulence, it is because their teachers have abdicated their responsibilities. Middle-class pupils may not suffer, because they learn to communicate in their own family; it is precisely the 'disadvantaged' who suffer when they do not acquire the disciplines inherent in successful communication – or, more broadly, in deliberate action.

Paradoxical as this may sound, a pupil learns to express himself not by talking about himself but by talking about other things; his interests, his concerns, his passions are what he is, and they are for the most part directed not towards himself but towards something outside himself. Except in a pathologically self-absorbed society, pupils will be largely uncommunicative about themselves, clear and vivid when they are talking about the objects of their affection. Similarly, when they show what they are by their mode of action, that action is other-directed; its expressiveness is revealed, not through any sort of self-concern, but through the style it displays, as the tennis-player shows what he is through the style of his play or a mechanic through the style of his work. This is the true sense in which 'le style, c'est moi': not that my style is something I arbitrarily choose but that the style reveals the man.

To emphasise capacities, however, still leaves one free to argue that the importance of the element of know-how, if 'in the first instance' essential, is in the long run limited and that to acquire it alone will often be either fruitless or dangerous. To have a capacity is one thing, to be willing to exercise it is quite another. I am not suggesting that there can never be any point in acquiring a capacity unless we propose to exercise it. Acquiring a capacity can help us to judge the capacity of others, to sympathise with their problems, to recognise their achievements. We may not wish to become scientists but still be glad that, in and through acquiring a measure of scientific capacity, we have learnt what it is like to be a scientist; we may not wish to become a footballer but still be glad that by learning how to play the game we have made of ourselves an informed spectator.

In a great many cases, however, teaching a 'know-how' is pointless unless the pupil is interested in exercising the capacity in question. The teacher cannot rest content, then, merely because the 'know-how' has been acquired. If it has been acquired resentfully, to satisfy an examiner, his work has almost certainly been in vain. ('Almost certainly', because what has been learnt resentfully is *sometimes* a source of satisfaction in later life.) A gym-instructor may compel his pupils to perform with some degree of adequacy a set of keep-fit exercises. But he has failed as a teacher if this is at the cost of persuading them that to be unfit is preferable to enduring the tedium of exercise. Neither can the science teacher be content if his pupils leave school convinced that science is the dreariest sort of pointless manipulation, even if they have mastered these manipulations. Teaching 'know-how' as if it were an end in itself can, indeed, be a source of deep antipathies not only to particular forms of activity but to schooling as a whole.

I have already granted, admittedly, that a pupil can develop an interest in an activity through acquiring a capacity in relation to it. The interest need not come first; the child can become interested by successfully doing – or perhaps by failing to do, if his failure presents a challenge to him. The medial stages in acquiring a capacity, furthermore, are often boring by their very nature, except to those for whom any sort of accomplishment is a personal triumph. However the child is taught, he cannot expect to acquire a capacity without being bored some of the time. But none of these considerations entitles the teacher to ignore the question whether he is developing in the child any interest, at least a spectatorial interest, in exercising the capacity he is acquiring.

Furthermore, the acquisition of know-how, divorced from wider concerns, can be not only useless but dangerous. That is most obvious in relation to communicative skills. The popular mistrust of glibness is not a mere prejudice; the salvationist, political or religious, the huckster, the media-created 'expert', are sufficient testimony to the damage that can be done by skills divorced from any sort of moral concern.

In Ancient Greece the great exponents of 'know-how' were the Sophists. Their emphasis on 'know-how' encouraged, so Plato argued, a mere cleverness which, divorced from scrupulousness, was a power for evil. Every 'know-how', Plato points out, is a 'capacity for opposites'. A doctor learns how to poison with drugs in the process of learning how to cure with their aid; a person trained in the analysis of propaganda is at the same time learning how best to be a propagandist. If a teacher thinks of the development of 'know-how' as his sole business, he runs the risk of unleashing monsters on the world. Or if not monsters, at best mere technical instruments. Although, as we admitted, the development in the child of habits, tastes, interests, knowledge, cannot be wholly divorced from the development of capacities, none of these is *reducible* to having such capacities. That is a point we shall often be emphasising in the chapters which follow.

The fact remains that the development of the child's capacities through training, if not by itself sufficient, is an important part of the teacher's work. The child needs to leave school having learnt to do certain things efficiently. This may seem to be so obvious as not to be worth saying. But in the non-Communist world to utter such a word as 'efficiency' is at once, in some quarters, to be self-exposed as a proponent of robot-schools. Let me, then, make another obvious remark. To argue that the schools have failed unless pupils learn how to perform efficiently some activities which they would not otherwise have performed so efficiently is not equivalent to maintaining that such efficiency is bound to be advantageous whatever the activities in question are, let alone that they ought to be job-oriented activities.[2]

Assuming, then, that one thing the school will do is to develop capacities, let us divide such capacities into two types: open and closed. A 'closed' capacity is distinguishable from an 'open' capacity in virtue of the fact that it allows of total mastery. Take, for example, the capacity to count. This anyone can learn to do, given adequate instruction and a modicum of intelligence, in such a way that no one could be better at it – quicker perhaps, but not better.

There are very many such closed capacities, some of them commonly learnt at home, others at school, others in the world at large. They are very important to us in our daily life. So the child learns at home to dress himself; at school to add and subtract; as he moves around he learns to find his way home to the place where he lives. All these capacities have to be learnt; an idiot may be unable to learn them; some people will exercise them more neatly, more expeditiously, more rapidly than others. But it would be absurd for a person to claim that he was 'better than anyone else in the world' in respect to them or, beyond a certain point, to go on trying to improve his performance.

In contrast, however good we are at exercising an 'open' capacity, somebody else – or ourselves at some other time – could do it better. Playing chess is an example, in contrast with playing noughts and crosses. It is possible completely to master noughts and crosses so that, except through sheer carelessness, one will never lose; it is impossible, in this sense, completely to master chess, although one can master certain types of opening and certain types of end-game. And yet chess is not, as is snakes and ladders, a game of chance. One can get better at playing chess as one cannot get better at playing snakes and ladders.

Not uncommonly, in connection with closed capacities, we can speak of 'learning the secret'. The small child, for example, does not realise that playing noughts and crosses is a closed capacity; but once he 'learns the secret' he can no longer lose. In the case of an open capacity there is no such secret to be learned. One cannot 'learn the secret' of writing poetry or of doing philosophy.

Closed capacities, it should be observed, can vary greatly in complexity. At the bottom level, they are what, following Ryle, we might call 'competencies'; the capacity to peel an apple, to tell the time, to use a calendar. At the top end, they may involve the mastery of relatively elaborate techniques, closed capacity may be piled on closed capacity. So, for example, the capacity to solve a class of extremely complex equations can be a closed competency, as can the capacity to paint in correct perspective or to operate a complicated machine.

To learn a closed capacity may therefore make considerable demands on students and require of them, during long periods of training, considerable concentration, vigilance and patience. Some of us may never master a particular closed capacity. Nevertheless, many closed capacities, unlike open capacities, can be converted with time into routines. So a worker in a factory can perform quite complex movements without thinking at all about what he is doing – even though at one time they took all his attention, as they would still take all *our* attention. In some cases, as in solving equations by a standard method, or indeed in adding up, human beings may never reach the stage of being able wholly to relax their vigilance. But the fact remains that a relatively simple machine can be programmed to carry out such tasks. It is only some imperfection on our part – some tendency to carelessness or absent-mindedness – which makes it impossible for us to act in a quasi-mechanical fashion, not the fact that we have to work out what we should do next in a quite fresh way.

How are closed capacities to be taught? The general answer is 'by training'. This involves giving the pupil opportunities for practice. He acquires capacities by acting; so far the slogan 'learn by doing' has its importance. But a pupil does not, of course, acquire competency *simply* by practice; he might go on forever practising the performance of a task in the wrong way, and so fail to acquire the capacity to perform it correctly. The teacher has a vital role: he does not simply say to the child: 'That is how to tell the time; now go away and practise.' He *demonstrates*: showing the child what to do. He *instructs*: saying what to do, perhaps with the aid of a general theory. He *corrects*: helping the child to see why he is wrong. He *praises*: letting the child know that what he is doing is correct. He *warns*: dissuading the child from acting in ways which will interfere with his acquiring the capacity in question.

Each of these tasks involves a great deal more judgment than is at first apparent. Take the case of *demonstration*. It is not enough, in most instances, to perform in front of pupils the act one wishes them to perform. When teaching children to write numbers, for example, a teacher does not simply go to a blackboard, write, and say to his class: 'Copy that.' He writes with a peculiar deliberateness, so as to make it clear, as rapid writing would not, how an 'eight' is formed, or a 'six'. Perhaps he talks as he demonstrates, talks about what he is doing. In demonstrating how to perform a chemical experiment, similarly, the teacher draws attention to the individual steps he is taking; he may describe them in words on the blackboard, or draw a sketch. 'Correction', similarly, may involve holding the child's hand as he writes a number, telling him what is wrong, or physically modifying the number the child has written. It is for the expert on teaching methods, not for the philosopher, to describe in detail such techniques of demonstration, instruction, correction, praise or warning, and to determine in what circumstances they are most effective. All I need remark is that training in closed capacities is itself an open capacity; there is always more to be learnt about how best to undertake it.

What about training in *open* capacities? That not uncommonly begins with training in closed capacities. It might be suggested, even, that this is as far as the teacher is able to go. For what is the test that a pupil has acquired an open capacity? The test is this: that the pupil can take steps which he has not been taught to take, which in some measure surprise the instructor, not necessarily in the sense they have never occurred to him or even in the sense that no other pupil has ever done such a thing before – such 'high-level' surprises are very rare – but in the sense that the teacher has not taught his pupil to take precisely that step and his taking it does not necessarily follow as an application of a principle in which the teacher has instructed him.* The pupil in other words has come to be, in respect to some exercise of some capacity, inventive. 'To do the unexpected, to do it

* There is an awkwardness here. One can speak of a person as having completely *mastered* a closed capacity. He has learnt how to count up to a hundred and that's that. But one cannot completely *master* an open capacity. Then at what point can one be said to have acquired it? At what point can it be accurately said of a pupil:

well, efficiently and at the right time' – these, according to an advertisement, are 'the hallmarks of a good Army officer' and, we might add, of any person who has acquired an open capacity.

Take the case of learning to speak French. On a traditional method of teaching, a child may for a long time simply do exercises. He repeats stock-sentences in stock-situations; he learns to say 'il fait beau' on fine days and 'il fait froid' on cold days, to point to the door and say 'la porte' or to the window and say 'la fenêtre'; given a sentence in French he learns to express it in the negative and to put it in the past tense. All these are closed competencies. A person can acquire them all, and many more, and yet still be incapable of speaking French. He can speak French only when he is not restricted to stock-phrases or a capacity to name objects but can use French to ask for what he wants, to express his own views, to issue his own instructions. This he does by uttering sentences he has never heard uttered. He has developed, we say, 'a feeling for the language', to however limited a degree. There are a great many comparable phrases – 'mathematical inventiveness', 'historical judgment', 'scientific imagination', 'literary sensitivity' – all of which suggest the acquisition of something other than a closed capacity, a capacity to act in a manner which is inventive.

These phrases, to some ears, have a quasi-mystical ring about them. So it is not surprising that their use has generated two very different reactions. The first, that they demonstrate the truth of the

---

'He can philosophise' or 'He can think like a mathematician' or 'He can write poetry'? Sometimes, a person says 'I can play chess' if he can do no more than go through a number of routine moves. So, similarly, a person might claim to be able to do mathematics if he can solve simultaneous equations, to philosophise if he can accurately reproduce a philosophical argument he has heard or to write poetry if he can compose a sonnet in regular form. But neither the mathematician, nor the philosopher, nor the poetry teacher would feel that such a pupil was as yet demonstrating his capacity to be a mathematician, a philosopher or a poet. We obviously wouldn't claim to be able to speak French merely on the ground that we can make proper use of the sentence: 'Je ne parle pas français.' On the other hand when we say that we can speak French we are not claiming that we understand every French sentence. No one is in that position. We may reply to the question 'Can you speak French?' in the affirmative if it is asked by a tourist who is in distress, in the negative if we are being asked to give an impromptu lecture in French. A school system has to make up its mind what level of capacity it is going to take as its objective. There is a minimum below which it has failed to teach the open capacity at all. But what the level ought to be, exactly when it should regard the pupil as having acquired a sufficient degree of capacity, is not something one can settle by an appeal to general principles. A student can be so trained in French that he can operate for himself in reading philosophy but without having the sort of training he would need to read a novel in contemporary argot or a particular dialect.

view I have already adumbrated – that open capacities cannot be taught. The teacher, it is then suggested, can prepare the way – by teaching closed capacities – for the pupil to develop various forms of 'feeling', 'sensitivity', 'judgment' but that is all he can do: these are inherent qualities, revealed by teaching, but not in any sense produced by it. This approach is naturally congenial to conservatives, who like to emphasise the part played in education by innate abilities. A second possible reaction comes from the other end of the spectrum: that all this talk about 'intuition' and 'sensitivity' is mere Romantic nonsense designed to conceal our ignorance. For the fact is, so the argument runs, that all capacities are, in principle, closed capacities. If some translations from the French, for example, are much better than others, this can only be, on this view, because the better translator has hit upon transformation-rules, naturally highly specific, which he himself, admittedly, cannot make explicit but which could in principle be formulated. They might, to take a case, have such a form as the following: when in French a person of a certain social class, in a particular social situation, uses the phrase, 'Mon Dieu', the correct English translation is not 'My God' but 'Well, I'm blessed'. With a different, definable, type of person and in a different, definable, situation it is 'Goodness me'.

When a philosopher argues[3] that it is always possible *in principle* to reduce an open capacity to a set of closed capacities, it is hard to frame a reply, as it always is when anybody says that something can be done *in principle*. One cannot but admit, furthermore, that the attempt to act in this way has had its great successes; many 'open capacities', or what appeared to be such, have been reduced to sets of closed capacities.

We can illustrate this point by an industrial example. In paper mills it is necessary to distinguish microscopically between paper samples in order to determine which is the better paper. This was once regarded as a 'connoisseurship' type of capacity. But it was broken down into a series of routine methods of discriminating. The effect is that instead of being wholly dependent on a few experts, the mills were able to employ large numbers of competent testers, relying not on 'connoisseurship' but on their capacity to carry out certain wholly masterable types of routine investigation. Quite generally, as science advances, 'science' in the broadest sense of the word, the number of closed capacities constantly increases, the area in which open capacities are called upon is correspondingly restricted. So in mathematics, let us say, even a very advanced pupil may still be learning new knacks. Is it anything more than an act of faith to claim that none the less not every form of capacity can be reduced to a complex set of closed capacities, that difference in level of mastery is not simply a difference in the number of closed capacities the greater master has, that inventiveness is not a mere temporary expedient?

To suggest, however, that there must be a masterable technique for coping with *every* type of situation is to commit oneself to the very large assumption that there is a limited range of possible cases and that it can always be immediately 'read off' what technique is the correct technique to apply in a given case. Consider even the very simple example cited above: the translation of the French 'Mon Dieu' into English. However many principles one tried to lay down for this translation, it is always logically possible for a new case to arise on which an individual decision has to be made. Changing social circumstances, or the imagination of a French novelist, can throw up new types of character for whom no provision has been made in the rules; changes in English conventions can make what used to be an appropriate translation into English no longer appropriate. 'Goodness me' may fade out of conversation; 'my God' may come to be more acceptable. What was at one time everybody's expletive can come to be the expletive of curates or, with a social movement in the opposite direction, only the expletive of the back-alleys. There are no general principles which would enable us to anticipate every such possible change and hence wholly to exclude the need for exercising a degree of judgment, or sensitivity, or a 'feeling for the language'. What linguistic principles could anticipate, to take an extreme example, the sentences of *Finnegans Wake* and lay down techniques in advance which a translator could automatically employ to translate them?

But if, for such reasons, it is not always possible to reduce closed capacities to open capacities, the question still remains, which we have raised but have not yet faced – and which still faces the teacher even if it be true that the distinction between closed and open capacities will, with the march of science, finally disappear – whether the teacher can do anything more than train in those closed capacities which are necessary, although by no means sufficient, for developing an open capacity. He can, let us say, teach a child how to play chess, in the sense that he can teach him how to put the pieces on a chess-board, what moves are permissible and what moves impermissible, how to be sure of winning – failure of concentration apart – from a certain end-position, how best immediately to follow up a particular opening. But beyond that point can he do anything more than say 'Now go ahead with my blessing', leaving the child to develop his chess-playing capacity by experience? Isn't it paradoxical to suppose that the teacher can teach a child to go beyond what he has been explicitly taught? Yet doesn't an open capacity involve precisely such a power of going beyond? This is the problem Ryle raised in his essay, 'Teaching and training'.[4]

It is clear, in the first place, that a child cannot be dragooned into making his own spontaneous moves. He can be compelled to follow a routine; he can be compelled, for example, to play football once a week. But he cannot be compelled to play an enterprising game of football. He has not begun to acquire an open, as distinct from a closed, capacity until he begins to take some pleasure in his achievement.

Liking, in some measure, what he is doing the child is prepared to try out new ways of acting. So he tries to read words he has not been taught to read; in the gymnasium he performs feats he has not been taught to perform. Even in acquiring the more complex sorts of closed capacity, such experimenting may no doubt facilitate learning. Yet it is not in the same degree essential. Although a child may learn how to solve simultaneous equations by inventing equations of his own and trying to solve them, he can do quite as well by coping with the examples set for him by his teacher or his textbook. But unless he 'tries his hand' at speaking French, tries to say things he wants, of his own accord, to say, he will never learn to speak the language, just as if he never writes English sentences which he has not previously read he will never learn to be a writer.

In the process, of course, he will make a great many mistakes. This is one point at which the teacher can help. Of the five methods of teaching closed competencies – demonstration, instruction, correction, praise and warning – the last three are as applicable to open as to closed capacities. In trying to acquire an open capacity, a child will almost certainly exhibit a certain degree of wildness, guessing beyond the points at which guessing is profitable, trying out tricks in a gymnasium which are physically dangerous, putting forward historical and scientific hypotheses which, in the light of the known facts, are merely reckless.

Here the teacher is faced with one of his greatest difficulties. He has himself to exercise judgment, not determined by any fixed rules or principles. On the one side, he has learnt from experience, or from his own teachers, or from reading, that certain procedures are wasteful or fruitless or dangerous. It would be wholly absurd, in the supposed interests of spontaneity, to let that experience count for nothing, to let the child discover by experience that chlorine is dangerous to the lungs or nitric acid to the hands. The child has to learn, and might as well be told, that writing is subject to conventions, that scientific and historical hypotheses are constrained by facts.

Yet, on the other side, too much prudence, too much determination to protect the child, may prevent him from acquiring a capacity. The child may never learn to ride a bicycle if he is wholly protected from falling; never develop any capacity as a scientist if his fresh ideas are denounced as reckless; never learn to write if his imaginative attempts to do so are too conscientiously corrected. In admonishing 'No, don't do it that way', the teacher, furthermore, will sometimes be at fault. The child, or more probably the undergraduate, may be opening up a new path. What the teacher supposes to be a fixed convention of writing that particular pupil will help to break down; what the teacher supposes to be a reliable test that particular pupil will show not to be reliable.

In recent times, we have become very conscious of the dangers involved in warning and correcting the young; we have so often had to face a situation in which established conventions have been overthrown, established theories rejected, generally accepted methods proved to be unreliable, that we have lost confidence in our capacity to distinguish between recklessness and daring, conventions and principles, the reliable and the unreliable. The Romantic obsession with spontaneity, originality, individuality has replaced the classical obsession with tradition, care and craftsmanship. 'Academic' has come to be a term of abuse, and the art-teacher's fear that he might stifle a rare genius in the bud disturbs his sleep much more than the fear that his pupils will learn nothing at all from his teaching.

There are no rules which will enable the teacher to determine when, and with what pupils, he needs above all to encourage, to inspire with confidence, and when, above all, he needs to warn, correct and advise. But if, in reaction to that fact, the teacher no longer warns, corrects and advises, he is abdicating his function as a teacher. He is not, in so doing, helping the child to develop an open capacity; to write English well, to read well, to discuss well, a pupil will *need* advice and correction.

The teacher, then, has at least a corrective role to play in helping the child to acquire open capacities. But that is not his sole function. Open capacities, we suggested, rest upon and incorporate closed capacities; these the child has to be taught. It does not follow that he must be taught them first. In the older tradition of teaching that was the assumption. In the school science course, the child was to acquire established techniques; later, it was supposed, he might blossom out into being an imaginative scientist. Writing school essays, he had to learn to conform to the established conventions, later he might blossom out into being an author. And so with mathematics, history, and the other subjects in the curriculum.

The effect, often enough, was that his pupils were so wearied by the endless preliminaries, or so disheartened by the teacher's criticisms, as 'premature', of any attempt to think for themselves, that they were completely bored by their school-life and certainly not attracted by the prospect of becoming scientists or writers. There is not the slightest reason why children should not learn disciplines and conventions, techniques and routines, in close connection with their attempts to act spontaneously.

Take a simple case. Before allowing a pupil to play a game of tennis, a tennis coach might insist on his spending months practising separate shots. Very roughly – except that the months often spread into years – this was how foreign languages were taught when the child was made to spend months, or years, learning how to translate individual English sentences into grammatical French sentences, without being allowed to speak or write continuous French. But a good tennis coach does not operate in this way. He intersperses attempts to develop certain closed capacities in his pupils – the capacity to hold their racquet in a certain way, to stand in the correct position to receive – with attempts on the pupils' part to play tennis, attempts in the course of which they will certainly, unless they are reluctant pupils, try to do things they have not done before. Nor will he try, as they display enterprise, at once to correct them at every step. Even should they be reluctant there is at least some hope that this experience of playing in a game will break down their reluctance, as hours of practice are unlikely to do.

In the same way, a science master can, from an early stage in his teaching, offer his pupils an opportunity to think up explanations for themselves, to try to think out ways of testing proposed explanations, to criticise suggested explanations. The English teacher can encourage spontaneous writing or spontaneous talk, adjusting his criticism to the stage the child has reached in his development. From the fact that the skilful practice of open capacities depends upon the mastery of closed capacities it does not follow, then, that the closed capacities must be taught first.

Neither the Romantic view that the child should simply be encouraged to go ahead, learning techniques, acquiring closed capacities as he feels the need for them, nor the traditional view that he should concentrate entirely on learning the closed capacities until he is 'mature enough' to exercise his own initiative, does justice to the pedagogical situation. It is as if the tennis coach were simply to let his pupils play until they asked him how to do this or that – by which time they will no doubt have already learnt to do many things the wrong way – or as if on the other hand he were to forbid them to enter the tennis court until they had spent years in practice. The exercise of initiative, the practice of techniques, ought to be thought of, rather, as alternating phases in the acquisition of an open capacity. Otherwise, the pupil may well leave school, or even university, without ever realising that, let us say, mathematics is anything but a set of closed capacities. Or alternatively he may leave without ever having acquired the closed capacities which he needs in order to exercise an open capacity as a means of solving problems, or cultivating an interest, or advancing his understanding.

Are demonstration and instruction only of use in relation to teaching a closed capacity? One is inclined, at first, to think so. For how is it possible to *demonstrate* to a child procedures one does not want him simply to imitate, or to *instruct* him how to go beyond anything he has been explicitly told to do? The fact remains that demonstration if in a somewhat special form has its part to play in the development of open capacities.

Take the use of demonstration in the teaching of painting. It is generally agreed that in an art school creative artists should spend part of their time doing their own work, in the presence of pupils. This is not in order to demonstrate how, let us say, to paint in perspective. Teaching a class how to produce a certain perspective effect, it will not worry the teacher if his pupils copy precisely what he is doing; that is exactly what he may want them to do. But he is certainly not teaching them to paint creatively if they go away from watching him paint and then paint exactly what he painted – any more than a philosopher is teaching a class to philosophise if as a result of having freely philosophised in front of them, they go away and reproduce exactly what he said and argued. The function of such a demonstration is to inspire, to show what it is like to paint or to philosophise, to generate a particular kind of excitement, to *be* an example as distinct from *setting* an example.

Instruction is of more limited usefulness in teaching open capacities. It tends, in practice, to take the form of exhortation. Heraclitus warns us to 'expect the unexpected'; a teacher may say as much to his pupils. He may say to them, too: 'Don't simply take it for granted that the methods I have taught you are the best methods'; 'Don't let yourself get into a rut.' But such exhortation is unlikely to be effective unless the teacher is at the same time demonstrating in his own person what it is like to be innovative.

Teaching is an open capacity, to which these general principles apply. We can look again at teacher-training in the light of this fact. In the first place, there is no question of anyone ever 'mastering' teaching, discovering a 'secret' which will rule out the possibility of his ever failing to teach a child successfully. There is no such thing as having nothing further to learn about teaching, or of the teacher reaching a point at which he has rules for dealing with every situation which can possibly arise. So it is no objection to a course of training that at the end of it a potential teacher has not completely mastered the art of teaching, any more than it is an objection to a tennis-coaching course that at the end of it the pupils have not mastered tennis.

Secondly, teachers must have an opportunity to practise, to 'try their hand'. Often enough, the period of 'practice-teaching' stops far too soon, partly as a consequence of the absurd presumption that at the end of his training a teacher should have completely mastered teaching, be in no need of further training.

Thirdly, even though teaching is an open capacity, teachers will need to be instructed in certain knacks, 'closed capacities'. How many such techniques there are in the case of teaching is another matter. Most of them, I have already suggested, are related to the teaching of special subjects or special classes of students rather than to teaching in general. So the mathematics teacher-in-training can be taught how best to introduce his pupils to the calculus; the foreign language teacher-in-training how best to improve the pronunciation of his pupils. Unlike books on repairing cars, books on 'teaching methods' do not contain very much in the way of definite techniques which the teacher can employ in a quasi-mechanical way. Some teachers object to the mere idea that there can be such techniques. But the discovery of a general technique is a considerable advance; it makes a method generally available, it raises the level of the weaker teachers. If the teacher-in-training could be better prepared in advance for the problems he is going to meet, as a doctor is prepared in advance for the treatment of medical problems, this could only be a service to him. This is so even though he cannot be prepared for *every* problem, cannot be put in a position in which he will never need to exercise his judgment.

Fourthly, highly generalised instruction is unlikely to be of much use to him, the sort of generalised instruction one finds in those textbooks on method which fall half way between the 'philosophy of teaching', in the popular rather than the professional sense of that phrase, and a practical handbook, with the vices of both and the virtues of neither. Demonstration, on the other hand, has a distinct usefulness. The trainer of teachers who instructs his pupils to be innovative but whose own classes are stodgy and conventional is unlikely to have any profound effect on them; from watching a good teacher, on the other hand, they can learn a great deal.

Like everyone else setting out to acquire an open capacity, teachers, too, can be warned and corrected, advised that particular methods will almost certainly produce undesirable effects. In this instance, no doubt, there are difficulties of a sort which do not attach to all open capacities. In the case of medicine, for example, there is almost complete agreement about what is to count as an undesirable effect. No one denies that doctors should be warned against a treatment for pneumonia which kills or incapacitates the patients who are submitted to it.

In special cases like psychiatry, however, the situation is by no means so clear. Teaching, in this respect, resembles psychiatry. In the eyes of conservative teachers, so to teach children as to encourage them to criticise the society in which they are living is to produce an undesirable effect, against which the potential teacher should be warned. Radical teachers see matters quite otherwise; for them, the potential teacher has rather to be warned that a particular way of teaching is likely to encourage docility, obedience to authority. All the same, there are corrections and warnings from which *any* potential teacher has something to gain, warnings and corrections which even the trail-blazer will need to take to heart. His writing on the board, his speech, can be criticised and improved; attention can be drawn to his mannerisms, to his tendency to do too much of the talking, to show favouritism, to ignore the quieter and duller child.

Finally, and most difficult of all, the trainer of teachers has to encourage, to communicate enthusiasm, to sustain interest, to counteract depression. In acquiring any open capacity, the pupil is subject to fits of discouragement when he seems to be making no further progress, to periods of frustration, boredom, or resentment. The art of training a teacher includes, as an important ingredient, a willingness to act, in such a situation, as a sympathetic counsellor. So much is true, of course, in all teaching.

I have still not faced the question what capacities the schools ought to try to develop. Nor, in its fullest extent do I propose to do so, to defend in detail a specific capacity-curriculum. There are, however, certain general criteria which have to be insisted upon; they flow from the character of capacities and the nature of learning as a lifetime activity.

From the standpoint of lifetime learning, open capacities obviously have distinct advantages over closed capacities. To have learnt to play chess is to be in a position to learn more over a lifetime about playing chess, in a sense in which having learnt to play noughts and crosses is not to be prepared to learn more, over a lifetime, about playing noughts and crosses. At the same time, the distinction between open and closed capacities is not the only one we need for our present purposes; there is also a distinction to be made – even if the boundaries, as the very terminology suggests, are not sharp – between 'broad' capacities and 'narrow' capacities.

The two modes of classification do not coincide in their membership. A capacity can be open but useful only in a narrow range of circumstances, closed but useful in a wide range of circumstances. Although chess is an open capacity, it is, on the face of it, a narrow capacity. It can be employed, that is, only in a narrow range of social situations, those in which one wishes to play an intellectually challenging game. No doubt, it has subsidiary employments – as, for example, the source of metaphors, analogies, illustrations. ('He was only a pawn in the great game of espionage.') But this use is relatively unimportant. In contrast, the capacity to count is both broad and closed.

Any educational curriculum which recognises the importance of preparing the child for life-long learning will particularly concentrate on capacities which are both open and broad. Not that it will entirely ignore closed capacities. For, as I have already emphasised, open capacities are normally founded upon closed capacities. And, as well, a particular closed capacity may be so broad that a school would be foolish to ignore it; the capacity 'to tell the time' is another obvious, elementary, instance.

Of course, there can be arguments about whether a capacity is in fact broad. There are educational systems in which chess-playing forms part of the normal curriculum. Learning to play chess, it is then supposed, prepares the child for acting rationally in a wide range of situations – all those situations which involve adopting a strategy.

From William James onwards, the concept of a 'transfer of training' which is here involved has, deservedly, been subjected to a great deal of criticism. It is often fraudulently appealed to in order to justify the retention of particular forms of capacity-development in the school curriculum when the original reasons for teaching them no longer hold good. At the same time, unless transfer of some sort is possible, even closed capacities could not be taught, or at least they could be taught only in such a ridiculously closed form as not to be worth teaching. 'In its broadest sense,' as this point has been put, '*transfer of learning is basic to the whole notion of schooling.*'[5] A child learns to add, not merely to add six and seven. And this is because he can transfer methods he has acquired in doing particular additions – or a principle he has learnt, if that is how he has been taught – to doing other additions. So one cannot rule out the possibility that when a school appears to be emphasising a narrow capacity, it is actually training in a broad capacity. But one should certainly demand direct evidence that this is so, that expert chess players, let us say, are in fact more skilled in making a wide range of decisions outside a chess-game than are those who have not studied chess, and that this does not derive from the fact that they have been initially selected in a particular way. To point to resemblances between solving chess problems and solving other sorts of problems does not suffice to demonstrate that practice in the former capacity will develop the latter capacity; the resemblances may simply not be perceived as such by the chess-player. On the face of it, directly to teach games-theory or decision-theory would be far more effective.

Of all broad capacities, the capacity to learn is educationally the most fundamental. And even though schools do not create that capacity, they can do a great deal to develop it. The fundamental importance of teaching the traditional 'three Rs' derives from the fact that they are so central to learning in many areas. To have no mathematical capacity, even of an elementary sort, is to be debarred from acquiring a great many other capacities; not to be able to read is to be similarly debarred; writing is an important way of learning as well as of communicating what has been learned.

There was for a time a strong reaction among educational theorists against the systematic teaching of the 'three R's'. This is a reaction which was commonly justified on a number of grounds. First, that the 'three R's' are a relic of a past age, that they have now lost their former value as high-roads to learning; secondly, that the teacher should concentrate on other things, like developing the child's personality; thirdly, that to teach the 'three R's' is to try to impose middle-class values on children. To reply to these justifications would carry us far afield. But we can attempt a few brief observations. On the first point, one can certainly admit that the schools have now to pay more attention to visual methods of learning and teaching, and that in the past they have often paid insufficient attention to oral communication. The 'three R's' are insufficient. Pupils need to be taught how to learn by listening or by looking or by discussing as well as by reading, to do so critically and effectively. But to be able to read is still a fundamentally important way of learning. So is being able to calculate.

On the second point, there is no conflict between teaching to read and developing the child's personality, whatever this may be taken to mean. Reading is a path to freedom; not to be able to read is to be restricted to what one is told or is allowed to look at. Nowhere in the world is it safe to rely, only, on what is made visible on the television screen. That is to say nothing of the importance of reading as a path of entry into literature, literature of every sort and description. Similarly, although it might seem plausible to argue that now there are calculators one need no longer learn how to add, to take that view is to be at the mercy of machines. As for middle-class values, however much we may wish to reform our society, it is also important, as Marx for one clearly saw, to try to preserve what is good in it. Accuracy in reading, clarity in writing may be, like hard work, bourgeois virtues. But it is far from following that in a socialist society, reading, calculating, writing would be useless capacities – unless, indeed, they came to be forbidden as the source of 'dangerous thoughts'.

The 'three R's', as we said, by no means exhaust the open and wide capacities which are fundamental to learning. Learning how to look things up, learning how to use books and libraries, are obvious examples of a closely related sort. So is learning to talk, both in one's own and in foreign languages. Here the objection to 'imposing middle-class values' is most loudly heard. And certainly learning to communicate by talking is one thing, learning to talk with a 'standard' accent or in a 'standard' grammar is quite another. Often enough, the emphasis has been on the second at the cost of the first. On the other hand, it is a great handicap to a child if he cannot talk a broadly comprehensible form of English; the school should not abandon the task of making children members of as large a language community as possible. Otherwise, they are confined within very narrow boundaries. There is nothing novel in the idea of teaching pupils and encouraging them to talk freely in the language they daily hear around them while at the same time teaching them a standard form of the language. It has for long been the case, let us say, that children from a particular region of Italy or Germany learn both the dialectal and the standard form.*

Systems of education can properly be rebuked for teaching too few of the broad and open capacities needed by a life-long learner, but not for teaching any one of them. What other capacities they need to teach is a matter for argument. But that every child should be taught how to learn on as broad a front as possible can scarcely be a matter of

---

* The problem is an acute one, however, in those schools in which the children have a variety of dialects, as has often happened in recent years as a result of the movement from countryside to city.

dispute. It would be as foolish to say that the school is a preparation for learning as it is to say that it is a preparation for life, foolish insofar as just as the child lives *at* school, so he learns *at* school. But the motto 'the school is a preparation for learning' at least serves to emphasise that teaching to learn is the school's special business. So far as preparing the child for the general conduct of life is concerned, the school is only one of many competing institutions. But teaching to learn is something only the school seriously attempts, however ignominiously it often fails even in that relatively narrow province. And it is in itself a preparation for life, a fundamentally important preparation.

To sum up then, training in capacities is an important part of the school's task although not its only task. Its special interest is in those capacities which are both broad and open – and within that class in teaching to learn. Such capacities as the 'three Rs' are basic to teaching to learn. Whatever more specialised capacities the school ought to teach, whatever form its curriculum ought to take, for it to neglect the 'three Rs' is for it to neglect its fundamental business. And if it did nothing more than teach them effectively, as it is far from doing now and as is indeed extremely difficult to do, it would thoroughly justify its existence. At what level it ought to teach them, how many languages a child ought to be able to read, how complicated the calculations are in which the child can be expected to be proficient, how well we can expect him to write – these are questions no philosophical discussion can settle. Indeed the answer to them will differ from child to child, from time to time, from society to society.

NOTES

[1] Max Black, 'Rules and routines', in R. Peters (ed.), *The Concept of Education*, (London 1967), p. 92.

[2] The pressure to make them that sort of capacity is, of course, powerful. See Peter Herbst, 'Work, labour and university education', in R.S. Peters (ed.), *The Philosophy of Education*, pp. 58-74.

[3] See the discussion of such a programme in W.K. Richmond, *Teachers and Machines* (London and Glasgow, 1965), p. 60. One may take Descartes to be arguing thus, in respect to thinking.

[4] Gilbert Ryle, 'Teaching and training', in R.S. Peters (ed)., *The Concept of Education*, pp. 105-19.

[5] M.L. Bigge, *Learning Theories for Teachers* (New York 1964), pp. 243-4.

Chapter Four

Teaching to Acquire Information

Every normal adult has at his disposal a store of information, although its nature varies from person to person. Some of it is trivial in the extreme, of interest only within a narrow family circle: 'Your Aunt Agatha never liked baked turnips'; 'That's the third time our cat has had kittens'. From this level of banality it may ascend to information about the abstract relationships described in modern physics: 'In a system of particles, the total number of nucleon charges is always constant.'

Some philosophers would wish to restrict the concept of 'information' to a rather narrower range. They would deny that, for example, propositions about the number of nucleon charges give us information, as distinct from providing us with a formula for making physical calculations. To that point we shall return in a later chapter. For the moment, the widest possible definition of 'information' will best serve our needs. So, with the *Shorter Oxford Dictionary*, let us count as information whatever a person can be 'apprised or told'. A pupil can certainly be 'apprised or told' that in a system of particles the total number of nucleon charges is always constant, just as he can be 'apprised or told' that the Battle of Waterloo was fought in 1815, or that Shakespeare wrote *Hamlet*, or that oxygen supports combustion.

Of course, what a pupil is apprised or told may not be true. The dictionary definition provides no ground for distinguishing between information and misinformation. So much the better. Information is acquired or imparted in exactly the same way as misinformation is acquired or imparted. (Except when the teacher is deliberately lying or concealing what he knows to be relevant facts.) As a result of listening, reading, reflecting on our experience, reasoning, we acquire both our information and our misinformation.

Philosophers, it is true, have often set out to discover an infallible method of acquiring information, a method by the use of which we could be confident of not acquiring misinformation. Some of them have thought that 'rational intuition' was such a method; others have placed complete confidence in 'pure observation'. But we may take it to be a principal outcome of recent philosophy that there is *no such method*. The risk of being wrong is a risk it is impossible to avoid taking; the risk in a particular case may be minimal – the teacher who tells his class that the French Revolution took place in 1789 need not seriously fear that he may be misinforming them – but no particular method of acquiring information carries with it a guarantee of success. We can go wrong when we observe; we can go wrong when we reason – whatever precautions we take. The teacher has simply to live with the fact that however scrupulous he is, some of what he imparts as information will actually be misinformation. Which is not, of course, a justification for not being scrupulous. However much care I take I shall sometimes go wrong; but I shall go wrong more often if I take less care. What it *does* suggest, once more, is that learning has to be a life-long business; we have not only to go on learning more than we did at school, we have to unlearn much that we learnt.

To talk about methods of acquiring information, then, is at the same time to talk about methods of acquiring misinformation. This understood, let us raise the general question: 'Where do we get our information from?'

John Locke, in his *Essay Concerning the Human Understanding*, answered this question in a direct and uncompromising way: 'In one word, from experience.' But this 'one word' will scarcely suffice. Suppose, for example, a boy has at his disposal a stock of information about the tribal organisation of Australian aborigines. When asked from what source he derived his information he replies 'from experience'. Asked further to particularise, he tells us that 'My experience consists in my having read a great many books about aborigines'. Then either he was attempting to deceive or making a rather pointless joke. For 'reading a book' does not, in such contexts, count as 'experience'. Yet, certainly, we can derive a great deal of information from books.

'Ultimately', the reply may come, even if not immediately, such information derives from experience – the experience of the authors of the books the boy has read. And if it be objected that they, too, acquired their information in a variety of different ways, only in part from experience, the same reply might be made: 'In the long run, too, these other sources of information must rest, insofar as they are reliable, on experience.' This epistemological regress, however, is of no pedagogical interest. The teacher is concerned with what goes on in the process of education, with how a particular person learns, and at this level it is highly important to distinguish between what he, as a particular person, can best learn from books and what he can best learn from experience. The fact that *someone else* has learnt from experience what *he* can best learn from a book is irrelevant.

Locke, of course, identifies having experiences with having sensations. And, certainly, to acquire information even from reading or listening, one must have sensations, visual sensations, auditory sensations. Our experience, however, is not of sensations, at least as the word 'experience' is used outside textbooks on epistemology. It consists, rather, in the variety and depth of our encounters with the world around us, even if these encounters are made possible by our capacity for having sensations.

When a headmaster asks an applicant for a teaching position 'what experience he has had', he does not expect him, in reply, to describe his past sensations; what the headmaster wants to know is what work the applicant has done, where and whom he has taught and for how long. To speak of a doctor or a teacher as 'experienced' is not to enumerate his sensations; it is to draw attention to the variety of problems he has encountered, the diversity of the situations in which he has found himself. In the course of a man's life, he goes to school, meets with success or failure, makes friends, falls in love, has children, takes jobs, works with tools, suffers the illness and death of those he loves. These are the experiences from which he principally learns. Sensations – the sensation of pain, for example, if he touches a hot object – form part, but only a small part, of his experience. Even when a child 'learns from experience' that fires burn, what he at first acquires is not information about sensations but a tendency to avoid touching fires. And when he does come to formulate what he has learnt as information, it is as 'fire burns' not as 'heat-sensations are painful'. So it is not merely arbitrary, although it does not accord with the usage of a considerable number of psychologists and philosophers, to proceed as we shall in what follows: to define experience not in terms of 'sensations', whatever these are taken to be, but, in Dewey's manner, in terms of the operations of an agent, his attempts to deal with the things around him.

In Dewey's manner, I said. But Dewey's definition of experience as trying to do something and having the thing perceptibly do something to one in return[1] is expressed, like most classical definitions of experience, in terms that are too egocentric. To learn from experience is not the same as to learn by trying to find out how things affect *oneself*. A child can learn from experience how to effect changes in things other than himself, including other people. And in so doing he is not necessarily thinking of the effects of these changes on himself. So let me say, simply, that we learn from experience by trying to do something and reflecting on what happens.

Once experience is defined in this way, it becomes quite implausible to suggest that all information is acquired from experience. When we learn from a book that Columbus sailed to America in 1492 we have not learnt this by trying to do something to Columbus and reflecting on what happens.

But *should*, even if normally it is not, all information be acquired in this way, should this information about Columbus be dismissed, therefore, as not worth learning? Is 'book-learning' necessarily inferior learning? Sometimes quite the contrary view has been taken, as by R.M.Hutchins when he argues that the schools should properly 'leave experience to other institutions and influences', so as to concentrate on 'intellectual training'.[2] But as against this, and as against, too, those progressivist disciples of Dewey who condemn the schools for actually doing what Hutchins says they ought to do, Dewey once wrote: 'It is a great mistake to suppose, even tacitly, that the traditional schoolroom was not a place in which pupils had experiences ... The proper line of attack is that the experiences which were had ... were largely of a wrong kind.'[3]

And this is certainly right. It is *impossible* to drive learning from experience out of the classroom. The schoolroom is not, cannot be, an intellectual cocoon, insulated from experience. Going to school, being taught by a particular sort of teacher in a particular class-room, having this or that class-mate – all of these form part of one's experience, an experience from which one inevitably learns. They constitute a 'form of life'.

The information the pupil acquires from his experience in a classroom will often not be information the teacher wants him to acquire. Some of this information is trivial; information about a particular teacher's weaknesses, derived by reflection upon the success or failure of the child's attempts to flatter, wheedle, or disobey. Some of it is anything but trivial; it may be of great importance to the whole future life of the child. From his experience at school, the child may acquire the 'information' that he is 'no good at mathematics', that good literature is boring, that the majority is always right, that 'authorities' are unquestionably correct. Or as Collingwood and his fellow students learnt, that 'any exhibition of interest in their studies was a sure way to get themselves disliked' so that 'they were not long in acquiring that pose of boredom towards learning and everything connected with it which is notoriously part of the English public school man's character'.[4] The information derived from experience often, as in this case, contributes to the formation of attitudes. It is an appalling fact that just as doctors and hospitals often make people ill, so it is at school that many young people learn to be suspicious of the imagination, distrustful of the intellect, cruel, cynical and conformist – not, for the most part, because the teacher wants them to turn out in this way but as a byproduct of their experience of teachers and the organisation of the school. So far, certainly, Dewey's insistence on the need to ensure that the pupil gets the 'right sort of experience' at school is amply justified. Yet, on the other side, to argue against Hutchins that all learning ought to be from experience is to fall into what Dewey himself calls the 'either ... or ...' trap.

Let us return, in the light of these remarks, to our original question: whence do we derive our information? No one-word answer will suffice. Indeed, a seven-fold distinction suggests itself: between what we learn by observation, what we learn from, or through, experience, what we 'pick up' from others, what we learn by study, what we derive by inference, and what is imparted to us by a teacher. All of these obviously involve the development, in the pupil, of a capacity which is both wide and open; the development of that capacity the teacher can assist or discourage. When we speak of the 'imparting of information', our principal emphasis, of course, is on the activities of the teacher rather than the activities of the learner; when we speak of observation, of learning from, or through, experience, our principal emphasis is on the activities of the learner rather than the activities of the teacher. But we should not be misled by this fact; in every case, the teacher is called upon to be active; in no case can the teacher successfully teach except by stimulating his pupils into activity.

First of all, then, for 'observation'. There is a certain amount of information which we acquire simply by looking at the things around us, as distinct from operating upon them. In short, we sometimes learn by being spectators. Traditional empiricists, Locke and his successors, often wrote as if this were our typical attitude to the world; they have been justly condemned, in England by Collingwood, in Germany by Heidegger, in America by Dewey, for adopting a 'spectator theory of knowledge'. For being a spectator is not, of course, our typical attitude; most of the time we are acting, not looking on. We encounter the things around us as tools or as obstacles, our fellow human-beings as helpers or competitors, not simply as objects to be looked at. For traditional empiricists, 'the grass is green', 'the table is in the room', 'that book is red' are the typical facts. But how often are we interested in such information? Much more typical cases are 'the grass needs cutting', 'the table is too low', 'that book is unreadable'.

Furthermore, even when we do adopt the attitude of a spectator we are not, as traditional empiricists commonly supposed, merely reflecting, passively, whatever happens to lie within our field of vision. Consider an extreme example of spectatorship. A man is sitting alone in a railway carriage, looking out of the window at the countryside as it flashes past. His powers of intervention are then at their minimum; he can do nothing to help the farmer load his hay, nothing to hinder the accident he sees as about to happen. What he observes in no way interferes with him, he can in no way act upon it. So, in relation to that world he sees outside the carriage window, he is purely a spectator.

But even then, he is not looking at the world with the degree of passivity ascribed to him by traditional empiricism. What he sees, and this is a fact of considerable pedagogical importance, will depend not only on its being there to be seen, on its being in his field of vision, but on his interests, his theories, his desires. It takes skill, knowledge, effort to observe the changing contours of the countryside, the variety in the crops, the factories, the livestock. No two spectators will, from such a carriage window, make the same observations, although what lies in their field of observation may be identical. If not in actuality, too, each of them *imaginatively* works upon what he sees. The keen gardener notices, and imaginatively prunes, an unkempt tree; the motoring enthusiast notices, and imaginatively drives, a rare Italian sports-car. Yet the fact remains that each is to this degree a mere spectator: he cannot *change* what he is looking at.

A child is in the same position when in a classroom he looks at a film of, say, life in an Indian city. He cannot give alms to the beggar; he cannot bargain with the street-trader; he cannot sell goods at the market. So far, he is a spectator. He is actively engaged in making sense of what he sees; he is not a mere 'recipient of sensations'; he may wholly misinterpret what is happening. But he cannot physically alter what he sees.

So one can understand why observation has so often been described as if it were wholly passive. Wholly passive it is certainly not, but it is *relatively* passive. Watching somebody prune a tree is relatively passive as compared with actually 'trying our hand' at doing so ourselves. And a child watching a film is relatively passive, as contrasted with a child playing a game, experimenting in a laboratory, or writing a play.[5] Even in such more elaborate forms of observation as dissection, when a zoologist has to operate upon an animal in order to observe it, his hope is to alter it as little as possible; he dissects only to be able to look more carefully at what lies inside, just as he adjusts a microscope only to see more accurately what a slide contains, whereas he may drop a chemical substance on to his specimen in order to discover what new behaviour it produces.

In nineteenth-century schools, or in such nineteenth-century schools as thought of themselves as being 'up to date', the teacher not uncommonly placed great emphasis on 'training the powers of observation' by the use of 'object-lessons'. This emphasis arose out of Pestalozzi's protest against 'verbalism', the sort of verbalism which Dickens so unforgettably caricatured in *Hard Times*, seventy years after Pestalozzi began to develop his views.[6] The account, in Dickens' *Hard Times*, of Mr Gradgrind's lesson on horses, makes it plain just how necessary that protest was.[7] In that novel Sissy Jupe, living her life among horses, is told by a school superintendent that 'she does not know what a horse is', because she is incapable of defining it formally, unlike her fellow-pupil Bitzer, who can confidently rattle off such horse-descriptions as 'Quadruped, Graminivorous. Forty teeth, namely twenty-four grinders, four eye-teeth and twelve incisive.' Object lessons emphasised looking at horses, and thereby learning to describe them, in contrast with learning by heart such formalised definitions. The child was to 'look for himself', as Dickens' Sissy Jupe had looked for herself, and the teacher was to train him to do so, rather than to learn descriptions by heart as her class-mate Bitzer can rattle off definitions of a horse. But object lessons – interpreted in a manner which would have horrified Pestalozzi – rapidly degenerated into an academic exercise no less boring than the learning of definitions.[8] Confronted with an odd array of objects, chosen, it would appear, at random, children were expected to draw them accurately or to describe them minutely, in a manner quite unrelated to any problem (whereas Sissy Jupe had learnt about horses by seeing them coped with). In 'nature-study' a tadpole might replace the piece of chalk used as an object in the drawing lesson or the English lesson but it was to be contemplated in the same manner. The underlying presumption was that there existed in the human mind something describable as 'the power of observation' which could be trained by exercise; Conan Doyle's Sherlock Holmes was the exemplar of what could, by this method, be achieved. So it did not matter what object the child observed, or how infinitely boring and unfruitful the observation of it was, how little related to anything the child wanted to know; the child's 'powers of observation' were none the less effectively being trained. Indeed, the duller the object to be observed, the purer was the exercise, the less contaminated by special interests or passionate concerns. Writing in 1893, W.T. Harris remarks that 'all writers uphold the Pestalozzian doctrine of instruction by object-lessons' and goes on to add that, as a result of Herbart's influence, this tendency was being counteracted by another, which emphasised 'not so much seeing and hearing and handling things, as recognising them and understanding them.'[9] The contrast is remarkable; it brings out the degree to which the object lesson was conceived of as teaching a kind of pure observation, quite independent of recognition and understanding.

Yet however futile the traditional object-lesson may have been and however untenable the theoretical considerations by which it was justified, this is no reason for denying, as Dewey does, that we sometimes do acquire information by simple observation in which we adopt the attitude of a spectator. 'Men have to *do* something to the things when they wish to find out something,' Dewey writes in *Democracy and Education*; 'they have to alter conditions. This is the lesson of the laboratory method, and the lesson all education has to learn.'[10] It is easy to understand why Dewey was led into these exaggerations. The 'spectator theory of knowledge' is his philosophical *bête noire*; again and again he pauses to denounce its iniquities. And the classroom in which the child's rôle is, as far as can be, restricted to spectatorship is no less his educational *bête noire*. But although it is possible to point to the rational grounds for Dewey's exaggerations and in a large measure to sympathise with them, it is none the less important to point out that they *are* exaggerations. I do not have to 'do something' to Venus in order to look at it through a telescope, or to the Acropolis in order to observe how it dominates the city of Athens – not at least in the sense in which in the chemistry laboratory I 'do something' to chemical solutions.

Neither, rejecting the view that the teacher can 'strengthen the powers of observation' of his pupils, should we be led to deny that the teacher can help them to learn by observation. Indeed, to some degree a teacher automatically helps his pupil to observe, merely in virtue of teaching his special subject, by arousing the child's interests and giving him information. So the geologist, the botanist, the geographer, the architect, looking through a train-window, may each of them acquire information by observation which he could not have acquired were it not for his special knowledge; the visitor to Italy who is already well acquainted with Italian history or the history of art will, as we say, 'get much more out of' a visit to Italy; the sociologist, the anthropologist, the archaeologist may, on a visit to Mexico, acquire information by observation which the normal tourist completely fails to acquire. In general, to learn is to be better prepared to learn by observation. As so often, we see how absurd it is to set up an antithesis between teaching a subject and teaching something else – in this case the 'power to observe'; teaching a subject *is* among other things, teaching to observe.

The teacher can assist his pupils to observe, too, by pointing out to them the kind of thing which they *need* to observe: the geologist does this in a field excursion, the anatomist in a laboratory, the medical tutor in a hospital, the art teacher in an art-gallery, the architect as he shows his slides. How do such lessons differ from the 'object-lesson'? Mainly in this respect; the 'object' is not now chosen at random with the intention of developing the students' general powers of observation; it is selected for special attention as the sort of thing which has to be observed in order to solve a particular kind of problem or to understand a particular kind of process. Increased powers of observation are in such teaching related, that is, to the student's developing interest in his subject. The medical tutor hopes that his pupils will improve their capacity for recognising, and for distinguishing between, the symptoms of diseases; he teaches them to observe, and to report what they have observed, as an ingredient in acquiring a particular skill. If, at the end of their training, they are still, in non-medical contexts, hopelessly unobservant this will neither surprise nor disturb him. Similarly, a geologist teaching his pupils to observe more carefully, as a clue to its structure and history, the contours of a landscape does not suffer from the illusion that he is at the same time helping them to observe more carefully the architectural details of a church-door or the composition of a painting. It will take an architect or critic to develop in them the capacity for making *that* sort of observation.

In a variety of other ways a teacher can help a pupil to acquire information by observation. There are many scientific instruments – the geologist's hammer, the botanist's microscope, the astronomer's telescope, the chemist's balance, the zoologist's dissecting knife – which facilitate observation. By teaching his pupils how to use these instruments and to avoid the 'classical errors' associated with them – errors, for example, arising out of a failure to protect a chemical balance from the effect of changes in air-pressure – the teacher can develop the capacity of his pupils to acquire by observation the sort of information it is important for them to acquire. Negatively, too, it will be worth his while to demonstrate to his pupils just how unreliable as a source of information what we 'see with our own eyes' can be; to what a degree we see what we expect to see. This point can be made, say, in a history lesson by comparing 'eye-witness' accounts of the same event. Here, as so often, the destruction of popular myths is not the least of the teacher's functions.

As I have already suggested, 'object-lessons' developed out of the teachings of Pestalozzi with his rejection of 'verbiage' and his insistence that 'man's knowledge must be founded on sense-impressions'. In the same spirit, teachers who aspire to break down the barrier between the schoolroom and 'life' not uncommonly take their pupils on various forms of excursion, to Parliament, to magistrates' courts, to factories. Their expectation is that the child will thus be enabled 'to see for himself' how society works, as distinct from 'merely being told about it by his teachers' or 'merely reading about it in books'.[11]

But it is wholly naive to believe that observation of this kind can serve as a substitute for, or is automatically superior to, book-learning. In the eighteenth century, the 'grand tour' was the typical form of excursion, from which, it was supposed, the traveller was bound to return with a greatly enlarged stock of information about countries, men, and manners. Rousseau, no lover of bookishness, raised the obvious objection: 'In order to learn it is not enough to traverse a country; you must travel in the right way ... There are many people who learn even less from travelling than from books, because they are ignorant of the art of thinking: in reading they are at least guided by the author, but in travelling they can see nothing for themselves.'[12] This does not mean, of course, that travel is never a source of information. But by itself – as distinct from the situation when it forms one ingredient within an education – it can easily be worse than useless: reinforcing prejudice, adding to the pupil's stock of misinformation, substituting mere visual vividness for understanding. A person who has been to Rome will almost certainly be able to picture it more vividly, assuming he has some capacity for visualisation, than a person who has merely read about it, in however much detail; it does not follow that he will have a better understanding, say, of the structure and function of the Roman Forum than the scholar whose information is entirely obtained from books.

The same is true of school expeditions. A child does not *necessarily* learn by attending carefully selected, aseptic, hearings in a magistrate's court, or by watching wheels turn in a factory, or by visiting museums. Many children are completely bored by such expeditions; they find them, and quite properly, more 'abstract', more 'remote from life', than what they can read in books. To read one of Churchill's wartime speeches is, indeed, to be brought 'closer to life' than one is brought by inspecting the panelling in the House of Commons. Knowing, from personal experience, what a magistrate's court looks like is very different from, and much inferior as 'life-awareness', to knowing what rôle such a court plays in a legal system, what its powers are, how magistrates are selected, what penalties they can inflict, in what ways their sentences can be appealed against, by what rules of evidence their procedures are governed. Few of these things can be learnt by a visit as such, although, of course, the teacher may use the occasion of a visit to impart information about them to his class. And if the teacher has carried his class to a point at which they *need* to observe a legal case, or a particular geological formation, or a certain kind of geographical region, in order more fully to understand what he has been teaching them, then certainly an 'excursion' can be of very great educational importance.

To sum up. It is certainly possible to acquire a great deal of information by observation. The teacher can do much to improve the pupils' capacity to acquire specific sorts of information by specific kinds of observation. Furthermore, he can supplement other forms of observation by, for example, arranging opportunities for outside excursions, or showing his class films or other audio-visual aids.[13] But the teacher should not presume that what the pupil learns by observation will necessarily be 'more real', more reliable, or more useful than what he learns by direct instruction or by reading. Indeed, the extent to which his pupils can acquire information by observation depends, to a large degree, on what they have already learnt – what skills, what information, what interests, they have already acquired, what theories they work with, what problems they have encountered.

Let us turn now to a second method of learning – by, from or through experience. Note the prepositional phrases. In ordinary English there is not, as far as I know, any rule which determines the choice between them. But there are distinctions to be made at this point, and the prepositional vagaries of the English language will provide us with a language in which to make them.[14]

Originally, the word 'experience' meant 'experiment' – as the French word 'expérience' still not uncommonly does. And it has something like this sense, we have already suggested, whenever we speak of someone as having learnt by, from, or through experience. This is particularly apparent in the case of learning *by* experience, which can most perspicuously be defined as learning by 'trying out', by attempting to act. To take the classical example, the baby learns by experience not to touch the fire, because when he tries to touch it he burns his finger, or is smacked, or is pulled away; a cat can learn by experience to open any door upon which it can exert leverage; a rat to escape from a maze. Each of them develops regular methods of procedure by trial and error.

As I am using the phrase, learning by experience is an important method of acquiring capacities. But as Aristotle long ago pointed out, it does not carry with it, of necessity, the acquisition of information. One can learn *by* experience how to ride a bicycle without having information about bicycle riding. Nevertheless, what human beings learn *by* experience they often convert into information which they can pass on to others or use to remind themselves how to act. They very frequently, although certainly not always, move from 'knowing how to', in Ryle's limited sense of the word, to 'knowing how to' in a rather different sense, which involves not only being able to act but being able to tell others how to act, being able to teach. So, for example, if their car is difficult to start on cold mornings, they may first learn by experience, by attempting with varying degrees of success a number of different procedures, how to start it. And then, perhaps in order to instruct their son how to start the car, they may formulate what they have learnt as information: 'In cold weather you will find it easier to start the car if you pump the accelerator before you turn on the ignition.' Let us say of such a person that he has not merely learnt *by* experience how to start his car, he has also learnt *from* experience that the car is most easily started under certain circumstances. Similarly, a child may learn *from* experience, and pass this information on to his friends, that on frozen ground it is dangerous to brake suddenly, or that a particular way of sitting on a bicycle makes it easier to control, or that a particular route to school is quicker than other routes.

Indeed, some people almost always reflect upon what they are learning *by* experience as they learn it; they conduct a conversation with themselves as they learn; they impart information to themselves, at once pupils and teachers. For them the difference between learning *by* experience and learning *from* experience is almost imperceptible. But, as is illustrated by the case of the baby, the cat, the bird, the cyclist, it is not at all the case that everybody who has learnt *by* experience has acquired information. A mechanic may be expert but inarticulate; he has developed, we say, a 'feel', for engines, but he has not sufficiently reflected on what he has done to be able to pass on what he has learnt as information to others. Every teacher has encountered situations in which he knows perfectly well how to act, but is incapable of telling his pupils what to do.

How does 'learning from experience' differ from 'learning by observing'? Ordinary usage does not sharply distinguish them, but we can scarcely expect ordinary usage to do more than suggest to us that there are epistemological distinctions we might wish to make. Differences like the difference between 'observing' and 'learning from experience' are not the sort of practically important distinctions which ordinary usage is likely to mark with firmness. But without undue arbitrariness we can put the matter thus: we 'observe' merely by looking, by being spectators; we 'learn from experience' by acting and then reflecting upon the consequences of our actions. So a pupil 'learns from experience' that teachers are bad-tempered on Friday afternoons if he is himself the sort of pupil who tests the teacher's temper; he learns by observation that his teacher is bad-tempered if he contents himself with timorously watching his teacher's reactions to the trials of a Friday afternoon, without himself adding to those trials.

Even if we reject as empty the classical conception of 'pure observation', it is educationally useful to distinguish, as we have done, a set of cases in which a pupil is in the position of being a spectator – although not a spectator who is devoid of expectations or information or does no more than passively 'receive sensations' – from those cases in which he learns by modifying what he has in front of him and reflecting on the outcome. In a science lesson, for example, the pupil may acquire information by watching a demonstration, whether in the laboratory or in a film. He will acquire such information only if he is in some measure interested, skilled and knowledgeable; his learning takes effort, absorbs his energies. But the demonstration rolls on before him; he cannot learn by modifying what he sees, by experiment. When he learns from experience, in contrast, he is himself the experimenter; he tries out various possibilities, he learns by way of reflection on his successes and his failures. He has still to observe; but he is not *simply* observing.

Exponents, from Rousseau on, of the 'discovery' method, with its central emphasis on learning from experience, often claim that information acquired from experience is more effectively learnt, more likely to be remembered and used, than information derived from, say, the reading of books. Whether this is so, is a matter for educational psychologists to settle. (As usual, the evidence seems to be inconclusive.)[15] Learning from experience certainly has one clear advantage; the child acquires capacities – the capacity, say, to handle chemical apparatus – in the course of acquiring information, as he does not by reading a book. One can admit this much without going anything like as far as Bruner when he writes: 'The schoolboy ... *is* a physicist, and it is easier for him to learn physics behaving like a physicist than doing something else.'[16] A pupil's school experimental courses inevitably simplify the actual situation in which a physicist finds himself and may well leave the pupil with a quite false impression of what scientific discovery is like. The notion that a child can somehow 'discover for himself' what it took physicists centuries to discover is manifest nonsense. Certainly, the child should be encouraged to experiment, to 'get the feel of doing science'. But he cannot entirely, or even substantially, learn his physics in this way. Indeed, every physicist has relied, and still relies, on a large body of book-learning; in teaching the child how to read scientific literature, just as much as by teaching him how to experiment, we are helping him to see what it is like to be a physicist.

If the teacher can encourage his pupils, to a limited degree, to learn from experience, he should also bring to their notice the difficulties and danger of this, as of any other, form of learning. The initial tendency of the child, still markedly characteristic of the uneducated adult, is rashly to generalise. Philosophers have sometimes written as if generalisation were something we very gradually learnt to do. On the contrary, it is something we very gradually learn *not* to do, or not always to do. Piaget refers to 'a very universal law of mental development, viz. that the desire to check results comes very much later in point of time than the faculty for inventing explanations'.[17] One can add that the desire to check generalisations comes much later than the desire to generalise. The teacher can help his pupils to see how important it is adequately to test the conclusions they draw from experience. Once more, the teacher automatically does this to some extent in the process of teaching subjects; to learn history or geography, for example, is to come to see to what a slight degree we can safely generalise about human beings from our experience of our own neighbourhood. But the teacher may also explicitly teach the child to appreciate the virtues of hypothesis-testing – in contrast with accepting immediate generalisations – as a method of acquiring information from experience. This will have to be done explicitly; the child will not pick it up automatically, in the process of doing school 'experiments' so set up as to suggest to the child that he has *proved*, let us say, Ohm's Law. (Some years ago, talking to a group of final year honours chemistry students, I found them reluctant to believe, to their teacher's horror, that hypotheses played any part at all in chemistry. 'We simply go into the laboratory and see what happens.')

As we have suggested, learning from experience and from observation are intimately related. One thing they have in common is that what we learn by means of them is something about the type of occurrence with which we are immediately confronted. So by trying to walk on it a child learns that ice is slippery; by looking carefully at a section of sea-side he notes the ways in which the growth of trees is affected by prevailing winds.

But there are other kinds of learning in which what we learn about is quite different in character from what we observe. It will be convenient to describe learning of this kind as learning *through* experience. In everyday usage, no doubt, learning *through* experience is most commonly used as a perhaps slightly more emphatic synonym for learning *from* experience: 'I have learnt through bitter experience,' a disillusioned English teacher might say, when he has tried and failed to do so, 'that it is impossible to interest the ordinary adolescent in the plays of Shakespeare.' In our terminology, he has learnt, rather, *from* experience. We shall reserve learning *through* experience for the special class of cases defined above, in which what we learn about is not the kind of thing which, in that learning-situation, we are directly observing.

The most obvious case of learning through experience is learning about geographical regions from a map. A map consists of lines, dots, arrangements of colours on paper, and we have, of course, first to observe these in order to learn from the map. If we merely read off from a map such information as that the dot marked Edinburgh lies above the dot marked London, or the coloured patch marked India is larger than the coloured patch marked London, then we are, of course, gaining information simply by observing the map itself. From such observation of a particular map we could learn about other maps. Taught on a particular map to pick out places a child can learn to do so with great accuracy, as also to pick them out on any other map on which they are marked, provided that it uses the same projection.

This, indeed, is what geography has often meant for schoolchildren: being able to name places and regions on maps, and to draw similar maps. So Froebel testifies that 'In physical geography we repeated our books parrot-wise, speaking much and saying nothing; for the teaching in this subject had not the least connection with real life, nor had it any actuality for us, although at the same time we could rightly name our little specks and particles of colour on the map.' Or, as a versifier has succinctly expressed the matter: 'History is about chaps, geography is about maps.'

But, very obviously, geography is not about maps, any more than history is about time-charts. Learning such facts as that 'there are lots of little dots in the area marked Pacific Ocean', or developing skill in placing the dots correctly on a map of the ocean and naming them correctly, is not learning geography. To learn geography is to learn not about maps, but about regions; not about the relationship between patches of colour but about the relationship between mountains, rivers and cities. But these are not actually before the child when he looks at the map; all he has before him are the dots and the patches of colour. There are many comparable instances; blueprints, graphs, molecular models in chemistry, diagrams in physics, cuisinaire rods in arithmetic and variously-shaped blocks in geometry. When pupils learn mathematics by way of experience with such maps and diagrams, such rods and blocks – drawing them, manipulating them, making constructions on them – they are learning *through* experience.

It is the teacher who, in large part, determines what his pupils learn *through* experience; the teacher sets before them models, diagrams, maps, or gets them to construct them in accordance with a predetermined plan. He teaches them, furthermore and most importantly, to *interpret* these objects. The view that all he needs to do is to confront the child with, let us say, wooden blocks, and then the child will automatically see mathematical relationships for himself will not stand a moment's investigation. Unless the blocks are part of a teaching programme, unless the child is directed to use the blocks in certain particular ways, they will remain for him coloured blocks.[18]

It is particularly necessary to emphasise at this point the difference between learning by observation and learning through experience. If we think of the child as simply *observing* rods of various lengths – or, as the technical language runs, 'having percepts' of them – and then somehow organising these 'percepts' into 'mathematical concepts' it becomes highly mysterious why he should be led to form the particular concepts the teacher wished him to possess. For it is always possible to organise a set of objects in a very large number of ways: why should the pupil arrive at that particular pattern of organisation the teacher wishes him to arrive at? But in fact the pupil *works with* the rods and blocks, works with them in imitation of the teacher or following his instructions. It is what he learns by working with them in a practical way, by the trials, the failures and the successes of his attempts, for example, to produce rods of equal length by joining rods of variable lengths, which prepares the way for his learning what a half is, or that six and four make ten.

Badly taught, the child may be left with the impression that geometry is about wooden blocks or, again, that atoms are small solid bodies joined by rods, just as he may be left with the impression that geography is about maps. At a somewhat more advanced level in comprehension he may fail fully to understand the method of projection employed by the map or model. Most people's ideas about the world are considerably confused as a result of the distortions inevitable in maps designed on Mercator's projection, which they suppose to present them with a sort of abstract photograph of the world. It is much more 'natural', one might say, to learn *from* experience or by observation than to learn *through* experience: it requires a very special effort by the teacher if the child is to engage in this latter kind of learning.

The process of learning through experience, then, is fraught with peril; it is certainly a debatable point, for example, whether the best approach to geometry is by way of manipulating blocks or cutting up paper, or whether this approach leads to a complete failure to comprehend the formal nature of geometrical relationships and the importance of proof in geometry.[19] All that can be said on this matter, in general terms, is that a teacher ought never merely to presume that his pupils are in fact learning through experience rather than by observation, that they are in fact learning about countries through maps rather than learning about maps, about geometrical relationships rather than about wooden blocks. He can hope to avoid this trap by constantly varying his pupils' experience, e.g. by having them construct maps on a variety of projections or by getting them to begin by mapping their own surroundings, so that they clearly understand how maps can be used, and what their limitations are.[20]

It must be admitted, of course, that the distinction between what is learnt 'from' and 'through' experience is sometimes a tenuous one. Suppose, for example, an engineer is studying the behaviour of a model plane in a wind-tunnel. Then, of course, what he is hoping to learn about is the behaviour of a large-scale plane under a variety of atmospheric conditions. But he reproduces in such detail in the wind-tunnel the physical relationships about which he hopes to acquire information that he might well think of himself as having learnt from, rather than through, his wind-tunnel investigations how an aeroplane behaves under stress. The more 'iconographic' the model, the greater the detail in which it pictures, the less significant the difference between learning from and through experience.

Furthermore, the distinction is in many respects a controversial one. Nobody, I suppose, would wish to deny that the child who is taught geography properly must learn about regions of the earth's surface, not about coloured patches on maps. But there is by no means the same agreement about what the child is to learn by working with cuisinaire rods or wooden blocks. For empiricist philosophers of mathematics, with J.S. Mill as their best-known representative, the child learns about the empirical, if very general, mathematical relationships which are exemplified in the relations he discovers between rods and blocks. When he puts the two halves of a rod together he learns that $\frac{1}{2} + \frac{1}{2} = 1$ in exactly the same manner in which he learns by putting a flame into a flask of gas that carbon-dioxide will not support combustion. Certainly, the child has to realise that he is not learning, simply, about *these* blocks or *these* rods, just as he has to realise that he is not learning, simply, about *this* flask of gas. But mathematics is learnt *from* experience, exactly as descriptive chemistry is; the precautions the teacher has to take are simply the normal precautions against rash generalisation on the one side or undue particularisation on the other. For a Mill-type empiricist, then, the distinction between what is learnt from and what is learnt through experience, in the sense in which we have described it, may have a certain utility in enabling us to distinguish between learning from maps and learning from travel, but that is the limit of its significance.

For the Platonists, at the opposite extreme, the distinction is vital. Empirical relationships, on their view, are never genuine examples of mathematical relationships; they embody them only imperfectly. The rods the child describes as equal are not *absolutely* equal, the point he makes with a pencil on a paper is not the geometer's point, just in virtue of the fact that however small it is, it has magnitude as well as position. The child may need experience and observation in order to understand mathematical relationships but he cannot learn about them *from* experience. So in Plato's *Meno*, Socrates is depicted as teaching a slave geometry; in the course of so doing he draws lines on the sand; but this is only, Plato and after him Descartes would argue, in order to stimulate the intellect to produce the mathematical ideas it already innately possesses. Here the contrast between learning *from* and *through* experience is a necessary one. Whereas in the map case what is learnt *through* experience of maps could also be learnt *from* experience of a region, mathematical relationships, according to Plato, cannot possibly be learnt *from* experience.

In an attempt to avoid both Mill's empiricism which, it is commonly argued, does not do justice to the peculiar certainty of mathematics and Plato's rationalism, with its conclusion that 'real' mathematical relationships exist in a timeless realm of ideal patterns, accessible only to the intellect, many mathematicians have been led to deny that mathematical propositions give us information at all, empirical or ideal; mathematics is rather, they say, in Wittgenstein's phrase, 'nothing but a bundle of techniques'. On this account of mathematics, it is a complete mistake to discuss the teaching of mathematics in a chapter which purports to be about methods of acquiring information, however broadly 'information' is interpreted; it belongs, only, to a chapter on the acquisition of competence and skills. Somewhat more conservatively, other mathematicianconventionalists have argued that the only information mathematics gives us is about the results of accepting certain particular mathematical conventions. So to take an example from a book designed to help parents to understand the 'new mathematics' it is, on this view, a mistake to suppose that a child who says that 3 + 4 = 12 is absolutely wrong; he would be right if he were using an arithmetic with different conventions, taking five as the base rather than ten.[21]

As the source of the last reference may suggest, these philosophical disputes about the character of mathematical information and its relation to experience can have important effects on the teaching of mathematics. Those who emphasise the connection between mathematics and experience are likely at the same time constantly to insist upon its practical and technical application and to employ methods of teaching mathematics which involve handling and working with objects; those who believe that mathematics is about 'eternal objects' are likely to feel that this approach conceals the formal structural character of mathematics; for some mathematicians the technique is the crucial thing; a conventionalist will tend to think of mathematics as in large part an exercise of the creative imagination. Only a philosophy of mathematics, it is fair to say, which does full justice both to the empirical relationships of mathematics, to its formal structure, and to its imaginative possibilities will be a wholly satisfactory foundation for mathematics teaching in the school. And no philosopher, it would I think be generally admitted, has yet succeeded in developing a philosophy of mathematics which does justice to these requirements. As things stand, mathematics courses in the schools tend to swing between a practical, a formalist and an 'imaginative' approach to mathematics. It is more than likely that none of these approaches will wholly satisfy the diverse aims of mathematics students. The formal-logical approach to mathematics which for a time swept the schools was soon under fire as failing either to provide the child with an adequate training in techniques or to satisfy the stricter demands of a formalistic approach. A merely practical approach dissatisfies the mathematicians, and so, often, does an approach through set-theory. These controversies are unlikely rapidly to die away.

So it seems that the distinction between what is learnt *from* and what is learnt *through* experience is both uncertain at the boundaries and highly controversial in its application to particular subjects. Yet it is of considerable educational importance, partly in order to warn of a real danger – the danger exemplified in the case of the geography student who learns about patches of colours rather than about regions of the earth's surface – partly to provide us with a mode of raising the issue of exactly what a teacher is trying to do when he teaches mathematics.

Much of the information we have at our disposal, as we have already suggested, is derived neither by observation nor from or through experience; it is 'picked up'. (Habits and attitudes, too, can be 'picked up'; that is a point to which we will have to revert.) In the modern world, especially, there is afloat a mass of miscellaneous information. Newspapers, commentators, periodicals, television programmes of the documentary sort, all set out to supply information, which is still further circulated by casual conversation, rumour, and second-hand oracles. But if, as a consequence of modern mass-communications, such free-floating information is now of unprecedented proportions, the picking-up method of acquiring information is not, in principle, a new one. The traveller, the wise-woman, the rumour-bearer, parents, doctors, tribal elders, all acted in the past, as they still act, as sources of information.

It is, however, an educationally important fact that there is so large a volume of information now available for the picking up; this may suggest that there is no longer the same need for the teacher deliberately to impart it. The nineteenth-century child, living, most likely, in a village or small town, or a very limited region of a city, with illiterate parents, no radio, no television, no cinema, no library, had very little opportunity to 'pick-up' information. If he was to acquire any information about forms of life outside his own limited sphere, it had to be imparted by a teacher, or, at least, acquired under his direction. The situation, now, is very different.

It does not follow, however, that the teacher is no longer necessary as an imparter of information. A characteristic feature of 'picked-up' information is its unreliability. The 'British empiricists', Locke and Hume, were both of them so conscious of this fact that they saw in picked-up information the principal source of error and confusion. 'Doctrines that have been derived from no better original than the superstition of a nurse, or the authority of an old woman,' Locke once wrote, 'may ... grow up to the dignity of *principles* in religion or morality'.[22] It is these principles, thus picked up, which form, so Locke thought, the greatest obstacle to clear thinking; we hear them appealed to so often that we are deluded into supposing that they have an absolute authority. Similarly David Hume ascribes 'more than one half of those opinions, that prevail among mankind' to what he calls 'education', and by this he means what we have described as 'picking up'.[23] For both Locke and Hume, intellectual progress takes the form of abandoning 'information' which has merely been picked up and replacing it by information derived from experience.

It is certainly part of the teacher's responsibility to get his pupils to see, in the manner of Locke and Hume, just how unreliable 'picked-up' information is. Indeed, much of his teaching in such subjects as elementary science, biology, or history will be directed precisely against the 'information' his pupils have 'picked up' from a variety of sources – the popular myths, accepted folklore, which still freely circulate as facts. He can help his pupils, in the course of his teaching, to distinguish between those sources of information which are likely to be reliable and those which are likely to be unreliable; he can draw attention to the tell-tale signals of unreliability – vague references, for example, to what 'your doctor will tell you', elusive authorities, misleading statistics and the like – and can thus in some degree provide them with a prophylactic against the cruder forms of deception. He can discuss the conditions under which journalists work, the requirements of television, as they affect reliability.

But only a foolish teacher will wholly condemn the flood of information which will continue to pour in upon his pupils during their whole life. Hume sometimes writes as if it would be better for people to believe nothing except what they have learnt for themselves from experience – in his rather special sense of 'experience' – but it would be absurd to carry experiential puritanism that far. To prepare them to learn from, to cope intelligently with, picked-up information, is certainly one of the most valuable tasks the teacher can undertake.[24] His problem, as so often, is to teach his pupils to be cautious and critical but not cynical. And he can best accomplish this end by getting them to see for themselves the degrees and kinds of unreliability possessed by different sources of information.

The difference between 'picking up' and deliberate study, considered as sources of information, is, of course, not a sharp one. But it is worth distinguishing between them. Study is a systematic, deliberate, attempt to acquire a particular kind of information – including, of course, practical information about the best way of acting in particular circumstances. It involves the practice of skills: skill in listening, in reading, in the use of indices, the following of arguments, the choice of books. That the teacher ought to train his pupils in such skills scarcely needs, one might think, to be argued. But in the course of an investigation into teaching in Australian universities, it emerged that some university teachers took the view that private study, as distinct from learning the information presented in the lectures and textbooks, was 'inefficient', and others that 'there is no time' for the student to work with any degree of independence; all his time will be taken up in learning what he is told to learn.[25]

Both these phrases – 'inefficient' and 'there is no time for' – deserve a little consideration. What is to be the test of efficiency? Efficiency is apparently being determined in the following way: that method of acquiring information is the most efficient which results in the student's having at his disposal the largest stock of information when he leaves the University. But clearly this is not the end of the matter. For a method which is efficient by this criterion may be less efficient than studying for oneself in a fundamental respect; namely, that in the course of studying for himself the student acquires, as he does not by cramming, those habits and skills which will enable him to obtain for himself the further information he will need in his later life.

Similar considerations apply to 'having no time'. When we say that 'we have no time to do x', this involves an implicit value-comparison, to the effect that what we are now doing, what now occupies our time, is more valuable than doing x would be, that it is, for example, more valuable to spend one's time giving lectures which students can cram for examination purposes than it is to teach them skill in 'information-retrieval'. The view that independent study is 'inefficient' and that 'there is no time for it' was, in the investigation referred to above, particularly expressed by University teachers engaged in teaching subjects of a professional, scientific, or technical nature. Yet it should be particularly apparent, in these cases, that a graduate who has not, in his undergraduate days, acquired skill in information-retrieval will rapidly cease to be an effective practitioner.[26]

A final point, of philosophical rather than pedagogical interest, but not wholly irrelevant to the practice of teaching. Is that form of independent study which consists in learning by reading assimilable to observation, or to learning from experience, or to learning through experience? There are certainly analogies worth insisting upon, in all three cases.

Sometimes what a pupil reads are eye-witness accounts as, let us say, Arthur Young's *Travels in France and Italy* is an eye-witness account of life in France before the French Revolution, or Pepys' *Diary* is an eye-witness account of the Great Fire of London, or as an anthropologist's account of life in a primitive society or a naturalist's of courting habits in birds are eye-witness accounts of human or animal behaviour. To read such an eye-witness account is, in some respects, like learning by observation. Like, because the eye-witness account, in the manner of our own observations as a spectator, is rich in detail; indeed, the eye-witness may notice details which, had we been present, we should not have noticed. But also he may have overlooked details which we would have observed, and for personal, political or literary reasons he may exaggerate, underplay or simply mis-report aspects of the situation which are of vital importance to us. So it would be misleading to think of reading an eye-witness account as equivalent to learning by observation – it is by its nature a vicarious form of learning.

Should we say, as we did (n. 13) of learning from films, that learning from eye-witness accounts is 'indirect' observation? There is a big difference between the two cases. It is true that a film, like an eye-witness account, can be designed to deceive us. But we can deliberately be deceived, too, in direct observation. The stage-magician, for example, deliberately arranges matters so that we shall see what he wants us to see, and not what he does not want us to see; what we observe when we visit a totalitarian country may have been deliberately put before our eyes as a 'show-piece', to deceive us about the country as a whole. The difference is that, presuming a photograph or a film has not been faked, we can 'see for ourselves' by looking at it what we would see if we were in the cameraman's situation. We can see, as we have already suggested, what the photographer himself may have completely failed to notice. In reading an eye-witness account, in contrast, we are entirely at the mercy of the witness as an observer. At best, we might describe reading as 'vicarious' observation, whereas looking at pictures is 'indirect' observation. But it is more sensible on the whole to treat it, simply, as learning by reading, as a manner of learning distinct from observation.

Reading a novel, or listening to a play, we may become quite as emotionally engaged in the fate of the characters and the situations in which they find themselves as we would be if we were ourselves participating in a comparable situation in everyday life. What we learn about human beings by reflection on what we have read in novels, or heard in a theatre, may for that reason be very like 'learning from experience'. It is indeed quite common, and not wholly unreasonable, to speak of a novel or a play as 'enlarging our experience'. But there is a difference; we cannot actively intervene in the conduct of affairs depicted in the novel; we cannot learn from our successes and our failures in so doing, although we can learn from the success or failure of the characters in the novel. So it is misleading to assimilate learning from reading novels to learning from experience, although important to see how alike they can be.

How is reading related to learning *through* experience? Here the situation is more complex. There are obvious analogies, and potent ones, between acquiring information through reading and acquiring it through experience. In the case of learning through experience, I said, what we learn about is not the physical object we see directly in front of us; similarly in reading, what we learn about is not (in general) the marks on paper in front of us. We speak quite as naturally of reading a map, or reading a blueprint, as we do of reading a book, and I referred to map-reading and blueprint-reading as examples of learning through experience. It was not entirely without justification that, in his *Tractatus Logico-Philosophicus*, Wittgenstein put forward the view that information-recording statements are all of them 'pictures', related to the facts they record, or purport to record, exactly as a model or a blueprint is related to what it depicts. 'A proposition,' he wrote 'is a picture of reality; a proposition is a model of reality as we imagine it' – even though, as he freely admitted, a proposition, an informative statement, 'at first sight ... does not seem to be a picture of the reality with which it is concerned'.[27]

But, once again, to assimilate information-statements to models is to push an analogy too far. It is interesting to observe, in the first place, that although, as I said, we so readily speak of reading a map, a blueprint, a musical score, we should *not* normally speak of 'reading' a molecular model or any other physical model, e.g. a model of a ship at sea. We also speak of 'reading' a thermometer and more generally, of 'reading' a calibration on an instrument, i.e. we use the verb 'reading' whenever we are involved in interpreting marks ordered in accordance with a rule or, as in the case of 'reading a palm', with what we take to be a rule.[28] But a statement does not act as a picture of what it says even in the extended sense in which the lines on a blueprint act as a picture of a house, or a map as a picture of a geographical terrain. In these latter cases we can point to a one-to-one correspondence between, for example, a line on a blueprint and the length of a room, a change of colour in a map and a change of altitude in a geographical terrain, and we at least suppose there to be a similar correspondence between the tiny bodies in a molecular model and the atoms in a molecule. We can set up relatively simple rules of projection which enable us to use the model as a way of learning about the properties of what it depicts. For example, by pencilling in new lines in the blueprint we can see how by altering the size of the rooms in a house we would affect the relationship between the house and the boundaries of the land on which it is sited, just as we can reshape a molecular model to study possible chemical changes, or can 'play around with' a map in order to see how, for example, diverting a river would affect the location of townships.

Statements are not like this. We cannot discover anything more about the Battle of Waterloo by scrutinising more carefully the sentence, 'The Battle of Waterloo was fought in 1815'. We can, of course, alter the sentence in various ways, and we can use it in arguments, draw conclusions with its help. But we cannot make use of it to try out alternative happenings, as we might manipulate a detailed model of the forces engaged in the battle and the terrain to see why Napoleon lost, and why it was impossible for him, even given a better strategy, to win. Wittgenstein himself grants that we cannot say what a sentence and the realities it depicts have in common; there is, on the contrary, no difficulty in saying what a blueprint and an (actual or projected) house or piece of machinery have in common. We can instruct a group of students: 'Here is a house: now construct a blueprint of it on a certain scale', and they should, if they undertake their work well, construct identical blueprints, assuming that they know the conventions. But if we say to them: 'Here is a house: now write a description of it', they may all write accurate descriptions, and yet none of these descriptions need have a single sentence in common.

In short, although there are analogies between acquiring information by reading and acquiring information by working with maps or blueprints, the two are none the less very different; working with maps or blueprints is much more like observing, much more like learning from experience, than is reading a book. To sum up, it is better to think of learning by study as a unique form of learning, possible only in highly developed societies, than to assimilate it either to observing, to learning from experience, or to learning through experience, although different types of reading are analogous to each of these. Reading is an alternative mode of learning with its own advantages and disadvantages; skill in reading is not identical with the ability to observe accurately, the ability to think reflectively about our experiences, the ability to see through our experiences to the formal relationships they illustrate, although it may be of great assistance to us in our attempts to do each and every one of these things.

There is one other way of acquiring information to which I have not so far specifically referred. We sometimes get information by inference. So, having learnt that Napoleon fought in the Battle of Waterloo and having learnt, too, that this battle was fought in 1815, we may infer that Napoleon was still alive in 1815. Or observing that a piece of litmus paper turns pink when we dip it into a certain solution, we may infer that the solution is acid. Or learning from experience that if we try to teach pupils certain procedures in logic, the unintelligent ones find them difficult to learn, we may infer that James will have difficulty in learning them.

As these examples will illustrate, information by inference can arise out of information derived by any other means. Philosophers have sometimes argued that it is impossible to derive genuinely fresh information by inference, since, they have said, if the inference is valid the conclusion we draw must be already 'contained' in the premises. This is too large and too difficult a question to be discussed in passing, nor is this the place to ask – although these are topics a teacher ought to consider – what kinds of inference there are and how they differ. It is enough for our purposes that a pupil can acquire by inference information he has not specifically been taught by his teacher, or read in a book, or acquired by observation or experience on a particular occasion. The effect is that information is to some degree 'open-ended'; in acquiring a piece of information we do not simply acquire *that* piece of information.

NOTES

[1] John Dewey, *Democracy and Education* (New York 1916), p. 163.

[2] R.M. Hutchins, *The Higher Learning in America* (New Haven 1936), p. 69.

[3] John Dewey, *Experience and Education* (New York 1938), p. 26.

[4] R.G. Collingwood, *Autobiography* (London 1939).

[5] There are special cases in which we deliberately assume the rôle of spectator. We refuse to intervene; we hold ourselves aloof. So a child may actively withdraw from a class, perhaps into 'dumb insolence'. In such instances, spectatorship is a form of social action, and may be deliberately embarked upon in order to study its consequences. But I am talking above about involuntary spectatorship, where we do not deliberately decide to be spectators, as a form of social experiment, but are forced to be spectators, in virtue of the situation in which we find ourselves.

[6] These views were not, of course, original to Pestalozzi. The Czech educator-mystic Comenius had been as vigorous an opponent of 'verbalism' as Pestalozzi and in his *Orbis Sensualium Pictus* (1658) had not merely advocated but employed 'visual aids' – in the form of wood-cuts – to extend the range of 'object lessons'. Francis Bacon, in his turn, had inspired Comenius. But Comenius' work was by the end of the seventeenth century almost entirely forgotten; neither Rousseau nor Pestalozzi seems even to have heard of him. To an extraordinary degree, the history of educational theory is a history of repeated fresh starts rather than of continuous progress.

[7] Charles Dickens, *Hard Times*, ch.2. This novel was first published in 1854. Pestalozzi developed his views from 1780 on. It took a long time for them to penetrate.

[8] Compare John Dewey, *How We Think* (London 1909), pp. 191-2. But I draw also on recollections of long hours of boredom in my own primary-school days, in the nineteen-twenties.

[9] W.T. Harris in the *Educational Review*, May 1893, p. 117.

[10] John Dewey, *Democracy and Education*, pp. 321-2.

[11] So Locke's disciple, Isaac Watts, in his *The Improvement of the Mind* (1741), exhorted the teacher to take his pupils 'to see the fields, the woods, the rivers, the dwellings, towers and cities distant from their own dwellings'. From their travels,

they are to 'bring home treasures of useful knowledge'. The school bus has made it easier to put these precepts into practice.

[12] J.J. Rousseau, *Emile*, trans. R.L. Archer, book V, pt.II (New York 1964), pp. 258, 9.

[13] What the child sees on a film or television I have counted as 'observation'. This might be questioned on the ground that the child is dependent on the observations made by the camera-man. For that reason we might prefer to speak, in such cases, of 'indirect observation'. Pupils should certainly be warned against the presumption as that 'the camera cannot lie', as against the argument 'he must know; he saw it with his own eyes'. But for the rest the distinction between watching, in a film, an insect alight on a flower and seeing the same through a glass screen is not of any great importance. The child can see what the cameraman did not notice.

[14] For a general discussion of the ways in which 'learning by experience' has been used by philosophers of education see John Hanson: 'Learning by Experience' in B.O. Smith and R.H. Ennis (eds), *Language and Concepts in Education*, (Chicago 1961). It will be clear from that article to what extent I am, in what follows, legislating for rather than describing usage.

[15] Compare David Ausubel, *Educational Psychology* (New York 1968), p. 497. On the discovery method in general, see R.F. Dearden, 'Instruction and learning by discovery', in *The Concept of Education*, pp. 135-55.

[16] J.S. Bruner, *The Process of Education* (Cambridge Mass. 1961), p. 14.

[17] Jean Piaget, *Judgment and Reasoning in the Child*, trans. M. Warden, (London 1928), p. 7.

[18] On this point see R.F. Dearden, 'Instruction and learning by discovery', in *The Concept of Education*. On the discovery method generally, see A.C. Hogg and J.K. Foster, *Understanding Teaching Procedures*, (Melbourne 1973).

[19] See, for example, D. Wheeler, 'The teaching of mathematics', in A.D.C. Petersen (ed.), *Techniques of Teaching*, (Oxford 1965), vol. 2, p. 39.

[20] For an account of the different types of confusion which arise from the use of maps, and the ways in which cartographers are trying to overcome them see E.B. Espenshade, 'Cartographic developments and new maps' in *New Viewpoints in Geography*, Twenty-Ninth Yearbook of the National Council for the Social Studies, ed. P.E. James (Washington 1959), pp. 93-111.

[21] R.T. Heimer and M.S. Newman, *The New Mathematics for Parents* (New York 1965).

[22] John Locke, *Essay Concerning the Human Understanding*, (Bk. 1, Ch. II, §22).

[23] David Hume, *Treatise of Human Nature*, (Bk. 1, Part III, §IX).

[24] So in *Suggestions for the Teaching of Classics*, Ministry of Education pamphlet No. 37 (London 1959), it is suggested that the classics master can 'by elaboration, explanation, and, where need be, correction' make use of television and radio programmes of popular archaeology, thereby converting 'fragmentary, half-absorbed impressions into valuable, informed interests' (p. 51). By such means the teacher can at the same time get his pupils to see both the usefulness and the limitations of such 'picked-up' knowledge.

[25] J.A. Passmore, S.W. Cohen, E. Roe, L. Short, *Teaching Methods in Australian Universities*, a report prepared for the Australian Vice-Chancellors' Committee, printed by Melbourne University Press, 1963. In my pamphlet *Reading and Remembering* (Melbourne 1963), I described methods of independent learning in more detail and at a more practical level.

[26] Several analyses have been made, one at the Case Institute of Technology, of the 'job-activities' of scientists. These indicate that, on the average, scientists spend about fourteen hours of a forty-hour week reading materials by, or writing materials

to be read by, persons who are not their professional peers. They spend an additional twelve hours reading materials by, or writing materials to be read by, their professional peers. See G.G. Mallinson, 'Developing competence in reading: science' in *Recent Developments in Reading* (Chicago 1965) p. 150. See also the Report of the U.S. President's Science Advisory Committee: *Science, government and information: the responsibilities of the technical community and the government in the transfer of information* (Washington 1963). Some chemistry departments in America required their students to take short courses in the reading of scientific literature; engineers, on the other hand, were, so the report found, frequently quite ignorant of the resources available to them. In his Inaugural Lecture at the University of Edinburgh, Professor T.L. Cottrell complained of British chemists in industry that they engage in quite unnecessary experiments when the information they need is readily available if they cared to consult the literature. It is rare to find an examination paper in *any* subject which asks the candidate, not for information as such, but what would be the best place to find a certain kind of information.

[27] Sections 4.01, 4.001.

[28] But not only in these cases, of course. One may also speak of someone as being able to 'read minds'.

Chapter Five
Imparting Information

There are, then, many different ways in which children acquire information – by observation, from and through experience, by picking it up, by private study, by reasoning. But these are not the child's sole sources of information. Much of the stock of information which he gradually acquires is, in our society, imparted to him by a teacher. How does imparting information differ from merely *offering* it, i.e. from simple 'telling'?

The teacher who tells his pupils that 'I once had an interesting holiday in Greece', or that 'I didn't own a television set until quite recently', will not be in the slightest degree perturbed if they immediately forget what he has told them; he may, indeed, prefer them to do so. If he tells them that 'the school sports day will be held on Saturday, May 30', or that 'the examination will be held in three weeks' ·time', he expects them, certainly, to remember this information for a short period of time, but only for that time. In contrast, he hopes, and tries to ensure, that they will remember for all time that 'Shakespeare wrote *Hamlet*' or that 'water is a compound of oxygen and hydrogen' – the sort of information which is staple to the subjects he is teaching. To attempt to impart information is to offer it in the manner most likely to ensure that it will be retained.

Merely to memorise a sentence without understanding its meaning is not to have acquired information. To take over an anecdote from William James, a child who has learnt to respond to the question 'What is the condition of the centre of the earth?' with the reply 'It is in an igneous condition' and yet cannot answer such questions as 'If a hole were dug towards the centre of the earth, would the temperature be higher or lower as the hole got deeper?' does not know that the centre of the earth is in an igneous condition.

Without understanding either the question or the answer, a child can learn to give the 'correct answer' to a set of questions in a religious or a political catechism, in the sense that if the question is asked in a certain set form, he can answer it in the corresponding set form. What the teacher has done in such an instance is not to impart information but to inculcate a habit, the habit of making a fixed response (the set answer) to a determinate stimulus (the set question). This can occur without the teacher at all realising that it is occurring; in other words, a teacher can wrongly believe that he has imparted information when he has not really done so. This is no new discovery; Montaigne long ago suggested that the teacher should demand of his pupils that they rephrase what they have been taught in their own words, so as to show that they understand 'the sense and substance of what they have learnt'. In all information-imparting, for the teacher to act thus is a bare minimum of pedagogical prudence. That he often does not impart information when he believes he has done so is not an objection to information-imparting as such.

How large a part of the teacher's concern is the imparting of information? Mr Gradgrind in a much-cited passage from Dickens' *Hard Times* had no doubts on this point:

'Now what I want,' he explains to a teacher in the school he controls, 'is Fact. Teach these boys and girls nothing but Facts. Facts alone are wanted in life. Plant nothing else, root out everything else. You can form the mind of reasoning animals upon Facts; nothing else will be of any service to them.'

The teacher to whom Mr Gradgrind thus addressed himself had been admirably trained to satisfy this demand; he had learnt, and proposed to teach his pupils: 'the Water Sheds of all the world; and all the histories of all the peoples, and all the names of all the rivers and all the mountains, and all the productions, manners and customs of all the peoples.' And Dickens is by no means engaging in parody. Well into the twentieth century many teachers shared Mr Gradgrind's ideal.

It is sometimes suggested that such information-imparting has now almost disappeared from our schools. So Ryle tells us that a 'vanishingly small fraction' of the ordinary teaching-day is devoted to the imparting of information, that the parental request 'Recite what you have learned in school today, Tommy' is now a wholly absurd one. Tommy has not learnt, he says, a specific piece, or specific pieces, of information; he has moved towards greater mastery or greater understanding but not by way of an additional item of 'knowledge that'.[1] After visiting a considerable number of classrooms in a large number of different countries, Martin Mayer came to a conclusion quite the contrary of Ryle's, namely that 'the programme of the intermediate years, in all countries, is designed primarily to give the children *information*'. And this, he goes on to suggest, is inevitably so. Children go to school, bright, lively, interested, but ignorant to a degree only the teacher fully realises. 'By the time the child [is twelve], however, he will have acquired an almost complete stock of "commonsense knowledge" about the world around him' – very largely as a result of the work of the schools.[2]

One of the best ways of finding out about what actually goes on in the schools, as distinct from what it is nice to think of as going on in them, is by inspecting the papers set in public examinations. In Australia, at least, the evidence from that source is decisive; the student is expected to acquire a great deal of information. This is so obviously true in history, in biology and in geography as scarcely to be worth illustrating. But economics students who are asked to describe the function and operations of the International Monetary Fund, the student of German who is asked to write half a page on Goethe, Beethoven, Dürer and Röntgen, the chemistry student who has to describe the nature and properties of sulphur dioxide, sulphurous acid, sulphuric acid, and hydrogen sulphide, are all of them being asked for information in the most limited sense of the word – information about the observable characteristics of a specific thing or kind of thing. Yet modern educational theorists are all but unanimous in objecting to information-imparting. Their objections fall under four heads – which I shall distinguish as moral, practical, activist, and structural.

1. Moral objections

The 'moral' objection is apparent in such 'progressivist' works as W.H. Kilpatrick's *Philosophy of Education*, in which he unreservedly attacks what he calls the 'Alexandrian' conception of education, the conception of it as a method of ensuring that the child acquires information. 'Education,' he writes in opposition to Alexandrianism, 'must primarily seek character and behaviour, all-round character of a kind to lead to proper behaviour.'[3]

The dispute between Kilpatrick and the 'Alexandrians' illustrates only too clearly one of the major sources of confusion in educational controversy – the attempt to establish 'an aim' for education, a single aim to which every act of teaching must be subordinated. For the 'Alexandrians', the Gradgrindists, it is the imparting of facts; for Kilpatrick it is the development of 'character of a kind to lead to proper behaviour' – whatever that may be. On the face of it, however, the educated man differs from the uneducated man in a great variety of ways, one of them being that he has at his disposal a stock of information, information of the sort he could not derive merely from reflection on his daily experience. However excellent his character, however democratic he may be, however practically competent, however imaginative, it would be highly misleading to describe him as 'educated' merely because he possesses these virtues in so eminent a degree; we have other words at our disposal for that purpose. Kilpatrick, and the very many educators who think as he does, have produced good reasons for objecting to such educationists as see in the imparting of information the *sole* business of the teacher; it requires considerably more argument than he has provided to sustain the view that it is not a *substantial part* of the teacher's business.

2. Practical objections

If, however, there is every reason for being suspicious of attempts to set up some single 'aim of education', there is one general assumption about teaching, in all of its forms, which I have taken for granted and which can scarcely be abandoned: that in all teaching the teacher sets out to produce upon his pupils a more than evanescent effect. The whole expensive apparatus of schooling makes no sense – except perhaps as a device for keeping children off the streets or as a conspiracy to *prevent* them from learning – unless it is presumed that the child changes for the better in some respects, whatever these respects are taken to be, during the course of his schooling, and in a way which influences his future conduct.

At this point, the *practical* objections to information-imparting come to the fore. Even before the investigations of educational psychologists, we all knew that we very rapidly forget a good deal of the information we daily acquire. As a result of their work we have come more fully to realise just how extensive that loss can be.

Experimental work in this field must, it is true, be regarded with a certain degree of scepticism. In the first place, much of it is concerned with the rote-learning of nonsense-syllables rather than with the intelligent learning of information; it is not obvious that what is true of rote-learning must also be true of the acquisition of information. Secondly, the experimental work seldom reproduces actual classroom conditions, in which the teacher tests and revises, makes his pupils use information in exercises, exerts his authority in a variety of ways. Thirdly, the question when it is proper to say of information that it has been 'forgotten' is not easy to settle; to identify remembering with being able to recall in detail is to impose tests which are altogether too stringent. A pupil may retain information in a recognition form, although not in a recall form. Asked 'What is the name of the author of *Moby Dick*?', he may be quite unable to answer or he may remember only that the author's name begins with 'M'. Yet to the question 'Was the name of the author of *Moby Dick*, Hawthorne, Melville, or Mark Twain?', he may unhesitatingly answer 'Melville'. Even more confusingly, he may be quite unable to recall the name 'Melville' on Monday, and yet it may 'come to him' on Tuesday; in a case of emergency he may recall what he cannot under normal circumstances recall; in circumstances similar to those in which the information was originally acquired he may recall what he thought he had forgotten. And, for certain purposes, this sort of limited remembering is all that he may need.

But however liberally 'remembering' is interpreted, it is quite impossible to deny that we forget a great deal of the information we have learnt, and often with disconcerting rapidity. What is the point of imparting information, it might well be asked, if it is forgotten at so striking a rate? Let the teacher rather concentrate on habits, on skills, on character-traits, where he can at least have some hope that his efforts will not be, in the long run, totally unavailing. A habit, once formed, can easily be slipped back into if it is for a time abandoned; skills get rusty but are unlikely, if thoroughly taught, to be wholly lost; people's characters can change but character traits are all the same remarkably persistent.

There are, however, practical objections to those other forms of learning as much as to the acquisition of information. The habits inculcated by the teacher may turn out to be useless, or even a serious hindrance, to the pupil in his later life; skills may be rendered unavailing by new inventions; character traits may be so rigid as to prove fatal to the pupil. That is one reason why it is important so to teach the child, or the undergraduate, that he will be prepared for changes. But without the help of information he will not be able to recognise, let alone effectively to cope with, those changes when they come.

A second practical objection to information-imparting is that, as I have already pointed out, much of what is taught as information is actually misinformation. In some subjects information has a particularly short life; what the doctor is taught as an undergraduate about the methods of treating disease, or even their symptoms, may later turn out to be completely erroneous. But the same is true even in such areas as history. Consider what contrary information about 'the Middle Ages' or 'the Renaissance' children have from time to time acquired. Once more, however, this only means that the teacher must be careful *how* he imparts information.

Undoubtedly the imparting of information lends itself to the use of authoritarian methods; the child may then tend to believe that what he was taught in school is true beyond all possibility of revision. But the two are not inevitably associated; information can be imparted in an intellectual atmosphere in which the child is constantly made aware that what he is being taught is not necessarily an eternal truth. This is one of the virtues of a genuinely historical approach – as distinct from what often passes for it, an occasional patronising reference to past errors, depicted as belonging to a darker age, when men still made mistakes.[4] If the child is brought to see – not in the case of every piece of information, of course, but now and then, as an antidote to complacency – just how and why intelligent men have been so badly led astray in the past, this may help to shake his own confidence that what he is now learning must be true. The practical objections to information-imparting, to sum up, are certainly serious but not quite as fatal as they are sometimes supposed to be.

3. Activist objections

To turn now to the 'activist' objections. Information-imparting is often associated with a kind of teaching in which, as Montaigne puts it, the teacher 'shouts into his pupils' ears as if he were pouring water into a funnel'. But this is *bad* information-imparting. If he is to have any hope of imparting information to his pupils, as distinct from merely talking to them or training them to respond to a set question with a set answer, the teacher must ensure that his pupils are actively involved, whether by reading a text, revising, writing essays, working out exercises, or sitting for examinations. These are all forms of activity, as is indeed *listening* when it is distinguished from merely sitting in a classroom in which a teacher is talking. The idea that in the old-fashioned schooling-system the student was merely passive, never active, is a wholly mistaken one.

It must be granted, however, that such forms of activity were wholly directed by the teacher and were undertaken by his pupils primarily in order to satisfy the teacher's demands. This, according to the 'activist' critics of traditional information-imparting, with Dewey as their leading spokesman, is its great weakness, and the reason why traditional information-imparting is educationally so unsatisfactory.It follows the contours of a systematically-organised subject; in that form it cannot be intellectually absorbed by the mind into its processes of reflection. To be educationally useful it must take as its point of departure the pupils' problems, not the traditional requirements of a 'subject'. 'Instruction in subject-matter that does not fit into any problem already stirring in the student's own experience,' Dewey writes, 'or that is not presented in such a way as to arouse a problem, is worse than useless for intellectual purposes. In that it fails to enter into any process of reflection, it is useless; in that it remains in the mind as so much lumber and débris, it is a barrier, an obstruction in the way of effective thinking when a problem arises.'⁵

But where is the pupil to get his problems from? So far as possible, Dewey replies, his problems should arise in 'what the learner has derived from more direct forms of experience'. The great mistake teachers make, he suggests, is in linking what is to be learnt at school this week with what was learnt last week, instead of bringing out its connexions with what the child is learning outside the school.⁶ School knowledge and ordinary experience are thus irretrievably sundered: 'Pupils are taught to live in two separate worlds, one the world of out-of-school experience, the other the world of books and lessons.'

With much of what Dewey says one can scarcely disagree. If the teacher is to have any prospect of being understood, as distinct from merely forcing formulae on his pupils, he must call upon their previous experience – including, however, their previous experience in the classroom; unless he touches his pupils' interests his teaching will not have any permanent effect upon them; if he can get them puzzled, and then get them to see what information they need and how badly they need it in order to resolve their puzzles, this is certainly the best possible context in which to impart information. As against the conception of teaching as consisting, wholly and desirably, in ramming facts into children, such of Dewey's earlier writings as *How We Think* are an admirable corrective.

One can scarcely deny, either, that school pupils brought up in the traditional way often thought of their out-of-school problems as one thing, their school-work as quite another. Many boys and girls left school without having ever grasped the idea of consulting books as a way of acquiring information of practical importance to them; book-learning, as they saw it, was one thing, the information they needed for the solution of practical problems quite another. They had no conception either of the theoretical value or the practical significance of mathematics and science. The literature they had officially studied at school, as distinct from what they read under the desk, was so jejune, so 'safe', so remote in time and place from their personal problems – their sexual problems, their problems in getting along with parents, their worries about drugs, or alcohol, or war – that they were left with the profound conviction that only in the comic-book, the cheap novel, the blood-and-guts thriller, are the 'real problems' of everyday life illustrated and illuminated.

Yet Dewey himself came to fear the consequences of his own teachings, and to dissociate himself from what he condemns as the extravagant, but which were often enough the perfectly natural, conclusions which were drawn from them:

'I am sure that you will appreciate what is meant,' he wrote in *Experience and Education*, 'when I say that many of the newer schools tend to make little or nothing of organised subject-matter of study; to proceed as if any form of direction and guidance by adults were an invasion of individual freedom, and as if the idea that education should be concerned with the present and future meant that acquaintance with the past has little or no role to play in education.'[7] He went on to describe the effects of such an education: 'Energy becomes dissipated and a person becomes scatterbrained. Each (school) experience may be lively, vivid and "interesting" and yet their disconnectedness may artificially generate dispersive, disintegrated, centrifugal habits.' There could scarcely be a more accurate description of the intellectual habits of a great many of the products of 'progressive' schools as they have become visible in our 'youth culture'. Television at once draws upon, and more firmly fixes, those intellectual habits.

The difficulties in Dewey's view, when it is interpreted as a programme for action, are indeed only too obvious. The experience of individual children is extremely disparate. In the one school – particularly in school-systems in which the children are not segregated on the basis of class-background or income – there are likely to be children from homes where money is a constant preoccupation, others in which it is scarcely mentioned; children from homes where the consulting of books is an everyday experience, others from homes where it never occurs; children from families which live in harmony, children from homes preoccupied with the problem of living together; children from homes where the only problems which are taken seriously are what and whether to buy; others from homes where political and social problems are the staple of everyday conversation.

In the most homogeneous of schools and the most homogeneous of societies, indeed, the teacher cannot presume any community of out-of-school problems in his classroom. This is true even in relation to practical problems – problems about what to do and how best to do it. As for theoretical problems, problems which arise out of an intellectual puzzle, the differences between individual children are even greater. One child may be puzzled about the manner in which a man-made satellite is put into orbit at a stage at which another child has not so much as heard of man-made satellites. What an individual child desperately wants to know is to another child a matter of indifference, or already familiar to him – sexual information is only the most obvious, not the sole, example of this phenomenon.

In these circumstances – and the more particularly as he often thinks it 'dangerous' to take as his starting-point many of the problems which most deeply disturb his pupils – the teacher is tempted to look for his 'out-of-school' problems in the detailed practical concerns of everyday life on the presumption that these, at least, must be of interest to all his pupils. A problem-solving approach to teaching is thus readily converted into a narrow, disorganised, vocational or social utilitarianism.

So for example, instead of learning chemistry or physics as an organised body of knowledge the child is introduced to a 'general science' course – I do not mean to suggest that all 'general science' courses are of this kind, but some certainly are[8] – in which he is expected to take an interest in a range of practical information related to personal hygiene, the pasteurisation of milk and the filtration of water supplies, the methods of extracting coal, iron, or oil, the best methods of growing crops and the mechanics of petrol engines. He is left with no impression whatsoever of science as a systematic body of knowledge, an exercise of the imagination, or a method of explanation.

Instead of being taught history, the child, similarly, is expected to learn – as 'social studies' – how elections are conducted or post-offices are run; the virtues of policemen, banks and the United Nations; why, and how, taxes are paid and pensions granted. Such 'social studies' may incorporate – or this may be a separate subject – 'current affairs' taught, as a gesture to 'immediate experience', not from text-books but from newspaper-cuttings and 'made more real' by uneasily patronising talks delivered by visiting officials, little accustomed to an audience of children. The child's interests, problems and needs are merely presumed, without adequate investigation, to be restricted to the current scene. (Compare old-fashioned 'practical arithmetic' with its assumption that the child is bound to be interested in the amount of wallpaper it takes to paper a room. What vistas of boredom the recollection of that sort of arithmetic and mensuration conjures up!)

'Current affairs' teaching tends in fact to be singularly *unreal*, unless the teacher is an unusually independent and courageous person. Even then he would probably think it improper to make the same sort of comment about a living President or a current political issue involving allegations of graft as he would about some comparable situation in the past. Political disputes, social controversies, as the teacher aseptically describes them, are very different from the rough-and-tumble disputes which the child may encounter in his own household. (Think of a boy like Stephen Daedalus in Joyce's *Portrait of the Artist as a Young Man* moving from bitter no-holds-barred family disputes about Parnell to school-lessons about the election system!) In contrast, a good history teacher can make intensely alive, with all its tragedy and squalor, the history of the past. As Martin Mayer puts it: 'Yesterday's paper is not so alive as Garibaldi's Red Shirts, or Catherine the Great, or Torquemada, or Scott at the South Pole. Imaginative teaching can make Elizabeth I of England a real woman and Thomas Jefferson a real man, but it would not be polite to take the same attitude towards [a living Queen of England, or contemporary President], who for purposes of conversation in a classroom must remain fictions and abstractions as long as they live.'[9] (The radicalisation of the schools in the nineteen-sixties, in some countries at least, rather changed this situation. But at the cost, often enough, of converting the teacher into a propagandist.)

We can at least express the matter thus: it is the merest presumption that the child is bound to be more interested in the world which actually lies around him than in the remote past or in distant parts of the globe; it is the merest presumption, again, that he is, or ought to be, interested only in what is 'in his interest' in the narrow practical sense of that phrase.[10] And once those presumptions are rejected, once the child is seen as a being who, to modify a phrase of Freud's, is 'polymorphously curious', then it is no longer at all plausible to identify 'real problems' with narrowly practical interests.

If this is to be his grounding principle, the teacher certainly must abandon all hope of introducing his pupil to the great traditions of science or scholarship. Science and scholarship are by their nature cumulative, systematic, not arising directly out of immediate and disparate practical needs. If the child is to learn to think systematically, to understand the great variety of ways in which problems arise, the very different types they fall into, the diversified way in which information can be brought to bear upon their solution, he must have under his control a considerable body of information. Such information he can only to a very slight degree obtain, as Dewey himself came more and more to recognise, from observation and experience. This does not mean that the information must at first be imparted to him as a global mass, only later to have questions raised about it; questions can be raised about it as it is imparted, problems set. So the child need not merely be told that the blood circulates in the body but asked what use to the organism this could possibly be; he need not merely be told that Elizabeth I persecuted Roman Catholics but can first be encouraged to ask himself what, in the light of the historic circumstances, her attitude to them was likely to be.

The teacher thus *creates* problem-situations, but can usually do so only by first imparting information. We can put the same point in terms of interests. The teacher has in some way to appeal to the child's interests in order to impart information, but by imparting information he can create new interests or greatly intensify existing interests. So, for example, he creates an interest in history by teaching the child history. Paradoxical as this may sound, to think of interests as given and the teacher's task as being merely to impart information by appealing to those fixed interests is to lay greater educational stress on information-imparting than to suppose that interests are not simply given but can be aroused by means of imparting information.

As for the supposed opposition between 'subjects' and 'problems', to teach history is to introduce the child to historical problems and their solution; to teach him to paint is to introduce him, among other things, to technical problems and their solution; to teach him to appreciate a novel is, among other things, to show him how the novelist has looked at certain human problems. The only question is whether the child's attention should be successively directed to a series of closely correlated problems which are tackled by closely related methods, or whether he should pass in a merely haphazard way from one problem to another as his uninformed fancy happens to dictate.

4. Structural objections

In many respects the 'structural' objection lies at the opposite extreme from the sort of objection raised by Dewey and his self-styled 'disciples'. Bruner, the leader of the 'structuralists', criticises Dewey very much along the lines we have suggested. 'In insisting upon the continuity of the school with the community ...,' he writes, 'Dewey overlooked the special function of education as an opener of new perspectives.'[11] Dewey failed to realise, Bruner further argues, what a great difference it makes that human societies are now literate; he assimilates the school system of a literate society to the merely practical institutions of preliterate society. Nevertheless, he agrees with Dewey in his opposition to the simple imparting of information, if only on what we called 'practical' grounds. 'Knowledge one has acquired without sufficient structure to tie it together,' he writes, 'is knowledge that is likely to be forgotten. An unconnected set of facts has a pitiably short half-life in memory. Organizing facts in terms of principles and ideas from which they may be inferred is the only known way of reducing the quick rate of loss of human memory.'[12]

In this comment of Bruner's, however, two different contentions are run together, which it is important to distinguish: the first that 'an unconnected set of facts has a pitifully short half-life in memory' and the second that 'organising facts in terms of principles and rules is the only known way of reducing the quick rates of loss of human memory'. What is here presumed, but not borne out in the examples Bruner goes on to give, is that to 'structure' information is identical with discovering rules and principles from which it can be inferred. In fact, however, information can be 'structured' in a variety of fashions; bringing it under principles and rules is not always possible.

In *Principles of Psychology*[13] William James distinguishes three different ways of making it easier to remember information: the mechanical, the ingenious and the judicious. 'Mechanical' methods include the familiar schoolroom procedures of repetition; 'ingenious' methods make use of arbitrary mnemonic devices; 'judicious' methods so reorganise the information to be remembered that it constitutes, in James's words, 'not so many odd facts, but a concept-system'.[14]

Let us look a little more closely at the distinction between 'ingenious' and 'judicious' methods. Suppose we need to remember, if only for examination purposes, what Sir Cyril Norwood took to be the aims of education: culture, athletics, religion, discipline, service. The initial letters of these words, as it happens, together make up the word 'cards'. 'Ingenious' systems of mnemonics make use of such accidental facts, working on the assumption that if we recall Norwood's aims as 'cards', it will be easier to remember what those aims are than if we set out to memorise them directly. Similarly we shall, it is thought, find it easier to recall the date of the discovery of America if we learn by heart the jingle 'In 1492, Columbus sailed the ocean blue' rather than if we try to recall the more prosaic sentence 'Columbus discovered America in 1492'. The rhyme with 'blue' helps us to remember that the date was 1492 rather than, say, 1497. The standard textbook in logic for some hundred and fifty years after its first publication in 1691, Aldrich's *Compendium Artis Logicae*, was very largely made up of such mnemonic rhymes and arbitrary devices – designed to assist the powers of recollection of Oxford undergraduates for whom logic was until 1831 a compulsory subject. In recent years they have fallen into disrepute, as encouraging the view that education consists in the rote-learning of rigmaroles, but as late as 1902 so notable a logician as C.S. Peirce wrote of them with respect.[15]

In 'judicious', as distinct from 'ingenious', devices for aiding the memory, the material to be remembered is also set out in an organised form. But whereas in Aldrich's *Logic*, say, the organisation of the material was determined by such accidental facts as that the Latin word for a particular logical process begins with 'r', judicious methods make use of forms of organisation which are inherent in the character and relationships of the information to be recalled. Obvious examples of such rational organisations of information are a family tree, a railway time-table, a time-chart, a graphical representation of economic fluctuations over a period of time.

James himself, following such of his contemporaries as Ernst Mach and Karl Pearson,[16] suggests that the whole of science is nothing more than an elaborate deployment of 'judicious' mnemonics. 'Judicious methods of remembering things,' he writes, 'are nothing but logical ways of conceiving them and working them into rational systems, classifying them, analysing them into parts, etc. etc. All the sciences are such methods.'[17] And although Bruner is less explicit on this point, he seems to work with the same assumption. He identifies, for example, the 'economy' of a scientific formula with the economy to be achieved by setting out a complex set of information in a tabular form.[18]

There is, however, a fundamental difference between the two cases. Compare the information contained in the laws of mechanics with the information set out in an astronomical almanac or ephemeris. The laws of mechanics are not simply a summary of the astronomical almanac. They assist us to make predictions not contained in the almanac, as the almanac itself does not; they assist us to understand and explain the movements of the heavenly bodies, as the almanac does not. That is the difference between Babylonian astronomy, which was content to construct ephemerides, and Greek astronomy which looked for celestial laws. On the other hand, the laws of mechanics do not by themselves tell us where any celestial object will be at a given time; they are utterly useless if this is what we want to know, unless they are supplemented by ephemeris-type information about the position of the heavenly bodies at some particular point of time, together with a great deal of other such detailed information. Astronomy is reducible to mechanics only if, in Plato's manner, we think of information about the actual position of the heavenly bodies as unworthy of acquisition. But that is certainly not the attitude of the astronomer himself, to say nothing of the navigator, the huntsman, or the astrologer. Even if it would be absurd to try to learn by heart the contents of the astronomical almanac for any given year, it is not equally absurd to learn which objects in the heaven are planets and which are fixed stars, what the principal constellations are called and how they appear in relation to one another.

Such information is certainly not deducible from scientific laws. Similarly there is no principle from which it can be deduced that Henry VIII broke with the Church of Rome, or how rapidly the population of India is increasing, or how many ribs a human being has, or when President Kennedy was assassinated, or how distant the moon is from the earth, or, even, that chloroform is an anaesthetic or that platypuses suckle their young.

What is the teacher to do about information of this sort, not deducible from laws? There are two possibilities. The first is to attempt to use whatever devices turn out to be most effective – mechanical, ingenious or judicious – in the hope that he will succeed in imparting it to his pupils. It is not deducible from a time-chart that the French Revolution broke out in 1789 but it may help the child to remember the date if he puts it in a time-chart. And at the same time that form of organisation may suggest problems, e.g. why so many revolutions occurred in 1848. The second alternative is for the teacher entirely to abandon the attempt to impart such information, concentrating all his attention on 'communicating structure' and reshaping the curriculum for that purpose. This is the alternative accepted by Bruner, and along with Bruner by a not inconsiderable number of contemporary educationists.

What is meant by 'communicating structures'? There are two senses of 'structure' which need to be distinguished. On the first interpretation, the 'structure' of a science consists of what is often called its 'logic', its methods of explanation, the types of theory it constructs, the ways in which it uses hypotheses. On the second interpretation, the structure of a science consists in its leading ideas, the conceptual system it employs, and, where this is applicable, the laws which relate them. Let us look at these interpretations in turn.

In his contribution to a discussion on the purposes and character of science teaching, the physicist E.M. Rogers complains that 'even those students who arrive at college with plans to become scientists usually bring a mistaken picture of science, something like a *stamp collection of facts* or a game of *getting the right answer*'.[19] This attitude of mind, he suggests, derives partly from the fact that high-school science courses consist partly of 'snippets of information', partly from the attempt to train pupils in the allocation of numerical values to general formulae. Neither procedure, he says, 'shows students how scientists work and think' – and of the many, no doubt laudable, aims set before the science-teacher, this is the only one, Rogers argues, he has a reasonable chance of achieving. Although he has no prospect, in the case of most of his students, of teaching them to be physicists or chemists, he can hope to give them 'an understanding of science and scientists – of what sort of thing they do and how they do it'. In this way the teacher can at once create 'a happier attitude towards scientists' among those high-school students and undergraduates who do not intend ever to become scientists, and provide a more adequate preparation than traditional science courses did for those few who will embark upon a scientific career.

It is very easy to sympathise with this approach to science-teaching, especially when one remembers just how futile the ordinary science course has so often been. It is certainly a minimum requirement of a science course that it should help students to understand what science is like as distinct from giving them that false impression that science is a bundle of tricks and isolated facts which some anti-scientists carry with them from their schooling to their grave. But the consequence, too often, is that instead of learning science the student learns something else – the philosophy of science with historical illustrations. Instead of learning by heart scientific formulae he learns by heart, often enough, definitions of theorem, hypothesis, experiment; instead of snippets of information about the behaviour of gases he acquires snippets of information about the behaviour of scientists. This result, it might be replied, is simply the outcome of bad teaching or bad curriculum design. Just how useful such a course *can be* in achieving the aims Rogers sets up for it is obviously a question which can only be settled experimentally.[20] But this much is clear: learning science is very different from learning what sort of thing science is.

Then should we say that the subject of a 'structure-centered' curriculum is not so much to give the pupil information about the nature of scientific thinking as to get him to 'think as a scientist does', to learn to solve his problems in the way in which a scientist solves them? These two objectives are often discussed as if they were one: it seems to be supposed that a 'structure-centered' curriculum will automatically develop the child's ability to solve problems – so that, as it were, Bruner and Dewey will be satisfied at a single blow.[21] But, of course, learning about science and learning to think like a scientist need to be carefully distinguished. It is one thing to teach a pupil, even with illustrations, that theoretical physicists proceed by constructing mathematical models and testing them in various ways; it is quite another thing to develop in him the capacity to construct such models and to test them. Learning about the general structure of scientific thinking consists in acquiring information about science; learning to think like a scientist involves acquiring habits, skills, character traits. And it involves, too, acquiring a great deal of information, information which at once raises problems and suggests where their solutions may lie.

To turn now to the second sense of 'structure', according to which the 'structure of science' consists in its leading ideas – in elementary biology, for example, such ideas as homeostasis, the life-cycle, adaptation, cellular structure, natural selection, inheritance and the general propositions relating them one to another. In this case, certainly, to learn structure is to learn science, not merely to learn about science. And we can grant that learning principles, learning concepts, the child has not the same need as he once had to acquire information, in the narrower sense of that word.[22] And to grasp these concepts is to be better prepared to understand the changes which take place in science. So, in this sense, we can fully agree that the child needs to learn the structure of science. The emphasis on structure, thus understood, is a healthy corrective to the information-cramming so typical of many traditional science-courses. But one can understand these concepts only within the matrix of a body of information. The concepts are empty unless we know how they are exemplified in particular cases. As so often, for a sensible view of the matter we can turn to Ernest Nagel: 'The materials of a discipline should be so presented that the logical principles controlling the analysis, the organisation, the validation, and the modification of scientific statements are kept in full view, and that the findings of the sciences are exhibited as the products of a creative but critical intelligence'. This, however, should not be 'in lieu of work in the substantive materials of the sciences'.[23] Teach so as to emphasise structure, select information with that in mind, in other words, but not in the belief that to do so is a substitute for imparting information.

Geography has been particularly subject to attempts to 'structuralise' it. It has sometimes been suggested, indeed, that geography should be entirely replaced by geophysics, since in virtue of its concern with 'the characteristics of particular places on the earth's surface' – to quote a recent definition – it is 'hopelessly unscientific'. At other times, under the influence of the doctrine that geography is 'a science of relationships' and the 'environmental determinism' which grew out of that view, it has been argued that geography, properly understood, is an attempt to discover a set of laws relating human behaviour to particular types of climate and to particular types of physical environment. But the present tendency of geographers is to reject all such views – to reaffirm that although it is possible to distinguish a number of general factors which operate in a region of a particular type, to understand any region in detail one must take into account such purely historical facts as that it was subject to a particular variety of human migration. 'I could perhaps understand early New England', so it has been said, 'without knowing the land, but never without knowing the Puritan immigrants.'[24] In fact, the geographer needs to know both land and people – the severity of the climate, the poverty of the land but, as well, the farming practices of the regions in England from which the Puritans came and their attitude to life. From general geographical principles very little indeed is deducible about the structure and climate of New England farming: that they did not grow pineapples, certainly, but not what they did grow or how they grew it.

Bruner, with his emphasis on structure, not surprisingly urges the replacement of 'information-laden' history and geography by a 'science of man',[25] a generalised anthropology which would take as its subject-matter such general concepts as language, tool-making, social organisation, child-rearing and mythology. It would study particular historical periods or particular geographical regions only as a way of illustrating the diversity of the forms in which such general concepts are exemplified. The object of such a course is not at all to impart information – 'it is only in a trivial sense,' Bruner writes, 'that one gives a course "to get something across", merely to impart information' – but rather to produce a set of highly generalised effects upon its pupils: to give them proper respect for and confidence in the powers of their own mind; to extend that respect and confidence to their power to think about the human condition, man's plight, and to social life; to provide a set of workable models that make it simple to analyse the social world in which we live and the conditions in which man finds himself; to impart a sense of respect for the capacities and humanity of man as a species; to leave the student with a sense of the unfinished business of man's evolution.[26] A not unambitious programme. Much more ambitious, certainly, than trying to get children to understand why the New England colony took the shape it did. How nice to be provided with 'a set of workable models that make it simple to analyse the social world in which we live'!

In an American analysis of the concepts of social science, some eighteen 'substantive concepts' have been distinguished – they include sovereignty, power, institution, social change – and some six 'value concepts', the dignity of man, empathy, loyalty, government by consent, freedom and equality.[27] To introduce a child analytically to such concepts as these is either to plunge him into the most difficult and most controversial problems in political philosophy, or else so grossly to oversimplify as to be a propagandist for a particular point of view rather than a teacher. How, devoid of information about what has actually happened in human society, is the child to choose between the view that government by consent is a fraud and the view that it is fully exemplified in representative democracies?

Unless, that is, all that is intended is to give the child a vocabulary. 'I looked at a sociology curriculum recently,' Michael Scriven has remarked, 'and came to the following conclusions. It teaches a vocabulary, but the net intellectual gain from it is indistinguishable from zero. If one wants to talk to sociologists it is splendid ...'[28] Of course, in learning any branch of science one is at the same time acquiring a vocabulary. To learn botany is, among other things, to learn how to use words like 'inflorescence' and 'monocotyledon', to learn chemistry is, among other things, to learn how to use words like 'halogen' or 'valency'. But in these instances the 'other things' are what are important – the new forms of organisation, the new kinds of relationship, which the use of these words helps us to investigate and to understand. This can happen in the social sciences, too. To learn to use the expression 'matrilineal society', for example, is at the same time to learn something new about forms of social organisation. But while the social sciences remain so theoretically inadequate, 'structural teaching' can easily collapse into mere verbalism.[29]

It is possible to imagine a curriculum-change which moved entirely in the structural direction. Accepting Lord Rutherford's dictum that science is either 'physics or stamp-collecting' it would teach no empirical science except physics, on the ground that physics alone exhibits the most general structures of the world; and for the rest only mathematics and logic. Or not carrying matters so far, it might replace traditional biology by genetics and molecular biology; geology by geophysics; history and social studies by a 'science of man'; the study of literature and art by aesthetics; the study of the English language by transformational and structural linguistics. In such a curriculum, the emphasis would be entirely centred on the most generalised kind of information. Attention would be drawn to specific differences only in order to exemplify and to illustrate structures.

Would such a curriculum be the ideal? On the face of it, the practical difficulties in remembering would be greatly lessened. For these general principles can be constantly re-exemplified; they lend themselves to non-repetitive revision, perhaps over several years of school-life, as they are made use of in a wide variety of circumstances. They are, or in principle can be, closely interconnected, rationally structured.

Yet before we throw away the kind of detailed analysis characteristic of history, two considerations at least might make us pause. The first is the fear that a thoroughly structured education might generate an attitude of mind with which we are already too familiar – an attitude which has been attacked by F.A. von Hayek and Karl Popper as 'scientism'.[30] Leaving aside the exaggerations which attach to Hayek's critique of 'scientism', we can at the same time recognise a real danger to which he has drawn attention, viz. the danger of presuming that the outcome of forms of social action ought to be deducible from general social laws much as the movements of a planet are deducible from general mechanical laws.[31] The detailed study of history and geography, in contrast with a generalised science of man, makes it clear just how complicated a matter it is to determine the consequences of social action, and just how dependent we are, if we hope to act sensibly, on the possession of a great deal of extremely detailed information. Indeed, the mistakes in American foreign policy since the Second World War largely derive from a too-powerful tendency to think conceptually and a weak appreciation of historical factors. Similar considerations apply, scarcely less obviously, to the practice of medicine or engineering; to think entirely in terms of general principles, without respect for the peculiarities of individual cases, is the path to disaster. Even in the case of mathematics, industrialists complain of a tendency to imagine that 'once an equation or formula has been produced, or even once it has only been shown that a solution exists, the problem is solved', where what the industrialist needs is numerical information.[32] In science generally, an emphasis on structure can lead to a neglect of that sort of detailed information which is essential for the adequate discussion of, let us say, environmental problems. It tends to cut off subjects one from another, as each possessing a structure peculiar to itself; it discourages cross-disciplinary investigations, the following-up of problems wherever they lead, as a breach in the tight walls of the structural subject.[33]

A second consideration is that general principles are, at least potentially, international in character. One has to add, 'at least potentially' for at a given historic period a particular nation may officially reject specific scientific principles. Einstein's theory of relativity, genetics, communication theory have, at various times, been rejected in the Soviet Union. But at least they are of international interest even when they are not internationally accepted.

In contrast, detailed information is often of interest only to the members of a particular community. It is no disgrace to an educated Frenchman that he has never heard of Patrick Henry or of Benedict Arnold, as it is to an educated American; the content of a botany course in Greenland will be significantly different from the content of a botany course in Australia; in every country an educated man can be expected to know something of the life and work of a Dante, a

Shakespeare, a Goethe, but an Englishman may reasonably be ignorant about Grillparzer, an Italian about Jane Austen, an American about Henry Lawson.

The advantage in this respect may be supposed entirely to lie with the structured 'international' subjects. But it is in and through the imparting of detailed information that the child is introduced to the traditions, the physical surroundings, the culture, of his own country or of those countries to whose civilisation his own is most closely allied. No doubt this has the effect that such detailed courses, especially in history, can be made the instruments of chauvinism. But however internationally-minded one may be, one can scarcely deny the importance of ensuring that the child has a special acquaintance with the traditions of his own country.[34] Nor is this sort of information likely to be forgotten with rapidity; it is subject to constant revision during the life of any person who participates at all actively in the culture of his community. It is hard to forget, in England, that Shakespeare wrote *Hamlet* or that Wellington defeated Napoleon.

For all that we forget so rapidly, indeed, many pieces of detailed information remain firmly fixed in our memory long after we would be hard put to it accurately to state, or effectively to employ, the most general principles of mechanics or of genetics. If I may judge by my own experience at least, it is by no means the case that detailed information is always forgotten or that it is less valuable to us in the conduct of our life than the general laws of physics. It is more than a little odd that 'structure' should be so emphasised at the cost of 'information' in a country like the United States where geographical and historical facts are of such great importance in understanding the assumptions, the population-shifts, the political institutions, the international attitudes which there prevail. Not to know that the United States was once a colony, that it once had a Civil War, that its black citizens were not free immigrants, that it has a large Jewish population, that many of its settlers were Puritans, is to find its actions and attitudes unintelligible.

At the same time, the teacher can certainly learn a great deal from the critics of information-imparting. He should ask himself, for example: 'Do I really need to impart this information? Is it not enough to try to ensure that my pupils will always be able to obtain it if they need to lay their hands on it?' As Bruner argues, he should try to ensure, in subjects where this is relevant, that his pupils carry away from a course of study the 'structure' which runs through the subject he is teaching, the ideas which will help them to analyse new situations as they arise, the general methods to employ, the general principles to apply. As Dewey argues, he should certainly do all he can to bring home to his pupils the ways in which information is relevant to the solution of problems; he should try to arouse their interest in problems, he should try to relate school-life to out-of-school life. But it by no means follows that he should entirely abandon the attempt to impart information, in order wholly to concentrate all his energies on the task of developing habits, attitudes and skills. If a boy is to understand geography, he must first learn that the earth is a globe that is surrounded by an atmosphere, that it contains more water than land; it is only too easy to forget, in the enthusiasm for new educational programmes, just how many such simple pieces of information the child has somehow to acquire and can most economically learn from a teacher. To such a degree has the word 'information' come to be a 'dirty' word, that geographers now sometimes refer to such elementary information as 'concepts'. But 'the localisation of industry' is a concept; that the world is a globe is information, pure and simple. To confuse between the two in order to make use of the aura of superiority which currently attaches to 'the teaching of concepts' is a device only too characteristic of educational writings and a principal means by which they generate intellectual muddle.[35]

NOTES

[1] Gilbert Ryle: 'Teaching and training', in *The Concept of Education*, p. 107.

[2] Martin Mayer, *The Schools* (New York 1961), p. 215. See also the emphasis on information – there called knowledge – in B.S. Bloom (ed.), *Taxonomy of Educational Objectives*, Handbook I (New York 1956), pp. 62-88.

[3] W.H. Kilpatrick, *Philosophy of Education* (New York 1951), p. 226.

[4] Both the history of philosophy and the history of science can, unfortunately, be so taught as to encourage the belief that what is now being taught is the once-and-for-all truth. See J. Agassi, 'Towards an historiography of science' in *History and Theory*, Beiheft 2, 1963, and J.A. Passmore, 'The idea of a history of philosophy', Beiheft 5, 1965.

[5] John Dewey, *How We Think* (London 1909), p. 199.

[6] Herbart and his followers had argued that 'instruction builds upon the foundation of experience already gained *in* or *out* of the school' (C. De Garmo, *Herbart and the Herbartians* (New York 1895) p. 77) (my italics). But in practice the lesson sequences constructed under the influence of Herbart – as I know from my own pedagogical training – were so designed as to form a closely knit logical sequence, leaving no room for that outside experience which to the more mechanical followers of Herbart could only appear as a disruption to a logically developed sequence. Many of Dewey's doctrines are best understood as an unduly violent reaction against the stress laid by the followers of Herbart on the importance of adhering to the systematic patterns of subjects. So where for a Herbartian a lesson begins by revising the previous lesson, for Dewey it begins with a reference to the

world outside the classroom. On Herbart's original view, however, it could begin in either or both of these ways, depending on the circumstances, and that is surely the more sensible approach.

⁷ *Experience and Education*, p. 22.

⁸ There is a sense in which 'general science' courses are premature. They rest on the presumption that 'science is a unity'. But 'the unity of science', at the present stage of scientific development, is a slogan rather than a description of the actual situation. If one tries to force a unity where there is none, the effect is very likely to be a mere agglomeration.

⁹ Martin Mayer, *The Schools*, p. 336.

¹⁰ The ambiguity of 'interest' is thoroughly explored by P.S. Wilson in his *Interest and Discipline in Education* (London 1971). The now irremediable confusion in meaning between 'disinterested' and 'uninterested' shows to what a degree this clarification is needed, how widely it is supposed that to consider something from a point of view other than our personal advantage is to take no interest in it. It is one thing to say that a form of activity is 'in the child's interests', quite another to say that the child is interested in it. The teacher who selects out of mathematics, as being bound to be interesting to the child, what it would be practically useful – 'in the child's interests', in the narrowest sense of the phrase – for him to learn may well find that the child is totally uninterested. Disinterested activities, in the old sense of that phrase, are more interesting to him.

¹¹ See Bruner's essay 'After John Dewey, What?' in *On Knowing* (Cambridge, Mass. 1962), p. 118.

¹² J.S. Bruner, *The Process of Education* (Cambridge, Mass. 1960), pp. 31-2.

¹³ William James, *Principles of Psychology* (London 1901), vol. 1, p. 668. This distinction between three ways of memorising is, he says, 'traditional', but I do not know its previous history.

¹⁴ Ibid., 1, p. 662.

¹⁵ See his article 'Mnemonic verses and words', in J.M. Baldwin, *Dictionary of Philosophy and Psychology* (New York 1902), Vol. 2, pp. 87-9.

¹⁶ See J.A. Passmore, *A Hundred Years of Philosophy*, 2nd ed. (London and New York 1966), ch. 14.

¹⁷ *Principles*, vol. 1, p. 668.

¹⁸ See especially J.S. Bruner, *Toward a Theory of Instruction* (Cambridge, Mass. 1966), pp. 46-8.

¹⁹ *Rethinking Science Education*, Fifty-ninth Year Book of the *National Society for the Study of Education*, pt. 1 (Chicago 1960) p. 19. See also Rogers' contribution (ch. 1) to E.J. McGrath (ed.) *Science in General Education* (Dubuque, Iowa 1948).

²⁰ See the critical comments of scientists reported by Bruner in *The Process of Education*, pp. 28-30. I have had some limited experience of lecturing in courses on the structure of science to classes consisting partly of students in the humanities and partly of students who had completed fairly advanced work in science. I seldom or never succeeded in getting Arts students to understand the balance between imagination and testing in science; almost invariably they over-emphasised one or the other. They had too little experience of science to understand what the lectures were all about. The science students experienced no such difficulty. But for them, of course, the lectures were not a substitute for detailed work in science but an auxiliary to it.

²¹ See especially L. Senesh, 'Organising a curriculum around social science concepts', in I. Morrisett *Concepts and Structure in the New Social Science Curricula* (New York 1967), together with the discussion reported on pp. 41-2.

²² Compare P.B. Medawar, *The Art of the Soluble* (London 1967), p. 114 and the discussion in Kwong Lee Dow, *Teaching Science in Australian Schools* (Melbourne 1971), esp. ch. 2. All the same the amount of sheer information is enormous even in a structure-minded text like Garrett Hardin and Carl Bajema, *Biology* (San Francisco, 3rd. ed. 1978).

²³ B. Blanshard (ed.) *Education in the Age of Science*, (New York 1959), pp. 203-4. The biology text by Garret Hardin and Carl Bajema, mentioned above, exemplifies this ideal in practice.

²⁴ The references to geography in the preceding paragraphs derive for the most part from *New Viewpoints in Geography*, the twenty-ninth year book of the National Council for the Social Studies (Washington 1959). The definition of geography is from the essay in that volume by Preston E. James: 'American geography at mid-century', 10; the remark about New England is quoted from Friedrich Patzel by J.O.M. Broek in his essay 'Progress in human geography', p. 36.

²⁵ 'Man, a course of study' in ch. 4 of *Toward a Theory of Instruction*. 'So much of social studies till now has been a congeries of facts. We should like to make the study more rational, more amenable to the use of mind in the large rather than mere memorising' (p. 96). If the emphasis is on 'more', one could well agree. But not if Bruner's remarks are read in the light of the proposals which follow.

²⁶ Ibid., p. 73, p. 101.

²⁷ See R.A. Price, G.R. Smith, W.L. Hickman, *Major Concepts for the Social Studies* (Syracuse 1965).

²⁸ In I. Morrissett (ed.), *Concepts and Structure in the New Social Science Curricula* (New York 1967), p. 148.

²⁹ The pressure is strong on the curriculum reformer to produce concepts, structures, and generalisations even when it would quite falsify the actual state of the subject in question to do so. Compare R. Hanvey, 'Anthropology in the High Schools', in *Concepts and Structure in the New Social Science Curricula*, pp. 95-104.

³⁰ See Karl Popper, *The Open Society and its Enemies*, 4th ed. revised (London 1962), note 4 in vol. 1, p. 285.

³¹ The points at issue are well brought out in a controversy between Hans Morgenthau and Ernest Nagel (B. Blanshard, (ed.) *Education in the Age of Science*, pp. 160-1). 'An enormous contribution could be made to political understanding,' writes Morgenthau, 'if American history were taught not simply as a recital of facts ... but as a manifestation of a universal human experience.' To this Nagel realistically replies: 'In the history of the human enterprise ... there is no unified body of theory in terms of which you can hope to understand the complexities of any one situation ... But to place the whole of history on the bed of Procrustes of some one allegedly definitive political truth or some one set of these, seems to me to be doing a serious disservice to political science.' Morgenthau is still dissatisfied: 'If there were no general truths about foreign policy, at least of an implicit kind, you would be unable to understand or learn from such a writer as Tacitus. Without the assumption of a set of political truths, which are true regardless of time and space, you couldn't hope to understand history.' The fact is, however, that we *can* understand history even though no one has brought forth a set of political truths which are more than commonplace. To understand, say, the assassination of Kennedy we have certainly to understand such sentences as 'Kennedy was assassinated by a fanatic', but we can do this without knowing any political truths which associate fanaticism and assassination. It is perfectly true that we can understand Tacitus only because some types of human and social situation recur, just as we can understand what a character in a Greek play means when he says 'It has started to rain' only because

certain types of weather situation recur. But we do not need to refer to meteorological laws in order to understand Greek references to the weather.

[32] *On Teaching Mathematics*, a report under the chairmanship of Bryan Thwaites (Oxford 1961), p. 10.

[33] Compare on this theme David Edge, 'On the purity of science' in W.R. Niblett (ed.), *The Sciences, the Humanities and the Technological Threat* (London 1975), pp. 42-64 and John Passmore, *Science and its Critics* (London and New York 1978), esp. ch. 3.

[34] Not however, to the degree which prevails in American elementary schools if it be true that 'except in geography, the textbooks and library materials rarely relate to anything outside our own country' (B. Blanshard, (ed.) *Education in the Age of Science*, p. 151). This is the sort of monstrous situation which gives rise, by way of reaction, to an equally absurd reaction into an empty kind of 'world history' with its jejune over-simplifications. In Germany, Herbartian educational principles combined with Fichte's doctrine of the nation to produce a curriculum centred on Germany to an astonishing degree. When *Robinson Crusoe* was used as a text in Dr Rein's Herbartian seminar, Robinson Crusoe's journey was re-routed to take him to Hamburg as his home port. The history course designed by Ziller, Herbart's most influential expositor, 'narrating the actual progress of the race' – the intent being moral – concentrated entirely on German history. A parallel course designed for the United States was no less North American in its emphasis, during the whole of its six grades. (See C. De Garmo, *Herbart and the Herbartians*, pp. 151, 119, 123.)

[35] See the lists of 'concepts' in C.B. Odell, 'The use of maps, globes and pictures in the classroom'. *New Viewpoints in Geography*, p. 200.

Chapter Six
Information and Capacities

In the course of discussing the acquisition and the imparting of information, I have already touched upon some of the ways in which information can be valuable – as, for example, a stage in the path towards acquiring a capacity. The doctor needs his anatomy, the agriculturalist his plant physiology. But since to emphasise the importance of information is to cut across the leading educational tendencies of our time, I should perhaps pause to consider a little more closely in what the value of information consists and what *kind* of information is likely to be particularly valuable. Only, of course, in general terms. To John Smith confronting a financial problem, a highly specific piece of information – that for example an unexpected cheque has been paid into his bank account – can be immensely valuable, for all that it is of no general interest whatsoever. The teacher will naturally concentrate on information which has a wider application.

Max Black has offered a temptingly straightforward answer to the question in what the value of information consists. Information, in his view, is valuable in so far as, and only in so far as, it enlarges our 'know-how'. 'Even "theoretical knowledge" of facts and principles,' he writes, 'if it is to be of any value, must be manifested in certain modes of activity.'[1]

This certainly does not accord with our everyday beliefs. We normally differentiate between that sort of theoretical knowledge which we suppose to have a purely intellectual value, to be worthy of our consideration for reasons quite other than its relation to action, to be worth contemplating for its own sake, and 'practical' information which, we are ready to admit, is valuable only insofar as it can be manifested in conduct. I have already described the way in which, having learnt how to perform a kind of action, we can in principle reflect on what we did and formulate our reflections as information which can serve others as advice. (We not only 'know how to' we know that '*this* is how to'.) Cookery books, gardening books, are replete with such information; it constitutes what we normally think of as 'practical' information and distinguish from 'theoretical' information. For theory, we look rather to science or to philosophy. And we do not ordinarily suppose that their value consists solely in their effect on our conduct. In their case, the proof is not, we commonly believe, in the eating, as it is with cookery recipes or advice on how to grow vegetables.

'Intellectual', as distinct from 'practical', information need not even be theoretical. We do not expect theory from a travel guide. Yet travel guides often draw a distinction between what they call 'practical' information, which tells us how to find our way to, let us say, Paris, and where to find a doctor when we get there, and another sort of information, of a different order, intellectually interesting, about the cathedrals of Paris or its history as a city.

Everyday distinctions are far from being sacrosanct. Perhaps, for all its prevalence, the distinction between intellectual and practical information is a distinction without a difference. Just as information about the addresses of doctors is valuable only if we need a doctor, so too, it might be argued, information about cathedrals or about the history of Paris is valuable only if it helps us to move around the city and to decide what we ought to look at. Again, just as the doctor needs anatomy only in order to help him to cure disease, so too, it might similarly be argued, physics and biology are valuable only in so far as they help us to cope with the world around us in a more effective manner.

Those who would thus subordinate information to action fall into two classes. The extremer proponents claim that *all* information is of value only in so far as it is manifested in modes of action. Others make this claim only about certain kinds of information – with a wider range, however, than what we would all freely grant to be 'practical' information. Let us make a crude distinction within the class of what is popularly regarded, whether in praise or dispraise, as 'intellectual' information, by distinguishing between 'theoretical' and 'historical' information, where both these epithets carry a somewhat extended sense. (The word 'information' is, of course, often *confined* to what I shall be calling 'historical' information; I should perhaps again emphasise that I am making use of a broad dictionary definition of information – 'that of which one can be told or apprised'.)

'Theoretical' information is universal in its scope. It tells us that certain relationships hold anywhere and everywhere, or in all circumstances in a fixed proportion of cases. Thus 'If a gas is heated, it expands' is theoretical information. So is 'Such and such a percentage of radium atoms decay, on the average, per second'. (I shall count as 'theoretical' propositions what are often distinguished from them as 'empirical generalisations'.)

As for historical information, that, as I am using the expression, may take any of such forms as 'the last American President was very devout' or 'Charles I of England was executed' or '95 per cent of Americans believe in free enterprise' – where this is read, unlike the statement about radium atoms, as being true only of Americans at a particular time in their history. 'Historical' information is either about a particular thing or a particular set of things at a particular time and place.

Making use of this distinction, with whatever qualms, we can now distinguish not two but three possible views – that *all* information is valuable only insofar as it is manifested in action, that this is true only of 'theoretical' information, that it is true only of 'historical' information.

To begin with the broadest doctrine, we can freely admit from the outset that all information *can in principle* be 'manifested in modes of activity', at least if we are prepared to interpret the phrase 'modes of activity' in a sufficiently encompassing fashion. This is by no means to demonstrate, of course, that it is *valuable* only for this reason. But it suggests, at least, how this view could arise and makes it plain that if we wish to stick by the distinction between 'learning that' and 'learning to' this cannot be on the ground that there is some information which is inevitably devoid of any effect on our actions.

If, for example, a child has acquired the historical information that 'the French Revolution broke out in 1789' he can normally answer questions, questions which he could not previously answer, such questions as 'When did the French Revolution break out?' He can normally, as he previously could not, obey such instructions as 'Tell me the date at which the French Revolution broke out'; with the aid of this and other pieces of information he can draw such conclusions as that 'Napoleon was a young man when the Revolution broke out' – conclusions at which, perhaps, he would not otherwise have arrived. If he can do none of these things then we should normally conclude that although he may have learnt to repeat that sentence parrot-wise he has not acquired the information that 'the French Revolution broke out in 1789'. And something similar is true of such 'theoretical' information as Boyle's Law. This enables the child to answer such questions as: 'What will happen to the volume of this gas if I increase the pressure on it?' and to tell other people how pressure is related to volume. It helps him, too, to infer what will happen when he pumps air into a tyre.

Let us call such capacities as the capacity to communicate, to answer questions, 'didactic capacities', and the capacity to draw conclusions from premises an 'inferential capacity'.[2] These capacities do not follow inevitably from the possession of information. That is why I used the word 'normally' throughout the previous paragraph. They have to be learnt, in the same way that other capacities are learnt.

As Piaget has made particularly clear, a child can have information at his disposal and yet be unable to draw from it conclusions which seem to us, as a result of our training, 'natural' and 'obvious'. His inferential capacities have not yet developed. The child who has learnt that A is longer than B need not draw the 'inevitable' conclusion that B is shorter than A. At a somewhat more advanced level, the expert mathematician may be startled at our failure, through lack of training, to draw from the mathematical equations which lie before us what seem to him to be obvious conclusions.[3]

Similarly with communication. A child has to learn to participate in the 'language games', to take over Wittgenstein's phrase, of answering questions, obeying instructions, communicating facts. He may have learnt a piece of information and yet still be unable to answer questions because he has not yet *acquired this sort of capacity*. We often find ourselves in this position with respect to a foreign language. We can understand what we are told, we have acquired a piece of information, but we cannot answer questions which are designed to test whether we have understood. A mature person, no doubt, receiving information in a language which he knows reasonably well is automatically able, provided he is not physically handicapped, both to answer questions relating to that information and to draw inferences from it. We may have no way of telling, furthermore, whether we have *in fact* communicated information to those who cannot exercise these capacities. 'I *think* he understands,' we say resignedly of a child or a foreigner, but without conviction. And by 'understands', in this case, we mean 'has acquired the information we are trying to offer him'.

It would be wrong, however, to conclude from the fact that in some circumstances we cannot tell whether a person has acquired information that under those circumstances it is nonsensical to say that he has acquired it. This kind of mistake has already created sufficient havoc in philosophy. Information, we can properly say, is always communicable *in principle*, and it is always possible *in principle* for it to act as a premise in an inference. But it does not follow that a particular child, in the course of acquiring information, is necessarily acquiring the capacity to communicate it or to draw conclusions from it. So even though the two are normally associated, acquiring information must not be identified with acquiring didactic and inferential capacities. Children have to be taught to infer, taught to communicate.

When it is suggested that the value of acquiring information always resides in its bestowing on the child a capacity for action, the reference, however, is not ordinarily to those didactic and communicative capacities which the acquisition of information normally carries with it. It would certainly be an absurd view that the value of *all* the information the child acquires lies in his being able to communicate it to other people or to derive further information from it. What would be the use, then, of passing on that information or deriving from it new information? Only so that it can be further passed on to have still more information derived from it? If a vicious infinite regress is to be avoided, it is obvious that *some* information must be valuable for reasons other than its capacity to be passed on or inferred from.

In a particular case, admittedly, a piece of information may be valuable to a particular person only as something to be communicated. So a teacher may value a piece of information only because he needs to acquire it in order to teach it to his pupils; a pupil only because he needs it to satisfy his examiners. There is, indeed, a real risk that the system of education will be clogged with information of this sort, which may properly be described as 'dead information'. Its practical value lies, purely and simply, in its transmissibility, and it has no intellectual value. The demand that information should offer the child 'know-how', where 'know-how' is taken to exclude such capacities as knowing how to pass examinations, arises as a not unnatural reaction against so absurd a pedagogical game. In reaction, 'live' information is defined as information which serves a practical end; information should be imparted, the conclusion then runs, only if it serves such an end.[4]

But it is one thing to argue that information which is of no value outside the school cycle of teaching and examining is not worth imparting, it is quite another thing to suggest that if information has any value other than this – or other than as a source of inferences, where again the mere fact that it makes inference possible, as every piece of information will, does not suffice to show that a piece of information has any value – this must be in virtue of the fact that it serves to modify our conduct. 'Historical' information, at least, can have a value of a different kind, not as a means to action but as a source of illumination. It can come to us as a revelation. That the stars are at immense distances from us; that at one time there were no men on the face of the earth; that men have lived, and still live, in conditions quite other than those to which we are accustomed, with different manners, different beliefs, different laws – none of this is information of which, ordinarily, the child will make any practical use. It is not, or not in any straightforward sense, manifested in his actions. But it destroys his illusions, compels him to remake his picture of the world, helps him to understand it better, stimulates his imagination. And that is just why it is so important.

What of 'theoretical' information, most clearly exemplified in scientific laws and the theories which contain or explain them? Are such laws and theories of interest and value only in so far as they enable us to act more efficiently? It is interesting to observe that this – the 'instrumentalist' – conception of scientific laws and theories which sees in them nothing more than instruments for practical ends arose, in the first place, out of hostility to science, or, at least, out of an attempt to limit its sphere of importance to the merely utilitarian. So it was suggested by Cardinal Bellarmine that we should not think of Galileo's theories as true but only as useful calculating devices. Bishop Berkeley, the first systematic instrumentalist, was alarmed at the encroachments of Newtonian science on theology. Science, Berkeley argued, does not tell us what the world is like, it does not give us understanding; that task is reserved for theology. All that science can do is to provide us with a set of 'dodges'. Its laws and theories are no more than devices to aid us in 'the conduct of life', useful fictions.

By an ironical historical twist, in the latter half of the nineteenth century and the first half of our own century this conception of science was taken over by scientists themselves (especially by scientists turned philosophers – most working scientists, it is fair to say, were *not* instrumentalists). Sometimes, in their case as in Berkeley's, this was to 'leave room for' theology; sometimes it was because they wrongly believed that an 'instrumentalist' account of science was the only alternative to objectionable, metaphysical theories about occult entities, 'ultimate realities', 'real natures'; sometimes because they themselves were preoccupied with prediction and control, rather than with understanding; sometimes because they were applying to the special case of scientific laws and theories a general pragmatic theory of knowledge, which they took over from Peirce, James and Dewey.[5] (This latter consideration especially applied to those teachers of science who had been influenced in the course of their training by the educational theories of John Dewey.)

Peirce himself, it is worth observing, came to be alarmed at instrumentalism in its pragmatic form. At one time, he admits, he had been inclined to subordinate knowing to doing, to such a degree as to suggest that the value of knowledge wholly depends upon the value of the actions it enables us to perform. But subsequent reflection persuaded him that the only activity which is desirable for its own sake 'is to render ideas and things reasonable', to see how they 'hang together', to attain to a theoretical understanding of them. Action, he came more and more to feel, is valuable only as a means to understanding; and science, pre-eminently, is valuable as a form of understanding, not as a guide to action.[6] Bertrand Russell, never amiably disposed towards pragmatism, went even further. He wrote an essay 'In defence of useless knowledge' – knowledge which lends perspective rather than enhances our power to act.

A decision on this point is of considerable pedagogical importance – especially, although by no means exclusively, in the teaching of science. Accepting Bacon's dictum that 'knowledge is power', John Locke laid it down that: 'He [the teacher] should make the child comprehend (as much as may be) the usefulness of what he teaches him; and let him see, by what he has learned, that he can do something which he could not do before, something which gives him some power and real advantage above others who are ignorant of it.'[7] In pursuit of this ideal, teachers have sometimes taught science in such a way as to lay great stress on its 'practical usefulness', the control it gives men over natural processes. Laws and theories, too, have been taught as formulae to be applied in the working of practical exercises. Teachers have supposed that by approaching science in this way they can arouse the child's interests as 'mere theories' cannot be expected to do.

One difficulty with this approach is that children, as we have already suggested, are often not at all interested in 'practical implications' and do not expect to use the laws they are taught in order to solve practical problems. Consider, for example, the formula which lays it down that the time a body takes to fall through a certain distance is a function of its initial velocity, the distance it has to fall and the force of gravity. Most of us learned this formula as part of our schooling. But how many of us have ever, in subsequent life, employed it in order to calculate the time a body will take to fall from a given point or the distance it has fallen, given that it has taken a certain time to do so? For the matter of that, how often have we *used* in this kind of way any of the principles of mechanics?

This is not to deny, of course, that such formulae *can be* practically useful, i.e., that many persons in many circumstances may employ them as part of the process of solving practical problems. Neither is there the slightest reason why the teacher should ignore that fact; the teaching strategies Locke recommends are by no means to be wholly despised, as the extremer sort of intellectualist might despise them. If a scientific law has applications in which children are genuinely interested, or can be brought to be interested, a teacher can properly draw his pupil's attention to them. By so doing he will bring out what is certainly an important aspect of science – the way in which it makes use of highly theoretical-looking principles in order to solve problems of great practical consequence. There is nothing Philistine in this; technology, the application of science, is itself an exercise of the human intelligence, the human imagination, the human gift for understanding. The pure mathematician who is reported to have rejoiced: 'Well, thank God, no one will ever find a use for *that* piece of mathematics' is as ridiculous a figure as the Philistine depicted by Matthew Arnold, with his monotonous refrain: 'What's in it for me?'

But the formula relating the time of fall to gravity has an interest which is quite independent of its practical usefulness. *It makes no mention of the mass of the falling body.* This cuts completely across the child's initial expectation, that heavy bodies will fall faster than light ones, a natural inference from his experience of falling leaves and falling stones. Again, to look through a microscope and see for oneself the Brownian movement, or in a glass of apparently clear water a multitude of forms of life – these are experiences which can have the force of a revelation. Not all discoveries, of course, are as spectacular as these. But science abounds in discoveries which, properly presented, can arouse the child's sense of wonder, disturb the complacency of his commonsense. If, to take the example cited in Skinner's *Walden Two*, twenty years after being taught physics a science teacher's pupils remember no physics but only that their teacher disliked Coca-cola, this is because *that* discovery disturbed and surprised them as his physics did not. But one could scarcely have a better indication that he was a bad science teacher.

The approach of the pragmatists and the instrumentalists certainly had its virtues. In part it was a thoroughly justified attack on mere verbalism, the mouthing of empty formulae, explanations of a verbal character which throw no light on what they professed to explain. To ask, as the empiricists did, 'What is the practical significance, the "cash-value", of believing that?' is itself a technique calculated to startle. This question may shock us into the realisation that a particular belief, perhaps one of our most cherished beliefs, is hollow, devoid of content.

But the classical rationalists, we may still wish to suggest, were drawing attention to features of the human situation which pragmatists have tended to ignore or underestimate. The delight in understanding, in seeing what the world is like, the disinterested search for truth – these are all, as Plato emphasised, specifically human traits, which most fully engage the mature intellect and can yet be discerned in embryo in the child. It is not merely a Romantic flourish to complain that teachers often destroy a child's 'sense of wonder'. Where the Romanticists go wrong is in supposing that this is a necessary consequence of emphasising such subjects as science and mathematics, that only a literary education can preserve the child's fresh curiosity. On the contrary, bad teaching of any sort, literary or scientific, can be in this respect equally fatal. The science teacher has, indeed, a special responsibility for developing the child's curiosity into a mature disinterested spirit of inquiry. It is as a result of the operation of such a spirit of inquiry that the world has emerged in so surprising and unexpected a light.

Once more, the difficulty is to chart a course between pedagogical extremes. Science teaching which degenerates into a series of exercises in showmanship, which leaves the pupils with no sense of the practical utility of science or of the degree to which it involves drudgery as well as imaginative enterprise, is as seriously falsifying as science teaching which leaves its pupils with the impression that science is only a matter of discovering practically useful formulae. Matthew Arnold's Mr Bootles, describing the teacher Mr Silverpump, is not, whether in Arnold's judgment or my own, describing the ideal teacher: 'Original man, Silverpump, fine mind! fine system! None of your antiquated rubbish – all practical work – latest discoveries in science – mind kept constantly excited – lots of interesting experiments – lights of all colours – fizz! fizz! bang! bang! That is what I call forming a man!' But neither is that teacher ideal whose pupils leave school with no notion of the way in which science has, again and again, destroyed commonplace assumptions, no conception of the way in which it enlarges our understanding and stretches our imagination. And the 'instrumentalist' conception of science can easily lead to that consequence.

We have rejected the view, then, that the value of information, whether theoretical or historical, consists only in the fact that we can use it to gain for ourselves practical advantages or, more generally, to modify our conduct. We have seen that information can be surprising, illuminating, that it can shock us out of our complacency. No doubt it then changes us, but not by providing us with a practical instrument. But we have also granted that surprisingness is not the sole criterion for deciding what information should be taught. What other criteria are there?

Adapting a distinction we made between capacities, even though the parallelism is anything but precise, we might say of 'theoretical' information that it is 'open' whereas 'historical' information is 'closed'. It is 'open' in the sense that the range of cases to which it applies is, in principle, unlimited or, if not in the case of empirical generalisations quite unlimited, at least very wide. This might suggest that school work should consist, insofar as it is concerned with information, with teaching the child theoretical information. (The proviso is, of course, important; schools are not only concerned with information.) For such theories help us to understand a great range of new phenomena, as fresh discoveries reveal them. By coming to understand them we both learn and prepare ourselves for future learning. We should then be reverting to Bruner's doctrine that the schools should concentrate on 'structures', at least if 'structures' is identified with 'theories'.

If 'theoretical' information is always open, however, it can also be 'narrow', 'narrow' in the sense that it has application only in a very limited range of types of situation. When theoretical information is described as 'highly specialised', this is what is meant. Information, let us say, about the embryology of the formation of the pouch in the platypus is 'open' in respect to all platypuses, in contrast with such information as that 'around Sydney, the platypus population is diminishing in numbers'. But it is still narrow, in the sense that it applies only to a relatively small number of members of the animal kingdom. In contrast, an 'historical' proposition, while inevitably 'closed', can be 'broad' in the sense of being relevant in a great variety of situations. That the earth is round is a case in point. And so is the information that the Soviet Union is ruled by the Communist Party or that there was a great depression in the 1930s. These are facts we shall often have to advert to in any attempt to understand the modern world – they form part of a person's 'general education'.

Of course, we can look up such facts in reference books. And so, it might be argued, we do not need to learn them at school. If, however, our school courses depreciate the value of information, then even if children are taught how to look up information, they may not in fact do so. There is a certain framework of facts, too, which reference books are accustomed to take for granted. So long as education was ruled by Mr Gradgrind this was a safe assumption. What was forgotten or never taught could be looked up. But not everything was forgotten and a good deal was taught. Lord Macaulay's 'every school boy knows who imprisoned Montezuma, and who strangled Atahualpa' was of course, a laughable exaggeration. Still, there was once a good deal that every schoolboy *did* know. Now, however, one simply does not know what one can assume to be a familiar fact, something one can take for granted as a starting point.

I am not suggesting that Mr Gradgrind was right after all. He *imparted* too much information. (The best teacher I ever had was one whose constant refrain was 'Look that up'.) He restricted himself too much to the imparting of information; he imagined himself to be imparting information when he was only cultivating verbal habits. But I also do not subscribe to the extreme anti-Gradgrindist view that there is no point in the child learning the basic facts about the structure of the world, about its major divisions, about its historical past. If anyone asks 'Why?', my answer is that he needs such information if he is going to have any understanding of what is happening. Not to have a 'world-chart' at one's disposal, temporal and spatial, is to be constantly at the mercy of propagandists. And, as I have already suggested, there is also a special value in a more localised world-chart, relating to one's culture, one's own civilisation.

The theories, let us say, of physics or of molecular biology, which are both broad and open, have a quite peculiar value as aids to understanding. But to dismiss 'historical' information merely because it is 'closed' is to overlook its breadth. Information, to sum up, can be valuable either because it is 'broad' and 'open', or because it stimulates the imagination, or because it is practically of great use, or because it offers us a framework of facts within which we can 'place' new developments. There is no single answer to the question why teachers should impart information or encourage their pupils to acquire it. It is not true either that only 'theoretical' or that only 'historical' information is worth imparting. On the view I have defended, to fail to impart either kind of information is to offer an inadequate schooling.

NOTES

[1] Max Black, 'Rules and routines', in *The Concept of Education*, p. 92.

[2] Compare Gilbert Ryle, *The Concept of Mind*, p. 286.

[3] See, for example, J. Piaget, *Judgment and Reasoning in the Child* (London 1928), trans. M. Warden, *passim*.

[4] As usual the case of mathematics is a difficult one. 'In Mathematics', so a mathematician tells us, 'knowledge of any value is never possession of information but "know-how". To know mathematics means to be able to do mathematics: to use mathematical language with some fluency, to do problems, to criticise arguments, to find proofs, and, what may be the most important activity, to recognise a mathematical concept in, or to extract it from, a given concrete situation' (L.V. Ahlfors, 'On the mathematics curriculum of the high school', *Mathematics Teacher*, 55, 1962, pp. 191-4, as quoted in H.B. Griffiths and A.G. Howson, *Mathematics*,

Society and Curricula, Cambridge 1974, p. 6). It is hard to know what to make of this claim. Of course, mathematicians have to be able to use mathematical language; of course they have to be able to solve problems; of course they have to be able to criticise arguments, to find proofs and to recognise mathematical relationships in given concrete situations. But something parallel can be said of any scientist. On the face of it, mathematicians also, like scientists, formulate propositions. And they can be very surprising; Thomas Hobbes, according to the familiar anecdote, found a proposition in Euclid so surprising that he was provoked into the response: 'By God, that's impossible.'

[5] For a brief history of this movement, see John Passmore, *A Hundred Years of Philosophy* (London, 2nd ed., 1966) and for some broader consideration of it *Science and Its Critics* (London and New Brunswick 1978). There is an important theoretical discussion in Karl Popper, 'Three views concerning human knowledge', reprinted in *Conjectures and Refutations* (London 1963).

[6] See specially Peirce's review of *Clark University in 1889-99*, first published in *Science*, 20 April 1900, pp. 620-2.

[7] John Locke, *Some Thoughts Concerning Education*, §167.

Chapter Seven
Cultivating Habits

For Locke, habit formation was the be-all and the end-all of
'education' – of 'education' in its broadest sense, 'bringing up'.
Rousseau was no less firmly convinced that the only habit the child
ought to form is the habit of forming no habits. Here is an opposition
quite absolute, totally uncompromising. And the issue is no means
dead. A line of filiation leads from Locke to Watson and B.F.
Skinner. Another line of filiation leads from Rousseau to the
'Romantic rebels' of the nineteen-sixties, with spontaneity,
creativity, as their catch-words and their fear of formal education as a
device for destroying individuality, imposing conformity. Sensibly to
explore this controversy we have first to make a number of quite
fundamental distinctions.

The word 'habit' can be used very broadly, in a manner sanctified
by the *Oxford English Dictionary*, to mean 'a settled disposition to act in
a certain way'. Used thus, it is by no means peculiar to human
beings. One can quite properly say of a plant that 'it has a habit of
dying out if the temperature drops suddenly' or of the weather that 'it
has a habit of turning nasty at this time of the year'. William James
went so far as to describe the laws of nature as nothing but 'the
immutable habits which the different elementary sorts of matter
follow in their actions and reactions upon each other'.[1] It is far from
surprising, then, that he also maintained that all living things are
'bundles of habits' and counted as human habits not only such
nervous tricks as snuffling or biting one's nails, such skills as fencing,
swimming, piano-playing, such acquired traits as the professional
mannerisms of the lawyer, the salesman and the doctor, but even
such intellectual capacities as the power to concentrate or the power
of critical judgment and such character traits as 'energetic volition'.
When 'habit' is understood in so generous a fashion, it would be
foolish, indeed, to deny that the teacher ought to cultivate habits –
such habits, at least, as the habit of thinking for oneself or the habit of
critical inquiry.

In *The Concept of Mind* Ryle protested against so multi-encompassing a definition of habit. It is 'tempting to argue', he freely granted, 'that competences and skills are just habits' – tempting because such competences as being able to tell the time and such skills as being able to play a musical instrument are, like habits, acquired dispositions.[2] But whereas the exercise of competence or skills demands intelligence, vigilance and self-criticism, to act out of habit, so Ryle argues, is, precisely, *not* to be vigilant, intelligent, self-critical. On this view, it is a contradiction in terms to describe someone as having formed the habit of thinking before he acts. Whereas, Ryle goes on, a habit is a determinate, inflexible, course of action, a skill is open-ended. A skilled musician can perform a piece of music he has never seen before, a skilled mechanic can repair an unfamiliar engine. (They are skilled in what I have called 'open capacities'.) But out of habit we can only do exactly what we have previously learnt to do. Pedagogically, Ryle further tells us, this difference is marked by the fact that a skill is taught by training, a habit by drill – where 'drill' is simple repetition and training includes the giving of reasons.

For all the importance of the distinctions Ryle is here making we cannot be content to let the matter rest at that point. Ryle oversimplifies. He is contrasting extremes: what he himself calls 'pure or blind habit' with such a relatively complex skill as mountaineering. The contrast between a 'blind habit' like nail-biting and a developed skill like mountaineering is so obvious that we automatically reject the suggestion that they belong to the same category. But the situation becomes distinctly more obscure once we recognise the need for distinguishing between different types of habit, of varying degrees of complexity. Then we shall be less confident that drill is always the appropriate method of establishing habits.

At the same time, it will merely confuse the issues to define habit as broadly as James did or the *Oxford English Dictionary* does; it will lead to our overlooking important pedagogical distinctions. Honesty, love, courage are each of them 'a settled disposition to act in a certain way', but it is best to classify them, for our purposes, as character traits rather than as habits. What distinguishes them from habits, as Ryle suggests, is that their operation in any particular case requires reflection, reflection on the peculiar circumstances of the case; they can never become automatic. Something similar is true of skills. They contain habits as an ingredient – the skilled tennis-player automatically grasps his racquet at a particular point – but they also involve a capacity to respond to unexpected circumstances. The skilled tennis-player has, no doubt, a settled disposition to act in certain ways, but those 'certain ways' include varying his actions as the circumstances require, with the style of his opponents, the weather conditions, the strength and readiness of his partner. He does not, as a player governed by habit would do, automatically take up a particular position on the court.

What about competencies? Very obviously, having a competence is one thing, habitually exercising it is quite another. 'I can drive to work' by no means has the same force as 'I habitually drive to work'. One must first have a competence in order to be able regularly to exercise it. But that is not a good reason for *identifying* the possession of the competence with its regular exercise. Whereas the habit, furthermore, is exercised in the appropriate circumstances without reflection, we often exercise a competence only after reflection.

So far, then, we can agree with Ryle. Indeed, not only with Ryle. For although James employs the concept of habit so widely, he nevertheless writes that 'in an habitual action mere sensation is a sufficient guide' or, again, that '*habit diminishes the conscious attention with which acts are performed*'.[3] This clearly does not apply to 'the habit of thinking before one acts'; it does not apply to skilful performance which requires concentration by the performer. For the most part we shall confine our attention to habits in this more limited sense, which excludes intellectual habits, competencies and skills, except insofar as they operate in a purely mechanical fashion. But from the fact that habits operate mechanically it ought not to be concluded that they are to be taught, solely, by mechanical drill. Some habits can be taught, we shall indeed be suggesting, by way of rules and reasons.

Let us begin, however, with such 'nervous' habits as nail-biting, snuffling, playing with paper-fasteners. These, certainly, are fully automatic. But they are acquired neither by drill nor by training. Their distinctive feature, from a teacher's point of view, is their complete irrationality. Perhaps Freud is right; perhaps nail-biting, snuffling, playing with a paper-fastener, satisfy an unconscious purpose, of considerable importance to the agent. But certainly it is fruitless to ask the nail-biter, as one can ask, say, a man who habitually prunes rose trees in late summer, 'Why do you do that?' in the expectation of receiving an answer which is in the least degree rational – whether in the form 'To make them grow better' or 'As part of a general cleaning-up programme' or 'Because this is the right time to shorten them'.

It follows that the nail-biter cannot be cured of his habit by persuading him that his reasons for biting his nails are bad ones, as we might persuade the rose-pruner that he would do better to prune his roses in early spring. For the nail-biter does not bite his nails for bad reasons; he has *no* reason for doing so. The best we can do is to offer him reasons for *not* biting his nails.

One scarcely need pause to argue that habits of this sort, the teacher will certainly not set out to cultivate. If they have a pedagogical importance, this is rather because teachers have sometimes spent an inordinate amount of time, and instituted reigns of terror, in unsuccessful attempts to eradicate them. An outbreak of nervous habits in his classroom may properly lead a teacher to suspect that something is wrong with his teaching. A good teacher may be able indirectly to reduce their incidence. But eradicating them is a task for the expert.

Closely associated with nervous habits, but much more serious, are what I shall call 'addictive' habits. Unlike nervous habits – unlike, say, the habit of running one's hand over one's head or rubbing one's hands together – addictive habits commonly begin from a conscious choice. There are exceptions to this: a person may become addicted to sleeping-pills because he has been given sleeping-pills in hospital. But, in general, it is by a deliberate act that a person first takes alcohol, or smokes, or takes drugs or works unduly hard. The basic test of a habit's being addictive is that the person in whom it is established suffers from 'withdrawal symptoms' if he cannot act in his habitual way. These withdrawal symptoms vary, of course, in kind and severity. So the heroin-addict suffers serious physical disorders if he cannot obtain heroin; the man who is addicted to working too hard develops a 'weekend neurosis' – anxiety, psychosomatic disturbance, depression – as soon as he ceases work. If breaking the habit does not give rise to withdrawal symptoms, then we might speak of it as being a 'gratuitous' habit rather than an 'addictive' habit – as when someone 'makes a habit' of having a drink before dinner, in the sense that he does not reflect before doing so, does not make a specific decision to drink, and would reply to the question 'Why are you drinking tonight?' with the answer 'I always do', but is not deeply disturbed if this routine is interrupted. (It is, of course, very easy to deceive oneself into believing that one can 'stop whenever one wants to', when this is not in fact the case.)

The duty is often imposed upon teachers of eradicating addictive habits. But experience suggests that teachers are rarely in this respect any more successful than they are in respect to nervous habits; the influence of 'peer-groups' is normally much more powerful. Teachers can, however, at least try so to act as not positively to encourage addiction. And they may easily do so unintentionally. It is part of their job, for example, to encourage their pupils to work hard. The risk is negligible, to put the matter mildly, that the vast majority of their pupils will ever become addicted, as a consequence, to hard work. But the teacher has certainly to take care lest the anxiety he inevitably arouses in encouraging hard work becomes unmasterable. (Other forms of addiction are often generated, as well, if this situation arises.)

Play can help to reduce the level of anxiety. Since the late nineteenth century, however, informal play has largely been replaced in schools by organised games. Of course, 'play' and 'games' are not irretrievably sundered; it is natural enough for us to talk, as we do, of 'playing games'. But in many schools games are developed to such a degree of organised seriousness that to speak of 'play' in connection with them is as misleading as it is to speak of a professional 'tennis-*player*'. Play has been converted into a form of work, as likely to become an addictive habit as any other form of work, involving the same heightened anxiety, the same competitiveness, and producing 'recreational drop-outs' who are unable to, or do not wish to, live up to the standards enforced by the games-master.

Plato perhaps initiated this tendency; in the *Laws* he argued that children's play must be disciplined and law-governed. He was desperately afraid, like many a school teacher after him, of any sort of spontaneity. In the nineteenth century, hostility to play came to be characteristic of the stricter forms of evangelical Christianity. 'Play of whatever sort,' a German educator once wrote, 'should be forbidden in all evangelical schools, and its vanity and folly should be explained to the children with warnings of how it turns the mind away from God and eternal life, and works destruction on their immortal souls.'[4]

But even without these theological and moral pressures, the natural tendency of a school is to convert any form of activity for which it takes responsibility into a form of work. Attempts to 'widen the curriculum' so as to 'let the child do what really interests him' may easily have the effect that forms of play in which the hard-working child found refuge from his school-work no longer serve as such. First, the contemporary novel, then films, now in the more 'up-to-date' schools television and the comic strips, become part of the curriculum. In search of pure play, the child is forced into drug-taking violence. The older, narrower curriculum, for all its defects, left the child more space for 'moral holidays' outside the school-room. There is a real problem in the modern world of finding forms of 'play' which do not turn into addictive habits. Play ought to be a 'gratuitous habit', something that people *can* do, leisure in the strict sense, as distinct from a different form of work. Such gratuitous habits, schools can try to encourage. But to do so does not come naturally to the teacher, or to the school as an institution. One hopes, rather, that gratuitous habits will be 'picked up' out of school, by children following their natural inclinations.

The teacher's principal positive concern, as distinct from his negative concern with nervous and addictive habits, is with a different class of habits, which I shall call 'routines', using the word 'routine' to mean an habitual mode of action which, unlike nervous, addictive or gratuitous habits, is 'governed by a rule'. We may 'make it a rule' to have a drink before dinner. But as 'make it' suggests, the rule does not then *govern* us. If it does the habit is not gratuitous. But how do we test whether an action is governed by a rule?

One way of doing so, of course, is to ask the agent. If we ask a soldier why he automatically salutes every senior officer he meets, we shall no doubt get the reply 'That is the rule in our army'. If his action has become habitual, it is a rule-governed habit – a routine. But sometimes a person's habitual actions are rule-governed without his being conscious of the rule which governs them. They are governed not by explicit but by implicit rules. Languages were spoken in accordance with rules before there were grammarians.

We might be tempted, then, to assimilate rule-governed behaviour to regular behaviour. For, in general, a rule survives only if it is regularly obeyed, and explicit rules often take the form of enjoining a form of conduct which, previous to its being enjoined, had been regularly performed. The explicit rule is designed to constrain a few dissentients, not to impose a quite new manner of behaviour on the community at large. Regular performance, all the same, is not equivalent to performance according to a rule. The habitual nail-biter, the addictive alcoholic, as we have already said, are not acting in accordance with a rule; neither, in most cases, is the child who regularly gets his sums wrong.

The last example is an illuminating one. A child *might* get his sums wrong because he is following a rule, although a wrong rule. How, short of asking him, can we distinguish this from the case when he regularly gets his sums wrong but without following a rule? Well, we might find that his mistakes make sense if we suppose him to be following the rule that to multiply by a fraction the fraction is first inverted. So, asked to multiply six by a half he gives the answer twelve, multiplying six by a quarter he gives the answer twenty-four. We may find, too, that sometimes when he has, at his first attempt, got his sum right, he goes back over it and inverts the fraction; it is obvious from his behaviour that he regards himself as having *made a mistake* by not inverting in a sense in which he does not rebuke himself for not having rubbed his hand across his head as he thinks. We understand his mistakes by adopting the hypothesis that he is following the wrong inversion-rule; he is not merely wrong, as he might be as a result of falling into a different mistake each time; he has formed a wrong habit, he has adopted a routine which is leading him astray.

Similarly, the anthropologist can judge whether, in a particular tribe in which men do not generally marry their cousins, this is only because they prefer women who are exotic and unfamiliar or is rather because to marry a cousin would be to infringe a taboo. He can watch their reaction to a story he tells them about somebody who does marry a cousin, can observe whether any special steps are taken to prevent cousins from being alone together, and so on. The regularity of certain behaviour no doubt *suggests the hypothesis* that the behaviour is rule-governed, but what settles the question is the kind of reaction which occurs when the regularity is for some reason threatened or breaks down.

Not all rule-governed behaviour, of course, is routine behaviour; to have adopted a routine is to follow a rule *habitually*, without deliberately deciding on each separate occasion to do so. Driving in a strange country, a driver may think to himself: 'Who gives way at this point? Ah, yes; the rule is to give way to the right, so I have to give way.' His giving way is rule-governed, but he has not *formed the habit* of giving way to the right until he ceases explicitly to refer to the rule. Obedience to a rule, then, comes to be habitual; it is not at first habitual, even when the rule is only an implicit one. To do something *from* a rule is not the same thing as to do it *as* a rule; these two are in fact quite independent of one another.[5]

The very same routine may be 'picked up' by one person, learnt as a result of teaching by another, adopted after rational consideration of alternatives by yet another. So, to take a simple example, a child in a chemistry laboratory might develop the habit of washing his crucible before filling it with a chemical substance either as a result of noticing that his teacher always does so, or because it forms part of the instructions laid down by his teacher, or because he has worked out for himself that it is desirable to wash it in order to avoid the risk that the crucible will contain chemical fragments left over from previous experiments.

Correspondingly, the teacher has at his disposal a number of very different methods of trying to establish habits in his pupils. One method, on which John Locke lays great stress, we might call 'example-setting'. 'Of all the ways whereby children are to be instructed,' Locke writes, 'and their manners formed, the plainest, easiest, and most efficacious, is to set before their eyes the examples of those things you would have them do or avoid.'[6] 'Example setting' consists in the deliberate use, as a method of establishing habits, of the tendency to imitate which plays so large a part in the 'untaught learning' of children – that kind of learning which grows out of the child's social experience, rather than as a result of the intervention of a teacher.

But Locke is very conscious of a major difficulty in simply leaving the child free to acquire habits by imitation, viz. that the child normally has before him, in any complex society, a variety of conflicting examples. Locke tries to overcome this difficulty by suggesting that the child must be surrounded by people who *deliberately* set an example of the desired sort. So, he says, children should not, as far as possible, be permitted contact with servants; they should be kept at home, not sent to school, so as to be spared any contact with 'vicious and ill-bred boys'; in choosing a tutor for his children a parent must be as circumspect as he would be in choosing for them a wife; in his relations to his children the parent must be careful constantly to set them an example. The object of these precautions is to ensure, by a kind of censorship, that the child encounters no models which it is undesirable for him to imitate.

These precautions have so little relevance to the conditions of modern life – or, indeed, the conditions of life of the ordinary boy, as distinct from the son of a wealthy landowner, in seventeenth-century England – that one is inclined to dismiss them as of merely historical interest.[7] But for Locke they are all-important, just because he lays such store in example-setting as a method of establishing routines; the precautions Locke is then forced to insist upon bring out very well the extreme difficulty of relying upon example-setting as a principal teaching technique.

The teacher not uncommonly finds, indeed, that in order to educate his pupils he has first to eradicate routines which have been established in them as a result of imitation. Even if we believe that the establishment of habits is a proper pedagogical task, we must still grant that teaching consists as much in trying to break as to establish habits. This is a permanent task for the teacher, not something he can do once and for all as a child enters school. For throughout his school life the child establishes new habits, habits which are in one way or another crippling, at least in the teacher's eye, as a result of imitating the practices of his peers, of his parents, or of actors on television.

Of course, there are some favoured parts of the world in which the teacher can still largely rely on the example of parents or friends to establish moral or linguistic habits or, even, intellectual routines. But this situation, it is fair to say, is the exception, not the rule; more often the routines the child is encouraged to acquire at school are in direct conflict with the routines he 'picks up' as a result of watching his friends and parents. The teacher's task is, under these circumstances, an immensely difficult one. He is not, in the manner Locke envisages, trying to establish routines in a wholly virginal mind – a 'blank sheet of paper' or 'piece of wax', to use Locke's favourite metaphors – but rather in a child who is already 'a bundle of habits', for many of which the teacher has to substitute new habits, as distinct from merely adding to the bundle. To those who condemn the teacher for failing to eradicate habits which are widespread in the community or for not establishing habits which are in fact almost nowhere exhibited, the teacher is tempted to reply, like King Canute to his courtiers, that his power does not extend to sweeping back an ocean with a broom.

Yet when a teacher is admired, his example can certainly be contagious. We can often recognise the pupils of a particular teacher: they take over, for good or ill, his stylistic mannerisms, his nervous habits, his habits of speech, as well as his intellectual and moral routines. That imitation reflects their admiration of him. They do not, in the same way, take over the habits of teachers for whom their admiration is less, and they may forcibly react against the habits of teachers they dislike or despise. And if the teacher, in trying to 'set an example', is led into hypocrisy, priggishness, or pedantry, his example is more likely to be met with derision than to be imitated.

A second method of establishing or eradicating habits is by a system of rewards and punishments. (For my present purposes, I shall use the words 'rewards' and 'punishments' in a very broad way, ignoring the differences between punishments and penalties.) Part of Locke's object in his *Thoughts Concerning Education* is to persuade his readers that physical punishment and physical reward are inferior methods of establishing habits, inferior not only to imitation but also to praise and blame. Corporal punishment, in his view, should be the last, rather than the first, resort of the teacher. The modern reader may be struck by the degree to which Locke would permit corporal punishment rather than by the limitations he places on its use. But it is only very recently that corporal punishment has been abandoned as the principal method both of eradicating and of establishing habits. (I was myself, at the age of ten, a member of a class in which we were caned whenever we got a sum wrong. The teacher was anything but a brute.)

Corporal punishment and the various varieties of what one might call 'moral punishment' – blame, the withdrawal of affection, loss of reputation – can be grouped together. They are all of them 'extrinsic', in the sense that they are deliberately imposed consequences of one's having acted in a certain way rather than intrinsic ingredients of that mode of acting. It is possible to escape them – for example, by concealing one's actions. People not uncommonly have 'private habits' which would expose them to blame, punishment, or loss of reputation if they were exposed to the public gaze, but which escape all such penalties in virtue of the success with which they are concealed.

But there are other sorts of rewards and punishments which are 'intrinsic', in the sense that they attach to the performance of the act even in private. These rewards and punishments again fall into two classes. To the first class belong what are commonly called 'pangs of conscience'. A routine may be so established in a child that he feels guilty when he does not perform it, even when no one could be aware of his omission. Similarly, the private performance of publicly approved acts can be 'its own reward'; to take a trivial instance, a child may 'feel better' when he cleans his teeth after a meal, even if there is nobody to rebuke him for not doing so. In such instances what was originally an extrinsic punishment has been internalised, so that it is now taken to be ingredient in the act itself that its performance involves punishments or rewards. Locke is particularly anxious to establish habits at the level at which rewards and punishments are 'intrinsic'. It is relatively easy, he says, to produce in children, by means of punishment, a superficial conformity to routine. But it is the teacher's object to establish habits which are 'woven into the very principles' of a child's nature – habits, that is, which will still govern the child's actions when there is nobody around to punish him for acting otherwise.

A second sort of 'intrinsic' punishment and reward is of a rather different character. The 'reward' derives merely from the successful performance of an act, and the 'punishment' from failure in it. A person may, for example, form the habit of doing the crossword puzzle in his daily newspaper. There is no public reward for success in 'getting it out', and no punishment for failing to do so. But the crossword-puzzle solver persists in his habit, because success in getting it out is its own reward. Should the character of the puzzle alter, should it for some reason become easier, or too difficult for him to have any hope of success, the habit will almost certainly be abandoned. In those classes of cases in which a person 'makes a habit' of regularly performing a certain kind of skilful act such 'intrinsic' rewards are of particular importance.

With the help of this conception of intrinsic rewards and punishments we can distinguish between, and relate, the formation, maintenance and eradication of habits by rewards and punishments and the process of conditioning, as when, in a laboratory, rats are conditioned to take a particular path through a maze. The resemblance between routine-formation and conditioning have often been insisted upon, especially by those, from Hartley on, who see in 'conditioning' the hope of forming a perfect society.[8] But there are educationally important differences between the conditioning of white rats and the inculcation by a teacher of habits in his pupils, even if it be true that to some degree habits *can* be produced in, or eradicated from, human beings by methods analogous to conditioning, by, for example, aversion therapy. (This sort of therapy is most likely to be useful exactly where the teacher fails, in the case of nervous or addictive habits.)

One important difference is that in a system of education the formation of habits is initiated by a person occupying an official role. Even when the teacher makes extensive use of rewards and punishments, his relationship to his pupils is significantly different from the laboratory experimenter's relationship to his animals. Suppose, for example, a teacher tries to develop in his pupils the habit – to take the simplest kind of instance – of writing the word 'I' with a capital letter. And suppose that he does this in the following way: he smacks any pupil who hands in a piece of written work which contains 'I' written with a small letter and he gives any pupil a piece of chocolate who writes 'I' with a capital letter. Then certainly the resemblance to animal conditioning is at its greatest. But even so the success of his method is profoundly affected by the relationship of his pupils to him, the degree of 'awe and affection' they feel for him, to use Locke's phrase. The white rat, in contrast, feels neither awe nor affection for the experimenter. Nor has the rat already developed a habit of obeying or disobeying him.

In fact, no question of obedience or disobedience arises in the relation between rat and experimenter. The teacher orders his class to write 'I' in a particular way, or to sit quietly; the experimenter does not order the white rat to take a certain route through the maze or to press a certain lever. The child is a participant in a social situation involving authority, the exercise of command; the white rat is not. It is completely unable to understand what is happening: the child may grasp what he is to do immediately. The rat does not feel a glow of satisfaction at being able to master the maze, in the sense in which the child can feel a glow of satisfaction at being able to do what he is asked to do. The rat does not know what is happening to him; he does not know it is the experimenter who is arranging to have pain inflicted on him, or who gives him things he wants for acting in the appropriate manner; the child connects the rewards and punishments with the person who inflicts them. He can anticipate, wait for, ask for rewards as the rat cannot. Indeed the rat knows nothing of rewards and punishments; for him, the question, only, is of getting something he wants or something he does not want. A punishment is not the same thing as a pain.

Finally, the experimenter has, in practice, complete control over his rats. He knows what habits they have already formed, and to what degree they have been reinforced; he does not have to meet the difficulty that there are social pressures operating in the precisely opposite direction, to produce aversive conditioning to the habits he is trying to reinforce – as when his fellow-children laugh at a child who enunciates more carefully than is customary in his social circle. This does not mean, of course, that there is an absolute break between the conditioning of animals and the formation of habits by rewards and punishments. For certain theoretical purposes, one may wish to insist upon the resemblances between different forms of routine-establishment; for our purposes we need to insist on the discontinuities.

In attempting to establish routines, the teacher has to take account of all these points of difference. He runs a real risk, for example, of only seeming to establish a habit of acting without really doing so. His pupils may deliberately decide to act in a certain way so long as he is there to reward and punish them, whether because they fear or because they love him, but with the firm intention of acting quite differently as soon as he is no longer present. Only if he succeeds in 'internalising' the rewards and punishments, it is fair to say, has he any real prospect of successfully establishing a habit. And this very often means that he has to arouse in his pupils a sense of guilt, so that if they fail to, let us say, set out their sums neatly they will feel emotionally disturbed. But he may be able to produce the same effect, without the risk of creating a neurotic condition, by making use of the child's sense of accomplishment.

One can easily imagine a teaching-machine intended to teach linguistic habits, which was so designed that when the pupil made a mistake he was given an electric shock, and when he gave the correct answer he was rewarded – perhaps by hearing a recording of his teacher saying 'That's a good boy', perhaps by some sort of financial reward. But the teaching-machine in fact makes use of a different kind of satisfaction and dissatisfaction; satisfaction in getting a task right, dissatisfaction on getting it wrong. (For some kind of students, however, the approval of class-mates and teacher is far more effective than the solitary satisfaction of 'beating the machine'.) This is one thing which differentiates a teaching machine from an animal-conditioning machine. The mere fact, too, that the machine programme is rule-structured, logically articulated, may be a source of satisfaction to the pupil and help him to establish a routine. That latter sort of satisfaction may only come in time. The unwilling recruit to the army is at first taught by simple drill; he is commanded to go through a certain sequence of actions and he does so with the minimum of enthusiasm and only under the influence of the fear of punishment. But his capacity to perform regular courses of action mechanically can come to be a source of pleasure to him.

Indeed, the fact that pupils can take pleasure in the mechanical competence which comes with the establishment of a routine can be a danger as well as an opportunity to the teacher. It helps the teacher to establish routines, but it may lead to an unwillingness on his pupil's part to pass beyond them. This is especially so if the child has first learnt his routines purely as procedures approved by the teacher, merely in response to a system of rewards and punishment. Even in such intellectual activities as mathematics, the establishment of routines has its dangers; the child who has acquired a particular mathematical routine may use it 'through force of habit' even when simpler methods are far more suitable.[9]

On the other side, the rewards-punishments method may develop in the child a deep resistance to the routine which the teacher hopes to establish in him. 'Let a child,' Locke writes, 'be but ordered to whip his top at a certain time every day, whether he has or has not a mind to it; let this be but required of him as a duty, wherein he must spend so many hours morning and afternoon, and see whether he will not soon be weary of any play at this rate.'[10] Human beings are resistant to conditioning and, by extension, to the conditioner, as laboratory animals, in general, are not. They are particularly resistant to the influence of punishment. And although I have spoken throughout of rewards *and* punishments, the traditional teacher and, interestingly enough, the traditional experimenter – although not Skinner and his followers – made use of punishments rather than rewards in order to establish habits. Delayed punishments, e.g. critical comments on written work received a long time previously, are peculiarly common in the schoolroom situation and particularly ineffective. But pupils may also rebel against rewards, either because they come to see them as insufferably patronising or begin to suspect them as a way of reinforcing, by bribery, an authority of which they have come to be suspicious, or merely because the reward itself begins to bore them.

A third method of establishing habits is by following instructions, explicit rules. Locke thought poorly of the attempt to form habits by teaching the child explicit rules, but this is partly, at least, because he drew a sharp antithesis between learning from rules and learning by practice. 'Pray remember,' he wrote; 'children are not to be taught by rules, which will be always slipping out of their memories. What you think necessary for them to do, settle in them by an indispensable practice ... This method of teaching children by a repeated practice, and the same action done over and over again, under the eye and direction of the tutor, till they have got the habit of doing it well, and not by relying on rules ... has so many advantages ... that I cannot but wonder ... how it could possibly be so much neglected.'

Locke particularly applies his preference for practice over rules, as so many of his successors have done, to the teaching of languages; he was an early advocate of the 'direct method'. French, he says, should be taught by conversation, not by grammatical rules, and even in teaching Latin, the method of the teacher should be to 'trouble the child with no grammar at all, but to have Latin, as English has been, without the perplexity of rules, talked into him'.[11]

Locke is certainly right in emphasising the importance of practice under a teacher's supervision – training – especially as against those teachers who confuse between teaching a rule as a piece of information – 'in Latin, the adjective agrees with noun in person, gender and number' – and establishing in his pupils a set of linguistic habits. It is not at all uncommon to find children who can recite by heart a set of rules governing the behaviour of words in a language, but who are yet quite incapable of writing and reading that language accurately. The total absurdity of a situation in which children can study a language for five years, can cite the rules governing it, and yet at the end of that time cannot speak, read or write it effectively is so obvious that it is natural to sympathise with attempts to find a different, more direct, method of teaching language.

There are no philosophical grounds on which it can be shown that it is the more effective to learn a language in one way rather than in another; that is a matter which – after it has been decided what the criteria for 'effective learning' are – can only be settled by observation and experiment. On one point, however, it is necessary to insist: there is no antithesis between learning by way of rules and engaging in constant practice. Even though one cannot learn a language without practice and even though learning to speak a language and learning, as pieces of information, the grammatical rules of that language are obviously not the same thing, it may still be the case that the child, in learning a new language, does best if he begins by learning the rules grammarians have discovered. It is certainly not possible for him, as the adherents of direct methods sometimes suppose, to learn a new language exactly as he has learnt his first language. In virtue of having learnt English, for example, he has established a set of linguistic habits which may well inhibit the habits he has to form in a new language. He has, for one thing, learnt to form sounds by means of certain kinds of movements of lip and tongue and this may inhibit his attempts to form sounds in a quite different way.[12] So he may need to pay deliberate attention to the lip movements he makes in forming sounds if he is accurately to pronounce a new language, as he did not need to do in learning his native tongue. And for similar reasons he may do best to pay attention to rules in order to learn the grammar of the language.

In any case, whatever the situation in regard to the learning of languages or – the case which particularly interested Locke – the acquisition of manners and moral habits, there are a great many instances in which the natural way of establishing a routine is by following instructions. It is a very important feature of our society that we have developed an elaborate mechanism of instruction-giving and instruction-following.

To take a simple instance: suppose I buy a new motor-mower. Accompanying it will be a set of instructions on how to start it. The instructions may run as follows: 'To start the mower, push the lever marked L in the accompanying diagram to the position "fully open"; then pull the knob marked K until it is fully extended etc., etc.' By following these instructions, and even without having any understanding of what happens in the engine when I push L or pull K, I can learn to start the motor. At first, I may need to consult the instruction book as I do so, but the starting-routine soon becomes 'a matter of habit'. This does not mean that it ceases to be 'rule-governed'; if the motor will not start, my first presumption is that I have absent-mindedly forgotten to push L or pull K. I criticise myself for carelessness or absent-mindedness if I find that this is so, i.e. I treat my routine as 'rule-governed'.

Developing habits by way of practice in following rules is an extremely useful and timesaving method of establishing them. Few of us would wish to have to find out how to start our new motor-mower by trial and error, or by working out the correct procedure with the help of general mechanical principles, or by observing a neighbour after having first decided that his routines are worthy of imitation.

If a pupil is to develop a habit as a result of following instructions, two conditions must, however, be fulfilled. First, he must be able to understand the instructions – not in the sense of being able to comprehend why they take the form they do, but in the sense of knowing what to do in order to follow them. This, of course, is not always easy. For all the importance of instruction-giving and instruction-following in our society, the process of instruction-giving is rarely taken seriously as a form of communication or the process of instruction-following as a form of literacy. Instructions are often couched in a form in which they are obscure, insufficiently detailed, or unduly technical. On the other side, many people find it difficult to follow even carefully-designed and clearly-expressed instructions. So confusion arises both inside the class-room – where teachers often give instructions which their pupils cannot follow – and outside it, where manufacturer's instructions, for example, are so poorly expressed that only those who do not need to be instructed are able to understand what they are supposed to do.

A second factor is that one must have confidence in the person giving the instructions. In general terms, to form a habit on the basis of instruction is to presume that the instructions are the best method, or the best method one is likely to meet with, of accomplishing what one is setting out to accomplish. So to form the habit, as a result of accepting a grammatical rule, of using a subjunctive in noun clauses following verbs like 'j' espère' is to presume that one needs to do this in order to communicate successfully in French; to adopt a mathematical technique as a habit is to presume it is the best method – at least, at a particular stage in one's mathematical development – of solving the class of problems to which it is applicable.

Of course, the child often has to follow instructions without having any real confidence in the person who issues them – either because that person is in a position of authority or because the child does not know what else to do. But he is unlikely, under such circumstances, to establish a habit of acting in the manner laid down by the instructions; he will retain a degree of vigilance, or wariness; he will not act 'by force of habit'.

A particularly difficult and, as it happens, educationally very important class of cases, involves modes of behaviour which are only *partly* rule-governed. Learning to read or to spell English is a case in point. As a result of these difficulties the teaching of reading has fluctuated wildly from time to time. It is often supposed that these fluctuations are characteristic only of our own age and arise out of our passion for experiment. But in fact all the major 'innovations' of the last half-century were already proposed and acted upon in the seventeenth century. This is a fact of more than historical importance; it suggests that there are certain dilemmas in the teaching of reading, dilemmas not lightly to be resolved.

The major difficulty is that there are some words – e.g. cat, mat, rat, sat – the spelling of which is rule-governed, and other words –

e.g. though, cough, bough, rough – which the child has simply to form the habit, by imitation, of spelling or pronouncing correctly. This leaves the teacher with three possibilities: the first, to teach the child to read phonically or phonetically – for our present purposes we can ignore this important distinction – making use of readers which contain only rule-governed words; the second, to teach him each word separately, by a 'look-say' method; the third, to teach him by way of a new alphabet.

In seventeenth-century France, the importance of teaching phonically was taken so seriously that in the traditional schools the child learned to read French by way of first learning to 'read' Latin, on the ground that Latin orthography is wholly rule-governed. (I use the word 'reading' in quotes to mean saying aloud what is written on the page, reading without quotes to mean *understanding* what is written there.) Children learnt, simply, that a certain set of sounds were represented on paper by a certain set of marks; later they were supposed to accommodate themselves to the peculiarities of French orthography as a set of 'exceptions' to established rules.

No one nowadays would dream of teaching children to read French or English by first teaching them to say Latin words aloud. Teachers may, however, try to teach reading with the help of 'readers' which are so constructed as to make use only of rule-governed English words. And then they are forced to use sentences which are little short of gibberish – 'the pig with a wig did a jig in the bog.'[13] It is next to impossible to provide reading material of any intrinsic interest to the child if the sentences in it have to be constructed out of 'rule-governed' words, where 'rule-governed' means governed by far-from-exceptionless phonic relationships.

The seventeenth-century Port-Royal educational innovators were divided on the teaching of reading. The philosopher Arnauld advocated the use of a phonic method, applying it, however, directly to French, as distinct from going to French by way of Latin. As might be expected, Arnauld was also the proponent of an improved alphabet, much along the lines of what has recently come to be called 'The Initial Teaching Alphabet'.[14] The teacher Guyot, in contrast, argued that the phonic method rested on a misguided attempt 'always to be logical with children and to show by rules something that depends entirely upon custom' – that children can in fact be taught to read 'only by habit and custom from having a given combination of letters shown to him and hearing it pronounced many times with the same sound'.[15]

The comments of Guyot are important; something of the impetus behind the phonic method, one more than suspects, derives from the feeling that language *ought* to be through-and-through rule-governed, that habits so fundamental as language habits ought to be rule-governed, not formed by simple imitation. (It is not surprising that Guyot later broke with the scientifically-minded Port Royalists and joined their old enemies, the Jesuits.) Only experiments, of course – and the experimentation is difficult largely because teachers, bored with elementary teaching, respond with enthusiasm for a time to any new method – will show which is the more effective method of teaching reading. Such experiments will need, however, carefully to distinguish between at least three questions: first, which method more rapidly enables children to read specially-designed phonic readers; secondly, which method more rapidly enables children to read a simple story in ordinary English; thirdly, which method is more likely to arouse and sustain in the child a habit of reading. The third question is, after all, the vital one. If the child is taught reading by a method which makes him bored with reading then however 'efficient' the method in quickly teaching him to read, it is not the method an educator would choose to employ.

For the rest one need only insist that there is no merit in pretending that habits can be acquired by way of instruction in rules, if they cannot in fact be so acquired. It is a variety of 'scientism' to presume that the phonic approach is somehow peculiarly 'scientific'. In fact a great many habits can only be acquired by imitation or by a reward-and-punishment method and there is no *a priori* reason why reading should not be one of them.[16]

Finally, habits can be established by reasoning. Locke placed great emphasis on this method; 'It will perhaps be wondered, that I mention reasoning with children; and yet I cannot but think that the true way of dealing with them.'[17] In recent years, Locke's emphasis on reasoning has come very much to the fore, especially in the teaching of mathematics. But what are we to understand by 'reasoning' in this context? How, in particular, does 'reasoning with a child' differ from 'instructing him by means of rules'?

Rules may be divided into two classes: arbitrary and rational. A rule is 'arbitrary' if it cannot be justified, except insofar as it constitutes a justification of a rule to say that it is 'what is done'. Many of the rules taught in schools are, in this sense, 'arbitrary'. So it is impossible to answer a pupil who asks: 'Why shouldn't I pronounce the French letter "*r*" in the way in which I pronounce the English letter "*r*"?', or 'Why should I say "please" when I ask for something?', except by replying 'That's the way in which the French, or we ourselves, act'. That is why citing rules does not always count as giving reasons.

Rational rules, on the contrary, can be justified, by showing that they are the best, or at least a good, means of achieving a certain end. So it is possible rationally to justify the rule that a child should wash his hands before eating a meal, or that in order to analyse a chemical solution of inorganic substances he should first add hydrochloric acid, or that long passages of prose should be broken up into paragraphs. The contrast between rational and arbitrary rules, when thus expressed, sounds absolute. But in practice there are a great many intermediate cases.

Sometimes a rule is arbitrary in the sense that there is no reason, except a historical reason, why there should be *that* rule, but is nevertheless rational in the rather different sense that there has to be *a* rule, and there is no reason why it should not be that one. So if an English child asks: 'Why does all traffic keep to the left?', he can be told: 'If the traffic were not to keep to one side of the road there would be complete chaos.' This answer does not, of course, explain why the traffic keeps to the left rather than to the right but does explain why it all keeps to one side. Many disciplinary rules, and many rules of etiquette, can to this degree be rationally justified.

Secondly, a rule may be rational in the sense that it can *in principle* be shown to be the best means of reaching a particular end, and yet it may in fact be impossible to show a particular person that it does achieve that end, let alone that it is the best method of doing so. For one thing, the consequences of habitually acting in accordance with the rule may be remote. So a child may be taught at school to adopt certain study habits, not because at that stage in his school career those habits are particularly advantageous to him but because when he reaches a later stage in his education, or when he leaves school, they will be helpful. Many of the habits a teacher tries to establish are only of such a long-distance usefulness; many of his difficulties in establishing a habit by reasoning derive from that fact. He is forced to use other, perhaps less effective, means of establishing the habit, because the consequences which make it rational are too remote from the child's present experience.

The 'reasons' we have so far mentioned are 'practical reasons'; a rule is supported by showing that it is productive of certain consequences. But that may still not satisfy a pupil; what he may be looking for is a *theoretical* justification.

Consider the case, in some ways the most difficult case, of mathematics. There are mathematical habits, e.g. the habit of putting signs of equality underneath one another, or of writing indices in small letters above the number to which they apply – of which the sole justification is practical: these habits reduce the risk of making certain kinds of error. But there are other mathematical procedures which have no such obvious practical justification, and which have commonly been taught as arbitrary rules. The effect has been that mathematics, the classical paradigm of rationality, has often been taught to schoolchildren as if it were the most arbitrary and irrational of subjects, in which success consists in establishing routines. So the child may acquire the habit, for example, of inverting a fraction when he divides by it, of setting out a long multiplication sum in a particular form, of employing a certain method of taking the square root of a large number, of using a logarithmic table to undertake certain forms of calculation, without having the slightest idea why he used this particular method. It is enough that the right answer 'comes out', by a kind of magic.[18] So long as this is true, he can only be drilled, not instructed. One can easily see why the general tendency of recent attempts to reform the teaching of mathematics has moved in the direction of attempting to rationalise it, as opposed to early 'reforms' which sought to make it 'more concrete' and 'more practical'. To compare a mathematics textbook of fifty years ago with a modern mathematics textbook is at once to be struck by the greater immediate intelligibility of the procedures the child is taught to adopt. Here, at least, the most inveterate of educational conservatives might be expected to rejoice at what has happened. Yet there are still difficulties.

One such difficulty is that the child may not be in a position to understand the justification for a habit at the time at which he needs to form it. So the temptation is to give him a reason which is, in the long run, mathematically indefensible, because, for example, although it works for rational integers it does not justify the application of the same techniques in dealing with irrational numbers. Suppose, for example, a child asks why he should count seven sixes as forty-two. Then it might be explained to him that seven sixes are forty-two 'because' if you begin from the number 6 and add 6 more 6's to it the result is 42. But when the child is introduced to irrational numbers 'no one annoys him by asking him to explain the multiplication of $\sqrt{5}$ by $\sqrt{7}$ as repeated addition'.[19]

The degree to which the teacher can give reasons, then, can depend upon the extent to which the child is called upon to develop manipulative habits before he can understand their justification. If the teacher takes the view that the child should not develop these habits before the stage at which he can understand their justification there is a real risk that he will never develop the habit in question. (Similar considerations apply to the acquisition of manipulative habits in, for example, chemistry.) Should the teacher adopt the principle, as some 'new mathematics' courses do, of presenting mathematics as a logical system, he may find that pupils never learn fundamental manipulative skills and never come to understand mathematical discovery as distinct from mathematical proof. The more 'rational' approach is not necessarily the best approach from every point of view, as both employers and mathematicians are now complaining.

The general situation, then, is that although the attempt to inculcate habits by showing them to be reasonable has obvious advantages, it also has its limitations. It can never, of course, be a substitute for practice; what it does, rather, is to provide a certain sort of motive for practising in a particular way, namely that it is a rational mode of acting. Not every habit can be 'founded' in this way, either because it has no 'reason' – unless 'That is what we do' counts as a reason – or because the 'reason' may not be intelligible to the child at the time at which the habit is to be established. We cannot explain to a small child why we want him to develop the habit of eating regularly except in terms too remote to be comprehensible to him at an age at which only *immediate* rewards and *immediate* penalties are comprehensible. If Piaget is right, then the child will not be able to understand reasons, they will not have any purchase on his mind, until well after he has established fundamental routines. Even such strong adherents of reason-giving as Richard Peters grant that the child will acquire moral habits before he can acquire the moral concepts which serve to make those habits rational.[20] The attempt to manufacture immediately intelligible reasons which are not in the long run good reasons leads to hypocrisy, or to a failure on the part of the child to realise just how large a part in life is played by the arbitrary.

To take up now the final question: what part does the teaching of habits play in the schools? In an authoritarian society, it is natural to lay great emphasis on the formation of habits; 'open-endedness' is feared above all else, because it may lead to the introduction of novelties, innovations, which lie beyond the ruler's control and may disrupt its established social pattern. In the State school systems set up in Europe during the eighteenth and nineteenth century, the emphasis on habit is everywhere apparent. That is why liberals like John Stuart Mill feared State education: 'A general State education,' he wrote, 'is a mere contrivance for moulding people to be exactly like one another.'[21] Whether or not this is an accurate description of State education systems, we can say this much with confidence: whenever the emphasis in a school-system is on the need for producing uniformity, it will lay great emphasis on habit-formation.

In contrast, educators who emphasise the importance of teaching the child to be creative, imaginative, sceptical, autonomous, will be ill-disposed towards the teaching of habits. They will think of the educator's task, in large part, as consisting in breaking-up old fixed habits and fighting against the tendency to form new fixed habits. 'What makes [educational] guidance necessary,' writes John Anderson, 'is our tendency to adhere to established modes of reaction, in spite of confusions and errors.'[22] Becoming educated, according to Anderson, is a matter of *unlearning* the fixed habits we have already formed – as the rulers, but only the rulers, in Plato's *Republic* are called upon to do.

Yet habits are important; we cannot be creative and imaginative all the time. Habits economise our energy: they leave us free to think in situations where it is desirable to think, by not forcing us to think about *everything* we are doing. We do not want daily to have to work out which shoe to put on first; what is the best route to the university; how to set out a multiplication sum; what to do first in analysing a chemical solution; how to shape our sentences. We should not care to be flown in a plane in which the pilot had not mastered his cockpit drill. The danger is that in acting through 'force of habit', we shall continue to act in ways which are no longer appropriate, or are not appropriate on some particular occasion, as when we persist in trying to take a certain route to the university during a period at which the road on that route is blocked, or persist in habits which served a function at an earlier stage in the history of society, or in our own earlier life, but are now wholly deleterious. Habit is neither the hero, nor the sole villain, in the educational scene; its rôle is at once modest and important. It plays some part in almost every human activity; it keeps us going from hour to hour, from day to day. A person all of whose actions are habitual would be a mere automaton, but a person with no habits could achieve nothing. James is right enough: 'We must make automatic and habitual, as nearly as possible, as many useful actions as we can ... There is no more miserable being than one to whom nothing is habitual but indecision' – or he is right enough except insofar as indecisiveness is a character trait rather than a habit.

My conclusions are unlikely to satisfy either the all-out proponents or the all-out critics of the inculcation of habits. I can set them out thus:

(1) Where it is possible to give a pupil good reasons, which he is in a position to understand, for adopting a habit, those reasons should be given.

(2) Pupils should not be given reasons for adopting habits which are actually *bad* reasons.

(3) Pupils will sometimes have to acquire habits when there is no reason for adopting them except that they are 'what is done' or when the reason for adopting them is not intelligible to them at the time at which they need to adopt them. This should be explained to them.

Whether, in a given case, it is *in fact* desirable for a pupil to acquire a habit, whether he *can* be given good reasons for adopting it, whether he can best acquire it by drill, by instruction or example-setting – these are questions which cannot be decided except by looking at the activity in question. That it can only be learned by drill is not *in itself* a decisive reason for refusing to inculcate a habit, if the habit is one which is educationally important, as are, for example, learning to read and learning to calculate. But it may be a decisive reason if by inculcating the habit the teacher will make his pupils less able to cope with changing circumstances, more apt to fall back upon automatic routines when they need to exercise their imagination. The pilot needs his cockpit drill, but not to be so drilled that he will be rendered incapable of flying a plane in which the drill is different. That is the teacher's problem, and a very serious one.

It should be added, finally, that the problem is one which will vary in nature and intensity from child to child. There are children who find it extremely difficult to learn what seem to them arbitrary rules. So Goethe found the rules of Latin grammar 'mere arbitrary law' and therefore almost impossible to learn.[23] Other children are not in the slightest degree bothered by their arbitrariness. They rejoice in rules as rules, are happy, as Goethe was not happy, to learn, as extra rules, their manifold exceptions. Some children, indeed, will have to be taught to be interested in the very concept of reason, so strongly are they attached to the arbitrary. Others will have to be persuaded that routines must sometimes be mastered, even in the absence of intelligible reasons, whether as a necessary preliminary to understanding those reasons, or because they do not *have* reasons but only historical causes, perhaps unknown. What must be avoided, in both cases, is a pretended rationality; the teacher ought not to spread error.

NOTES

[1] William James, *Principles of Psychology* (New York 1890), p. 104.
[2] Gilbert Ryle, *The Concept of Mind*, p. 42.
[3] William James, *Principles of Psychology*, Vol. I, pp. 115, 114.
[4] For more on this theme see *The Perfectibility of Man*, p. 320.

[5] For more on the ambiguity of 'rule' see S.E. Toulmin, 'Rules and their relevance for understanding human behaviour' in Theodore Mischel (ed.), *Understanding Other Persons* (Oxford 1974), pp. 185-215.

[6] John Locke, *Some Thoughts Concerning Education* (London 1962), §82. There is, of course, no novelty in this emphasis on imitation. See, for example, Plato's *Laws* (729b,c) where Plato argues that precepts are in moral training relatively inefficacious. 'For the best instruction lies not in precept but in the constant practice of what we preach.' After Locke it is strongly emphasised by William James. 'Each of us is in fact what he is,' James is prepared to say, 'almost exclusively by virtue of his imitativeness' (*Talks to Teachers*, 1899, p. 48).

[7] Perhaps it is a testimony to the domestic circles in which Locke moved – at once cultivated and Puritanical – that Locke placed such stress on home education. Quintilian, in contrast, had no illusions about the kind of atmosphere the child was likely to encounter in upper-class Roman circles: 'They see our mistresses, our male objects of affection; every feast rings with impure songs' (1.2.8). The child, in his view, must be kept *away* from home.

[8] For further historical detail on this point, see J.A. Passmore, 'The malleability of man in eighteenth-century thought' in Earl R. Wasserman (ed.), *Aspects of the Eighteenth Century*, (Baltimore 1965).

[9] Compare the experimental work of A.S. Luchins: 'Mechanisation in problem solving' (*Psychological Monographs*, vol. 54, 1942) and 'New experimental attempts at preventing mechanisation in problem solving' (*Journal of General Psychology*, vol. 42, 1950, pp. 279-97).

[10] *Some Thoughts Concerning Education* (§73).

[11] Ibid., §66, 165.

[12] Compare D.A. Wilkins, *Linguistics in Language Teaching* (London 1974), ch. 7.

[13] See F.J. Schonell, *The Psychology and Teaching of Reading* (London 1945) – from which this example is taken – for an attack on the phonic method and a defence of the 'look-say' method.

[14] See A. Arnauld and C. Lancelot, *General and Rational Grammar: the Port-Royal Grammar*, ed. and trans., J. Rieux and B.E. Rollin (The Hague 1975). On the Port-Royalists in general see H.C. Barnard, *The Port-Royalists on Education* (Cambridge 1918) and for the comparable story in England C.C. Fries, *Linguistics and Reading* (New York 1962). On the Initial Teaching Alphabet see J.A. Downing, *The Initial Teaching Alphabet* (London 1967); F.W. Warburton and Vera Southgate, *I.T.A.: An Independent Evaluation* (London 1969).

[15] For Guyot, See Barnard, op.cit., pp. 146-8.

[16] 'Although language is systematic and follows certain rules, one masters a language best by behaving in it and having his behaviour reinforced rather than by learning the rules.' So W.F. Marquardt reports the general conclusion of linguistics in 'Linguistics and reading instruction' (Conference on Reading, University of Chicago: H.A. Robinson (ed.), *Recent Developments in Reading*, 1965, p. 115). His conclusion is sometimes contradicted. But at least there is nothing absurd in supposing that even though a kind of behaviour is rule-governed, the best way of establishing that kind of behaviour as a habit is not by teaching the rules but by punishment-and-reward techniques. This controversy, however, can touch on deep human concerns; perhaps that is one reason why it is so hard to settle. So in his *Syntaxis* (Nuremberg 1565) Luther's associate Philip Melanchthon argued that the direct method has a harmful effect on society by breeding contempt for rules. See the discussion on this sixteenth-century controversy in V. Jelinek (ed. and trans.), *The Analytical Didactic of Comenius* (Chicago 1953), pp. 48-57. Andrea Corvinus, Professor

of Rhetoric at Leipzig announced in a letter in 1634 a plan for teaching languages by first teaching 'a universal grammar or metaphysics of languages'. More recently Noam Chomsky, a vigorous critic of habituation theories of language learning, has argued that 'the child approaches the [linguistic] data with the presumption that they are drawn from a language of a certain antecedently well-defined type, his problem being to determine which of the (humanly) possible languages is that of the community in which he is placed', *Aspects of the Theory of Syntax* (Cambridge, Mass. 1965), p. 27. The question 'How does a child learn a language?' is of quite central importance both to philosophy in general and to the philosophy of teaching in particular. For a broad discussion, with bibliographies, of language-use generally, see Department of Education and Science, *A Language for life* (London 1975). A more radical view is presented in Frank Smith, *Reading* (Cambridge 1978).

[17] *Some Thoughts Concerning Education,* §81.

[18] Compare E. Stones, *An Introduction to Educational Psychology* (London 1966), on 'superstitious learning' in mathematics (p. 198). Abraham Flexner concluded thus: 'Even when a certain degree of success [in mathematics] is attained it often happens that it is quite unintelligent; children mechanically carry out certain operations in algebra, guided by arbitrary signs and models; or they learn *memoriter* a series of propositions in geometry. The hollowness of both performances ... is evident the moment a mathematical problem takes an unfamiliar turn' (*A Modern School*, New York 1916, reprinted in *A Modern College and a Modern School*, New York 1923, p. 113.)

[19] R.Beatley, 'Rule and reason in mathematics and algebra', *The Mathematics Teacher*, vol. 47, no. 5, 1954, reprinted in I. Scheffler (ed.), *Philosophy and Education* (Boston 1958), p. 211. My discussion at this point is considerably indebted to Professor Beatley's article.

[20] Richard Peters, 'Reason and habit: the paradox of moral education' in W.R. Niblett (ed.) *Moral Education in a Changing Society* (London 1963).

[21] J.S. Mill, *Utilitarianism, Liberty and Representative Government* (London 1910), p. 161.

[22] John Anderson, 'Socrates as an educator' in *Studies in Empirical Philosophy*, (Sydney 1962), p. 211.

[23] I should confess that in this respect, if in no other, I resemble Goethe. During many of my mathematics lessons, as well as in learning languages, I was in a state of fury at the arbitrariness of what I was doing. Not until I read Whitehead did I have the slightest idea, for example, what the point was in solving algebraic equations graphically, when algebraic methods were at hand. In advocating habit-formation, so far as I have done so in this chapter, I am advocating something I have always found extremely difficult. The reader should, I think, know this; it may affect my arguments.

Chapter Eight

Cultivating Imagination

'I have come very strongly to believe,' writes philosopher and sometime headmistress Mary Warnock, 'that it is the cultivation of imagination which should be the chief aim of education, and in which our present systems of education most conspicuously fail, where they do fail.'[1] We have learnt to regard with some suspicion anyone who, like Mary Warnock, claims that this rather than that is *the* chief aim of education or *the* respect in which our education systems are deficient. But such enthusiasts can usefully direct our attention to *an* important outcome of education or *a* respect in which it is defective.

Then, too, Mary Warnock by no means stands alone in thus emphasising the cultivation of imagination. We expect such an emphasis from those who would wish to enlarge the role of the arts in education. And there we certainly find it, but by no means uniquely. Consider, for example, this at first sight somewhat surprising pronouncement by Viscount Goschen, late nineteenth-century statesman and financier, addressing a group of Liverpool business-men: 'I hold,' he wrote, 'that the cultivation of the imagination amongst all classes whom such an education can reach is not only important to the young themselves as increasing their happiness, but important to the nation as qualifying them to become better citizens and fitting them to take a useful and noble part in our national duties.'[2]

The association Goschen here suggests between the cultivation of imagination and the education of 'better citizens' who will 'take a useful and noble part in our national duties' is in striking antithesis to Plato's *Republic*. Although 'education for citizenship' is central to that dialogue, the imagination is systematically down-graded. Habit formation, certainly not the cultivation of the imagination, is in Plato's eyes the great educational objective so far as the bulk of the population is concerned. As for the élite, the philosopher-kings, dialectical power, not imagination, is what Plato seeks to cultivate in them. And Plato is far from being a solitary dissenter. If in the eyes of

Warnock and Goschen the cultivation of imagination ought to be a teacher's primary concern, most books on education are silent on the subject. An educational psychologist may single out for special thanks in his preface those among his teachers who encouraged him 'to think imaginatively about educational problems' and yet still, in the course of his book on learning and teaching, say nothing at all about the cultivation of such imaginative thinking.[3]

One need not be surprised that educationists should differ so notably. Their conflicts of judgment reflect the fact that in the history of thought in general, and especially over the last three hundred years, 'imagination' has been one of the most Protean of concepts, even in the usage of a single writer. So Thomas Hobbes, like Plato before him, officially defines imagination as 'decaying sense'. Yet in another place, now in the modern, not the Platonic, spirit, he ascribes to its operations 'whatever distinguishes the civility of Europe from the barbarity of the American savages'. In Hume's philosophy, such startling fluctuations in judgment are no less conspicuous.[4] Everyday speech betrays the same uncertainties, not only about the nature but about the value of imagination. 'That's only imaginary' is a dismissal-phrase, as is 'You must have imagined it' or 'That's a figment of the imagination'. 'He has a powerful imagination' is often a polite way of saying 'He's a liar'. Yet 'a powerful imagination' 'exceptionally imaginative' are, in other contexts, terms of commendation.

Obviously, there are troubled waters ahead. Like 'education' and unlike 'teaching', 'imagination' is so penetrated by confusion-creating ambiguities that we shall have to establish for ourselves a usage, even if to do so cuts across, in some measure, the grain of ordinary practice. Let us begin, then, by distinguishing between imaging, imagining, and being imaginative.

By imaging I mean, simply, the capacity to visualise – or to do what corresponds to visualisation in the case of other sense modalities by, for example, 'running through a dialogue in one's head' or 'mentally humming a tune'. (In what follows, I shall concentrate on visualisation, as most writers do.)

Imaging and imagining are often identified. The imagination, it is then said, is nothing more or less than the capacity to form images. But this will not do. When we visualise, we are as often as not remembering rather than imagining, or are engaged in that kind of expectation in which we simply transfer the past to the future. It is a minimum requirement for imagining that we go beyond anything we have actually observed or experienced – even if not every form of 'going beyond', deduction for example, counts as imagining.[5]

So much I can, I hope, take for granted. But the question still remains whether it is possible to imagine without imaging. That disputed question – disputed because the opposite view has been taken by philosophers otherwise so disparate as Ryle and Sartre – we can fortunately set aside. We can sink it in a rather different question, more germane to our present purposes. Is it possible to imagine *effectively* without being able *vividly* to visualise? If the answer to that question is in the negative, then a teacher who sets out to cultivate the imagination will, inevitably, be attempting to develop his pupils' capacity to visualise. And that is precisely what a good many books on teaching have assumed to be the case.

So teachers have been told that 'if we wish to produce imagination we must first see to it that our pupils have a large number of vivid images to be scrapped or recombined'. Or, even beyond this, that teachers themselves 'should seek by practice to develop powers of vivid imagery', acquiring by such means a capacity to use 'vivid coloured words' which will, in their turn, arouse vivid images in their pupils. Reading to a class, teachers are also told, they should think of themselves as trying to generate 'a cinematographic picture' in the minds of their audience.[6] Only then, the suggestion is, can their pupils achieve imaginative comprehension.

Very obviously, this pedagogical advice rests on a number of empirical assumptions – over and above the assumption that the capacity vividly to image can be improved by practice. The first assumption is that a child can imagine only if he has a 'large number of vivid images'; a second assumption is that there is a close connection between having vivid images and using vivid words; a third assumption is that a child who is responding with imagination to a literary text will necessarily be engaged in an activity very like looking at a film, except in so far as that film is entirely 'in his mind'.

Are these assumptions justified? Well, as I said, this is an empirical question. However, as Galton long ago pointed out in his classical study of imagery, it is an empirical question of a rather special sort, insofar as it is very difficult for those who vividly image to bring themselves to believe that other people do not, and vice versa.

Kant writes with scorn of 'a representation such as painters ... profess to carry in their heads, and which they treat as being incommunicable shadowy images of their creations'.[7] Imagery, on his view, could never be more than a 'blurred sketch'. So we can take it that he at least, an imaginative thinker if ever there was one, did not visualise vividly. But he may, none the less, be mistaken in supposing that those artists who profess to have clear images in their heads, which help them to paint imaginatively, must be misleading themselves. The only thing that seems to be reasonably plain is that some people are able to 'see' or 'hear' what they imagine, or indeed what they remember, in a way in which some of us cannot. It is by no means so clear whether this capacity is a help or a hindrance to them, whether a teacher should seek to encourage or to discourage it. The psychologist Humphrey tells us that 'the images which hinder thinking are all of a high degree of clearness'. 'Those which further thinking,' he adds, 'are less and less concrete.'[8] If this be so, then the vivid imager will be handicapped when it comes to imaginative *thinking*. One can easily see why this might be so; the very vividness with which a possibility is envisaged could prevent other possibilities from being properly taken into account. A teacher reading aloud a philosophical essay to a class and wanting them to respond to it imaginatively would not hope to generate in his class a flow of vivid images – far from it. Even in responding imaginatively to poetry, a child might be handicapped if he vividly visualises a metaphor, which then becomes quite ludicrous. On the other hand, there are some distinguished artists, some distinguished scientists, who visualise in great detail and in a manner which appears to contribute to their capacity to imagine. Even within so abstract a sphere as mathematics, those French mathematicians who write under the name of 'Bourbaki' tell us that to be good mathematicians we must think in 'mental pictures'.

In the light of this conflicting evidence, let us assume that teachers will normally be confronted by pupils some of whom imagine by vividly imaging, some of whom, while not being fatally unimaginative, image only in a sketchy and blurred fashion. Some methods of cultivating the imagination are likely, for that reason, to be effective with some pupils, ineffective with others. In some subjects, furthermore, the non-visualiser may find it hard to be imaginative – perhaps, for example, in coping with geometrical problems – in other subjects, his imaginativeness may readily be cultivated. These conclusions will surprise nobody, except those who find it impossible to believe that anybody's mind can work in a manner which is substantially different from the way in which their own mind works, or that a person can be imaginative in one area, unimaginative in another. But they obviously present a problem to the class-teacher. There was a time at which, so great was the emphasis on imagery, it was seriously proposed that separate classes be formed for visualisers, motiles, audiles. But the class-teacher will naturally prefer methods of cultivating the imagination which are broadly effective. Even though they suppose otherwise, the methods suggested by educational psychologists as a way of improving the capacity to visualise all fall into this class.

They tell us, for example, that a child should be presented with a diversity of experiences. On their interpretation of the situation a particular mechanism then comes into operation: the diverse experiences create vivid images, which the child, if he is imaginative, will decompose and recombine in a variety of ways. But we do not have to suppose the existence of this mechanism in order to understand how a diversity of experiences can cultivate a pupil's imagination. A diversity of experiences helps to destroy the belief, natural to the child, that there is, and can be, only one way of living, one way of talking, one way of doing things, one sort of object worth creating. It promotes, or can promote, a feeling for alternatives. And by so doing it enlarges his power to imagine, whether or not he vividly visualises these alternatives.

A diversity of facts can have the same effect as a diversity of experiences. Just for that reason, it is quite wrong to draw a sharp antithesis between imparting facts and fostering imagination. Dewey realised as much. 'The feeling that instruction in "facts", "facts", produces a narrow Gradgrind,' he once wrote, 'is justified not because facts in themselves are limiting, but because facts are dealt out as such hard and fast ready-made articles as to leave no room for imagination. Let the facts be presented so as to stimulate imagination, and culture ensues naturally enough'.[9] To insist, as I have already insisted, that there are facts which everybody needs to know is not to suggest that such facts have always to be taught as something which 'just happened', which are 'simply there'. They can be taught, sometimes at least, as that possibility which, out of other possibilities, came to be realised; they can be presented in a way which invokes a fruitful reflection on what might have been, the sort of reflection which leads to a deeper understanding of what in fact is. So, to take a banal example, pupils can be taught when and where Columbus landed in America in a way which raises questions about what would have happened had he landed elsewhere in America, or at a somewhat different time, or under different national auspices. These are real alternatives which help the child to understand the effects of Columbus's landing when and where he did, help him to understand by calling upon his imagination.

On the other hand, as Dewey goes on to argue, to contemplate the *purely* imaginary – what is not, in my phrase, a 'real alternative' – is not thus fruitful. It is a 'real alternative' that Columbus should have not landed at all, or should have landed elsewhere, or should have landed at a different time, or should have failed to gain support from the Spanish court, as it is not a 'real alternative' that he should have arrived in America by jet-plane. Without attempting the task of trying to define 'real alternatives', we can roughly exemplify the contrast thus: for Columbus to have arrived by jet-plane, the entire historical situation would have had to be different in almost every respect. By imagining this to have happened, therefore, we throw no light on the actual situation. On the other hand, a relatively slight, then possible, change in the weather or in the political situation would have had the effect that his fleet sank, arrived elsewhere, or did not set out. To envisage the possibility of these things happening is to enlarge rather than to weaken our power of understanding; it brings home to us the precariousness of his exploit.

Something similar is even more obviously true in relation to the future. The question 'What would happen if supplies of mineral fuels were to run out?' casts light on our present situation and what we need to do. 'What would happen if engines could run without fuel?' does not in the same way advance our understanding. 'Imagination,' as Dewey writes, 'supplements and deepens observation; only when it turns into the fanciful does it become a substitute for observation and lose logical force.' Now we are well on the way to that other distinction we foreshadowed, between imagining and imaginativeness. Imagination, as such, has no boundaries, or more accurately its boundaries are set only by the fact that it has to have some, however remote, connection with our prior experience. 'Nothing could be more free,' as Hume once put it, 'than that faculty', even if at the same time he also recognised that imagination could never cut *all* connexion with experience. In his less sceptical moods, Hume also saw that there were two different sorts of imagination. We can roughly distinguish them – the terminology is not Hume's – as the mind at play and the mind at work.[10] Let us call the first 'fancy' and the second 'imaginativeness'. (Coleridge's famous distinction between 'the fancy' and 'the imagination' is not identical with, but in some passages in his writings runs close to, the distinction I am here making. At other times, as in his official definition of 'the fancy', he means by it, rather, that sort of unimaginative imaging to which I previously referred, imaging which is, in Coleridge's words, 'no other than a mode of Memory emancipated from the order of time and space'.)[11]

Using this terminology, we can say that Montessori when she forbade the reading of fairy-tales to young children, Kant when he laid it down that the young should not read 'novels' (i.e. romances), Dewey when he is suspicious of 'a flight into the purely fanciful and the unreal', were all of them hostile to the fancy. So far, they were

Puritanical, in the manner of those evangelical educators, to whom we already referred, who would drive play of any sort out of the school. But they were not at all opposed, quite the contrary, to *imaginativeness*, to the exercise of the imagination within a form of work.[12]

Dewey, to be sure, rejects the distinction, at the child's level, between work and play. But this is only because he identifies play with doing what is enjoyable and work with doing what is useful. He is quite rightly arguing that the useful can also be enjoyable. (Work with no enjoyment I should prefer to describe as 'toil'.)[13] But when I speak here of 'play' I have in mind a mode of acting which is quite unconstrained by any sort of objective restraint. Imaginativeness is 'work', not pure play, insofar as, unlike pure play, unlike fancy, it has an objective. It entertains possibilities which have not been realised, or which we do not know to have been realised, in the interests of problem-solving, understanding, creating.

The purest form of fancy is a day-dream. A day-dream toys with possibilities which are not 'real alternatives'; its sole function is as a relief from reality, it is not a path to problem-solving, understanding, creating. The weakling boy dreams of himself as a great footballer, the mediocre scientist as winning the Nobel Prize, without the dream in either case helping him to become something other than he is. Such fantasies can take shape also as romances; the romance-writer or the film-maker then does our dreaming for us. This is the sort of imagining Montessori and Kant wished to expel from the child's life.[14]

There are two questions here: the first, whether pupils should be *allowed* to exercise their fancy, the second whether their teachers should set out to cultivate it. Many of us would wish to argue that fancies, even of the most absurd, the crudest, kind have a part to play in human life; they cannot, and ought not to be, expunged. We should not ban, for that reason, either the romantic or the pornographic novel, although we should try to ensure that they were nobody's *sole* reading. We remember, too, what was previously said, that the boundaries of 'real alternatives' are not sharply defined. 'Imagine,' we might say in astonishment, 'Jimmy Carter being President of the United States.' And we mean that this is something which, before the event, we should have dismissed as a flight of pure fancy. But Jimmy Carter did not dismiss it thus; he exercised his imagination in order to become President; he did not merely have fancies, he was *imaginative*. The deeply imaginative have not uncommonly been dismissed as 'mere dreamers'.

The very difficulty of drawing the distinction, in particular cases, between the exceptionally imaginative child and the 'mere dreamer' suggests that imagination and fancy have a common root; they cannot be sharply sundered, as Coleridge wished to sunder them, into 'two distinct and widely different faculties', as distinct from 'the lower and higher degree of one and the same power'.[15] They are both, indeed, ways of imagining, exercises of the imagination. Both when he is day-dreaming and when he is acting imaginatively the pupil goes beyond what he has observed, what he has experienced, what he has been taught to do. We can argue rightly enough that the special responsibility of the school is to develop imaginativeness. But some children are so deprived, by rigorous routine-governed parents, that their fancy will need to be encouraged rather than disciplined. (Not all deprived children, by any means, are deprived in virtue of their poverty.) Even if the school tries to teach its pupils to think things through it has to begin by encouraging them to think things up.

Fancy can be destroyed only by rigorously confining the child's education to dogmatically-presented facts, habit formation, closed capacities. And to act thus is at the same time to destroy inventiveness. As Quintilian long ago pointed out, the teacher has the task of curbing and controlling but not of drying up the child's flow of imagination – when it does flow. It is very easy for him accidentally, unintentionally, so to act as to produce such a desiccation. Imaginativeness, the teacher therefore needs always to remember, is disciplined fancy, not something wholly antithetical to fancy, much as a game is disciplined play and turns into toil if the element of play is ever removed from it.

An alternative way of describing imagination, alternative to the description of it as going beyond what we have specifically been told, have experienced, or have been taught to do, is Ryle's way, in terms of make-believe. Such an approach is worth exploring, as a way of underlining the points we have been making.

It is sometimes fiercely contested, as robbing the imagination of any value: 'If imagination were confused with make-believe,' Collingwood once wrote, 'a theory identifying art with imagination would seem to imply that the artist is a kind of liar; a skilful, ingenious, pleasant or even salutary liar, perhaps, but still a liar.'[16] In fact, it implies nothing of the sort, even in respect to imagination in general, let alone that particular exercise of the imagination we call 'being imaginative'. A child make-believing he is a bear is not trying to deceive, as a liar tries to deceive us; he is pretending, to be sure, but not as a confidence-man pretends. By the very act of stepping on to a stage – as distinct from a platform – an actor differentiates himself from a mountebank, a vendor of patent medicines, a lying politician. Occasionally, no doubt, a novelist may set out to deceive us, pretending that his novel is a genuine biography or, on the other side, pretending it to be a work of the imagination when in fact it is a transcript of actual happenings, actual conversations. But such cases are rare. When a person 'make-believes' he does not normally set out to make us believe. At most, he demands from us, in Coleridge's famous phrase, 'a willing suspension of disbelief'. To imagine, whether or not in an imaginative way, is to allow ourselves, in the language of phenomenology, temporarily to 'bracket' the way things are, or, at least, the way we ordinarily take them to be. (By exercising our imagination, we may discover that how we ordinarily suppose them to be is not how they actually are.) In short, make-believing is not lying, even if we can use it in order to lie, whether to others or to ourselves about ourselves.

But if not a kind of lying, the reply might come, make-believing is at best a kind of play, whereas we have supposed imagination to be capable of being exercised in work. For a developed view of this sort we can turn to G.F. Stout's *Manual of Psychology*. He there draws a distinction between make-belief, which he links with imagining, and belief in the full sense, which he links with work. What Stout calls 'full belief', with no imaginative ingredient, can be found in its purest form, he says, in practical activity directed towards the pursuit of specific ends. It is characteristic of belief in its pure form that it is wholly governed by what it takes to be objectively the case, and rejects outright whatever is not taken to be objectively possible. If, for example, a teacher has it as his object to teach French to his pupils, he will work with various beliefs about his pupils' capacities; those beliefs guide his actions; they will be, or ought to be, discarded if they turn out to be false. In imagination, however, he can think of himself as being confronted by a class of children who are all of the highest intelligence and enthusiastically devoted to learning French.

Belief, it will be plain, is on this view a form of work, part of the process of dealing with the world; imagination, in contrast, is for Stout, as make-belief, a form of play. 'Even the savage,' Stout writes, 'is by no means always in a strenuous practical mood. He has his time for play as well as for work; and among other forms of play, he indulges in the play of ideas. When he is comfortable and idle it gives him pleasure to represent things not as they are, have been, or will be, but as he would like them to be, or in any way which may happen to interest him. He may communicate his imaginings to his comrades, and they may be handed down from generation to generation. Such works as the plays by Shakespeare ... are ... the most advanced development of this mode of mental activity.'[17]

The great point about imagination, on this view, is that it is, in Stout's phrase, 'pleasure-yielding', this pleasure arising from the absence of obstacles. 'We need introduce no obstacles,' he writes, 'into the flow of imaginative activity, except such as can easily be overcome by imaginary conditions and so serve to enhance our pleasure on the whole'[18] – as when a small boy imagines himself as meeting exceptionally stalwart opponents on the football-field only in order that he can the more triumphantly conquer them. In the language Freud has made familiar, belief, it would then appear, is governed by the 'reality-principle', imagination by the 'pleasure principle'. And we can readily understand those who would argue that it is the teacher's task to ensure that the child is governed by the reality-principle, not by the pleasure-principle, that television will sufficiently ensure that the pleasure-principle has its rights.

It is an interesting fact, however, that Stout quite naturally uses the phrase 'such *works* as the plays of Shakespeare'. There are, it is true, those who refuse to believe that writing of any sort is work, just as there are those who, as can happen in relation to any other activity, do not *work at* their writing. But both of those can be dismissed, the first as ignorant, the second as parasitic. That point made, we can safely deny that Shakespeare's writings are *simply* forms of play; Shakespeare worked at them. It is not true, furthermore, that in writing his plays Shakespeare had no obstacles to confront except such as he himself created in his imagination and could therefore overcome in his imagination. If, in Sartre's words, a dramatist's tragedy is simply 'a dream under his control', the control is set by circumstances which he does *not* control. Shakespeare faced a great many circumstances of this sort. The need to carry through a plot, to cope with the peculiarities of his stage, his theatre, his audience, to be consistent with what he and they took to be true of human beings, to write lines of verse – all of these constitute *objective* obstacles Shakespeare could overcome only by imaginative thinking, imaginative work, not idly, by pure play.

To carry this argument further, it is also not true that imagination is exercised only after practical needs have been met. Imaginativeness can be exercised by the paleolithic hunter in hunting as much as when he is painting on cave-walls; his imaginativeness is then exercised in the service of his practical needs. Indeed, it could easily be the case that his cave-painting was unimaginative and his hunting imaginative, that in his painting he simply copied what he had seen other painters do whereas in his hunting he devised new methods of attracting or capturing his prey.

Returning from paleolithic times to our own times, consider novel-writing and engineering as activities which are often sharply contrasted with one another, the first as purely imaginative and the second as merely practical. It would be odd, certainly, to describe an engineering achievement, let us say a bridge, as 'a work of the imagination', whereas it is very natural to describe a novel, even a bad one, in these terms. For what we have in mind, most often, when we call something 'a work of the imagination' is that it has a peculiar relationship to what we think of as being 'the real world', that in some sense it does not form part of it. (A novel considered as a physical object, as a set of printed pages, of course forms part of that world, but not its characters or its events.) It is not just that it is made rather than found; that is as true of engineering innovations as it is of the novel. Rather, although the constituents of such a 'work of the imagination' as a novel are, in a certain sense, persons and events, they are not persons about whom certain types of questions can sensibly be asked or events in relation to which certain forms of action can sensibly be undertaken. (We laugh at Partridge in Fielding's *Tom Jones* when he reacts to 'events' in *Hamlet* as he would have done to similar events in 'real life'.) In contrast, a technological invention, like a television set, constitutes, once it has been made, a part of the 'real world'; it is in the same position, ontologically speaking, as any other physical object; we do not raise questions about its ontological status as we do raise questions about the ontological status of a character in a novel. ('In what sense does Tom Sawyer *exist*?')

But even if, for these reasons, we do not normally describe a bridge or an automobile as a 'work of the imagination', it is quite natural to describe some such objects as 'imaginatively designed', others as 'unimaginatively designed'. Indeed, many of the most imaginative creations of our time are the work of engineers. Granted that, in the sense I have recently explained, every novel is 'a work of the imagination', the fact remains that most novels are conventional, unimaginative, drearily machined to a pattern. So, too, are most of the engineer's products. But imaginative engineering is at least as common as imaginative novel-writing.

The teacher need not be perturbed, then, that in cultivating imagination he is cultivating make-believing. That does not imply either that he is encouraging lying or that he is encouraging mere fantasies. The engineer's model is a make-believe bridge; the teacher's task is to encourage his pupils to work imaginatively – thinking is, of course, a form of work – or, if we like to use the Freudian terminology, to put the pleasure principle to work in the interests of the reality principle. This will sound impossible only if we suppose that it is impossible to take pleasure in creating, in understanding, or in finding out how things really are. 'Playfulness, warmth, openness and freedom to entertain the fanciful,' writes Richard Jones, describing the attitudes a perhaps exceptional teacher was able to engender in her children, 'were not just childish things to be put away some day; they went well with purpose, skill, work, and being in control of things.'[19]

One may nevertheless have qualms about classifying imaginativeness as a form of make-believing. This is because 'make-believing' has to be considerably stretched if it is to cover all cases of being imaginative. It is easy enough to see how a scientific hypothesis, or a mathematical hypothesis, or a philosophical hypothesis, even the construction of an engineering model, can be thought of as a form of 'make-believe'. The scientist, the mathematician, the philosopher 'make-believe' that the universe began with a big bang or that the rules of language are in some sense innate or that a line has been projected in a certain way or a bridge built in a particular manner. They then try out their make-believing; they test it in one way or another, perhaps by 'thought-experiments' which are themselves a form of make-believe. In the end they have formed a new belief, either that a particular hypothesis is acceptable or that it has to be rejected. A mere fancy can in no way be brought to the test, but imaginative make-believing can be.

If, however, we call Mozart a more imaginative composer than Haydn, it would be more than a little odd to say that this is because he thinks up more fruitful ways of make-believing than Haydn does. No doubt, we might, under pressure, take this view; Mozart is better, we would then say, at make-believing that his music goes in a certain way and trying out this make-believing. But there is something factitious about any such interpretation, as there is indeed about the suggestion that a person who is imaginative in his teaching is imaginative only in virtue of being better at make-believing than the unimaginative teacher. It will be more sensible to turn, at this point, to a different way of thinking about imaginativeness, to describe imaginative work as work which deviates from routine in certain special ways, of which make-believing is one, but only one. The peculiarly pedagogical problems in cultivating imagination can be more effectively brought to light if 'being imaginative' is thus contrasted with 'behaving in a routine fashion'.

It will also be more obvious that to be imaginative one must have knowledge – knowledge, to begin with, of what is ordinarily believed or done. There is no question of the teacher's cultivating a faculty, 'the imagination', which the pupil can then exercise at will whenever and wheresoever he chooses to do so. What the pupil can learn – allowing for transfers of the usual, limited, sort – is *how to do a certain kind of thing imaginatively*. That is why a person can be an imaginative scientist but be wholly conventional, or wildly fanciful, when he talks about social questions. The view that scientists should read literature in order to cultivate their imagination has no empirical foundation; what they need to read, rather, is imaginative science. I do not mean that they can *never* be imaginatively stimulated in their science by reading outside it; this is far from being true. But only from imaginative *science* will their daily inspirations come.

Of course, we must not *define* 'being imaginative' as 'proceeding in a way which is not routine'. A child may deviate from a routine out of laziness or inadvertence or sheer 'bloody-mindedness', because he has been inadequately trained, or because he is not capable of picking up the routine. A historian does not demonstrate his imaginativeness, except in an ironic sense of the word, by failing to consult sources or to check his facts. Neither does a scientist by failing to take routine precautions against error. The imaginativeness of the historian would be shown, rather, in his finding new sources or a new way of making use of old sources; the scientist's imaginativeness comes out in his formulating new hypotheses, in his finding ways of doing new things, or new ways of doing familiar things.

The emphasis, all the same, is in each such case on novelty, on making a break with routine, on doing something unconventional. Fancy need not be unconventional. To revert to an earlier example, the mediocre scientist who dreams of himself as being a Nobel Prize winner is being as conventional as anyone could possibly be. Imaginativeness, in contrast, *has to be* unconventional.

'Unconventional', however, might suggest an absolute break with tradition. Very few examples of imaginative work are of this character. Great break-throughs are extremely rare, the sort of break-throughs, that is, which one associates with such names as Plato or Galileo or Darwin or Freud or Marx. Most of us, whether as husbands or wives or parents, as workers or employers, as artists or scientists or philosophers, are imaginative only within narrow limits. We make minor innovations within a tradition; we do not try to establish a new tradition, we do not even question, in fundamentals, the tradition to which we adhere. Indeed, if this were not so, it is doubtful whether human society could survive. Most of the time, indeed, we are not being imaginative at all – when we go beyond what we are perceiving we do so by invoking a familiar principle, a familiar rule, in a purely routine fashion. Or we do so unthinkingly, as a matter of habit.

The concept of imaginativeness has been greatly damaged by those who have confused it with mere fancy. They have supposed that in order to be imaginative one must break not only with routines but with the restraints imposed by the very character of an enterprise and its relationship to the social and physical world surrounding it. They have condemned application, conscientiousness, carefulness, as obstacles to imaginativeness whereas in fact they are characteristics of which the imaginative person has particular need if he is not to collapse into fantasy.

It will by this time be obvious that there are close connexions between what I have called 'imaginativeness' and what some psychologists have called 'creativity' or have distinguished as 'divergent' thinking from 'convergent' thinking. Imaginativeness, I have said, can be shown in the capacity for making use of old things in a new way. The Chicago creativity tests emphasise the capacity of the child to think of unconventional ways of using objects as tools. We can properly object that this is not the only way of being imaginative. We can object, too, that the tests do not always sufficiently distinguish between the imaginative – the creative in a strict sense – and the merely fanciful. Nevertheless, what the tests are testing is certainly imaginativeness, if only imaginativeness of a particular sort. A generalised 'creativity' is as mythical as a generalised 'imaginativeness'.[20]

The modes of imaginativeness, as we have already suggested, are indeed extremely diverse. Teaching itself can be imaginative or unimaginative, in either of two ways. First, the teacher may be imaginative in thinking up new ways of teaching his pupils. By so doing he does not necessarily cultivate their imagination. Indeed, he may use his imagination in order to think up new ways of imposing routines on them, as Plato and Locke, in their very different ways, substantially did. It is only if his 'new ways' are new ways of cultivating the imagination that an imaginative teacher, in this sense of the phrase, will stimulate the imagination of his pupils. Secondly, the teacher may be imaginative in respect to the subject he is teaching; he may see it as, show it to his pupils as, an imaginative enterprise. They will not all of them grasp what he is doing; some of them will dislike his proceeding thus. But a few at least are likely to 'catch' his imaginativeness.

As I have already suggested, there is no form of enterprise that cannot be conducted imaginatively. Equally, there is no subject that cannot be taught imaginatively or unimaginatively. Art is often taken to be the example *par excellence* of a subject in which imagination is cultivated. But this need not be so at all. 'For eight solid years,' says one of Heinrich Böll's characters, speaking for many of us, 'I had drawn vases and practised lettering ... I had loathed these lessons more than anything else in school, for hours on end I had suffered unutterable boredom.'[21] It needs no demonstration that such art teaching did nothing to cultivate the imagination; one can easily understand how it come to be replaced by the teaching of art as 'free expression'. But 'free expression', however valuable it may be as a therapy and even although it can issue in paintings which have a certain charm, is not, as it stands, a form of learning to paint. The child does not learn from it either how to paint or what it is like to be a painter, why painting can be a source of such agony, such depression, as well as of delight. His fancy, but not his imagination is stimulated, unless, as fortunately happens as often as not, the teacher, for all his pretence of doing so, does not in fact abdicate his responsibility to discipline the fancy.[22]

It is sufficiently obvious that science cannot be so taught as to suffer from this defect of encouraging the fancy rather than imaginativeness. Discipline, apprenticeship, respect for the tradition of workmanship, are more obviously inherent in science than they are in painting. But the opposite supposition is more plausible, that far from cultivating imaginativeness, it – along with mathematics – by its very nature kills imagination. Many humanists, with miserable memories of school science and mathematics courses, take this to be so. They would grant that art and literature *can* be taught so as to weaken imaginativeness but still argue this is *inevitably* the case with mathematics and science.

Yet science is one of the great triumphs of imaginativeness. The problem, however, is that, like mathematics, it has been, from the point of view of the teacher who seeks to cultivate imaginativeness, somewhat *too* successful in discovering routine methods of doing things, so successful that one can proceed quite a long way in the subject without encountering a point at which it is sensible to try to think up alternative methods. Science courses can easily leave pupils with the impression that these routines were discovered in the manner in which they are now set out; indeed, the child is often enough told that a particular classical experiment 'proves a law beyond doubt'.[23] He is then left with the impression that there is no room for speculation in science, no room for an imaginative moving beyond what is known, that any 'moving beyond' which takes place is strictly rational. Mathematics courses can have the same effect. Mathematics lectures, so it has been said, tend to 'unfold before their listeners with inevitable logic, and often with a clarity that is fine for a certain kind of listener'. The effect, too often, is that 'their exposition does not convey the mathematical *insight* that it should'; that indeed such teachers 'fail to teach'.[24] Children can leave school with no impression of how difficult it was to see for the first time what are now presented to them as obvious mathematical relationships, no sense of what it is like to make a mathematical discovery.

One can certainly grant, then, that certain subjects are particularly liable so to be taught as not to cultivate the imagination whereas other subjects peculiarly lend themselves to such cultivation. At a very early stage in his English courses, the child is encouraged to write imaginatively; at an early stage, too, he encounters imaginative writing of a high order. In science, in contrast, he generally learns from a text-book, not from the imaginative writings of great scientists.[25] In discussing scientific discoveries, furthermore, his text-book often proceeds as if these discoveries were either 'inductions' from experiments or deductions from general principles, on the false assumption that the only sort of 'going beyond' which is permissible in science is strict inference. (Some text-books have tried to correct this situation.)

Even the distinction between English and science, no doubt, must not be made too sharply. Much of what is called 'imaginative writing' is nothing but a routine reproduction of a conventionally-designed story which the child has read or seen on television. That is one reason, indeed, why the child is now so often encouraged to write about his own experiences rather than 'to make something up'. What he 'makes up' is too often a stale repetition of literary clichés; he does not know what the clichés are for his own experiences; he has to look at those experiences freshly.[26] But a certain style of imaginativeness, the thinking up of alternative 'possible worlds', is then abandoned in favour of the recording of experience. The child needs to learn 'making up', whatever difficulties this pedagogical task may impose on the teacher.

To talk about imagination in relation to the teaching of literature is at once to be reminded of a special kind of imaginativeness, on which great stress is sometimes laid. Mill describes this sort of imaginativeness in the course of admonishing Bentham for his lack of it. It is the power of feeling as we would feel if circumstances were different. And this, Mill says, 'is the power by which one human being enters into the mind and circumstances of another'; it is the kind of imaginative power possessed preeminently by the poet, the dramatist, and the historian. Without this power, Mill continues, we do not even know our own nature, except in so far as 'circumstances have actually tried it and called it out'. Still less can we know anything about our fellow human-beings, except for such generalisations as we can make by observing 'their outward conduct'.[27]

When Mill goes on to explain why Bentham lacked this power, he offers the explanation that Bentham had 'little experience'; he did not himself know what it was to be passionate, or ill, or depressed. This would make it appear that our knowledge of how other people feel is a matter of inference rather than of imagination. Bentham does not know how other men feel merely because he has not himself felt in that way. Mill's more general view, however, is that in imagination we can go beyond anything we have actually experienced. We can contemplate how we would feel if circumstances were quite different from what they are and, hence, how other people are now feeling in their actual circumstances. So we are not wholly confined to our actual experience and to inferences from it.

The cultivation of this sort of imagination is often taken to be the peculiar province of the literature-teacher. The novelist, the dramatist, the poet introduce us to a 'possible world'; they help us to see, by their capacity for describing such a 'possible world' in detail, what it would be like to be persons quite other than we are. For our present purposes, however, the fictional persons and events of literature do not differ sharply from what is described to us as an 'actual world' by an anthropologist or a historian, when the society or the period the anthropologist and the historian describe does not form part of our own everyday 'life-world'. They interest us, or can interest us, as alternative 'life-worlds', which we can partly understand by cross-identifying with the human beings who lived in them. By this means they stimulate our imaginativeness.

It is a much disputed question whether such an imaginative identification with members of past societies or with characters in novels – an identification sometimes described, as in theories of 'empathy', as *feeling* with them or sometimes, with Collingwood, as 'thinking their thoughts' – is *essential* to the understanding of other persons, and indeed of ourselves, as distinct from being a heuristic device.[28] In his criticism of Bentham, Mill, some would say, grasped a truth which was other than what he was officially asserting: the truth that we understand ourselves directly and understand other people by inference from ourselves. Others would maintain that those generalisations about human beings which Mill mentions only in parenthesis are all that we need in order to understand, even if they need not be wholly derived from our observation of *external* behaviour. For others again, 'empathy' is totally distinct from any sort of inference.

Setting aside this large topic, let us be content to emphasise that a pupil, in and through the imaginative act of putting himself in another's place, by treating it as a 'real possibility' that he himself, or someone with some of his leading characteristics, should be in a place or at a time quite other than the place and time he actually occupies, should be in 'someone else's shoes', can come better to understand other people, past and present, real and fictional. There is, of course, much that he cannot come to understand by this method. The pupil may understand, as a historical character did not understand, exactly what was happening to that character when, stricken by epilepsy, he felt himself to be possessed. About the historical character's prospects of success, equally, the pupil may know more than the historical character himself did, or about the nature of the forces which surrounded him. I am saying no more than that there is *something* to be learnt in this way, that imaginativeness can be an aid to understanding.

People sometimes fear the imagination. And one can certainly see why they might fear this particular, imaginative, way of coming to understand. They are afraid, let us say, of social studies courses which try to get children to see the world as cannibals have seen it; they fear that the pupils may come to see the world in that way, too. Plato objected to literature on this ground, except where the child could put himself in the shoes of a good man, with honourable thoughts and honourable feelings. But if it is carefully kept in mind that the object of the imaginative exercise is to gain *understanding*, not to *sympathise with*, then this fear, if not wholly groundless – for children can come to identify with characters in a sense which the teacher does not seek – is at least mitigated. (The teacher cannot do *anything* which is not, for some children, a possible source of danger.)

How can imaginativeness be encouraged, in science or elsewhere? It is encouraged, to a degree, whenever an open capacity is taught; a child can play an imaginative game of chess as he cannot play an imaginative game of noughts and crosses. Whenever the solution of problems replaces the doing of exercises, there is some room, too, for imaginativeness; that is one virtue in 'problem-centred' education. (It does not matter, of course, if a routine way of solving the problem is already known to his teacher, provided that the child does not know the method.) The teacher, as I have already argued, can impart information in such a way as to suggest that there are genuine alternatives, in a manner which can set the imagination to work. He can teach routines, too, as something which had to be imaginatively worked out; he can encourage the child to reflect on possible alternatives to them. Through the teaching of literature, of history, of social sciences, of foreign languages, the teacher can introduce the pupil to 'possible worlds', opening up his mind to alternative modes of feeling, of living. Through the study of art he can help the child to see the world differently, breaking down the child's conviction that it must be seen in one particular manner, with the particular kind of practical emphasis characteristic of his society, and in that way alone. In teaching mathematics and science, he can bring home to the child the importance of imaginative leaps, enlarge the child's sense of wonder, show him that the world cannot be taken for granted. Technical training, even, can encourage imaginativeness, as the Bauhaus sought to do in its training of artist-craftsmen.[29] In no field is imaginativeness out of place; everywhere it can be encouraged or discouraged. Whether it is a question of building up out of fragments, in the manner of the archaeologist, of developing hypotheses, in the manner of a scientist, of thinking out new ways of doing things, in the manner of a technologist, of seeing the world differently, in the manner of a painter, the child can acquire – in and through learning a discipline, not in utter opposition to discipline – the capacity to move beyond his everyday observations, his everyday experiences, his everyday inferences.

A great deal depends, however, not only on how a subject is taught but on the atmosphere of the classroom and, beyond that, of the school. Imaginativeness is a form of courage; it is generally safer to stick to an established way of doing things. If the atmosphere of the class and the school is one in which prudence, disguised as 'rationality', is the supreme virtue, the child is unlikely to be imaginative. Plato was right, from his own totalitarian point of view, to fear imaginativeness.

Furthermore, the school, and even the university, is often enough thought of as a place where students are taught 'a job'. Even in areas like philosophy, 'being a good professional' has come to count for more than displaying imagination. The notion of the university, let alone the school, as a place from which innovations ought to come, new ways of thinking, is now, I suspect, more than ever under threat, brought into disrepute by the wild fancies which masqueraded in the nineteen-sixties as imaginativeness. As so often, the 'radical' extremists have opened the way for the bureaucrats, always present on the sidelines, ready to take over. To teach in a way which emphasises at once the need to be careful, to be critical, and to exercise the imagination is extraordinarily difficult. The two extremes of woolliness and pedantry, in a broad sense of that word, are much easier to develop in the child than a genuine imaginativeness, as I have defined it. But the teacher cannot be fully satisfied with any lesser ambition, at least unless he is prepared to be a mere servant of an authority bent on preserving at every point the established order of things, whether that authority be the State, a Church, or, what can be quite as authoritarian, a profession. Imaginativeness, disciplined fancy, lies at the very centre of a free society. For all the educational sins that have in recent years been committed in the name of the imagination, for all that routines have to be learnt, information acquired, habits formed, capacities developed, we must not allow ourselves, out of that weariness with the responsibilities and the risks of freedom which now threatens the Western world, to fall back on an education in which nothing counts except getting pupils to do well what they are told to do, getting them to conform to a pattern. That is the path to despotism.

NOTES

[1] Mary Warnock, *Imagination* (Berkeley 1976), Preface, p. 9.

[2] C.J. Goschen, 'The cultivation and use of imagination', in *Addresses on Educational and Economical Subjects* (Edinburgh 1885), pp. 7-8.

[3] James Thyne, *The Psychology of Learning and Techniques of Teaching*, Preface, p. 8.

[4] For further detail on the fluctuations of 'imagination' see J.A. Passmore, *Art, Science and the Imagination* (Sydney 1975).

[5] In a somewhat different context, with a purely epistemological purpose, we might need to reconsider this antithesis. For both Hume and Kant, certainly, every observation, every experience, already involves the imagination. But the imagination then operates as a 'blind but indispensable function of the soul' over which we have no control; it cannot be cultivated. Our interest lies in that class of imaginative operations which *can* be cultivated; these are what concern the teacher. The teacher does not have to cultivate the child's capacity to see a desk as a three-dimensional external object, even if it be true that to see it thus is already to bring the imagination into play. Neither does he have to cultivate the child's capacity to infer from a loud bang that someone has slammed a door. For our present purposes, we need to draw a relatively sharp distinction between observation and imagination, between inference and imagination, however uncertain the boundaries may be.

[6] The first quotation is from M.W. Keatinge, *A Study in Education* (Oxford 1926), p. 173, the others from a much reprinted teachers' manual A.G. Hughes and E.H. Hughes, *Learning and Teaching* 3rd. ed. revised (London 1965), pp. 136-7.

[7] Kant, *Critique of Pure Reason*, A571, B599, trans. N. Kemp Smith.

[8] George Humphrey, *Thinking* (London 1951), p. 287. He is following Willwoll.

[9] John Dewey, *How We Think*, pp. 223-4.

[10] For a defence of this interpretation of Hume see J.A. Passmore, *Hume's Intentions*, 2nd ed. (London 1968).

[11] S.T. Coleridge, *Biographia Literaria*, ch. 12; ch. 13, p. 146.

[12] Dewey is often, as by Gordon Hullfish and P.G. Smith in their *Reflective Thinking: The method of Education* (New York 1964, p. 36), taken to be hostile to the imagination. It will be apparent from the passages I have already quoted that this is not so.

[13] Compare John Passmore, *The Perfectibility of Man*, chs. 14, 15.

[14] For a discussion of imagination in its broadest sense see M.B. Sutherland, *Everyday Imagining and Education* (London 1971).

[15] S.T. Coleridge, *Biographia Literaria*, ch. 4, p. 42.

[16] R.G. Collingwood, *The Principles of Art* (Oxford 1938), p. 286.

[17] G.F. Stout, *Manual of Psychology*, 2nd. ed., (London 1904), bk. 4, ch. 8, §2, p. 565.

[18] ibid., bk. 4, ch. 9, p. 592.

[19] Richard M. Jones, *Fantasy and Feeling in Education* (New York 1968), p. 255; Pelican edition (Harmondsworth 1972), p. 214.

[20] Compare on this theme Liam Hudson, *Contrary Imaginations* (London 1966).

[21] Heinrich Böll, *Children are Civilians Too*, trans. Leila Vennewitz (Harmondsworth 1970), pp. 45-6.

[22] The better books on child art recognise this. See, for example, K. Holmes and Hugh Collinson, *Child Art Grows Up* (London 1952).

[23] Compare Paul Gardner, 'Science and the structure of knowledge' in P.L. Gardner (ed.), *The Structure of Science Education* (Melbourne 1975), pp. 37-8.

[24] H.B. Griffiths and A.G. Howson, *Mathematics, Society and Curricula*, p. 214. For more on mathematics, considered critically from this point of view, see Imre Lakatos, *Proofs and Refutations* (Cambridge 1976).

[25] Compare John Passmore, *Science and Its Critics*, pp. 78-9.

[26] Compare J.L.P. Creber, *Sense and Sensitivity* (London 1965).

[27] J.S. Mill, 'Bentham' in J.W.M. Gibbs (ed.), *Early Essays by John Stuart Mill* (London 1897), pp. 348-9.

[28] Some of the points at issue are canvassed in Theodore Mischel (ed.), *Understanding Other Persons* (Oxford 1974).

[29] Compare H. Bayer, W. Gropius, Ise Gropius, *Bauhaus 1919-1928* (Museum of Modern Art, New York 1938.)

Chapter Nine
Teaching to be Critical

What is it to teach a child to be critical, and how can we tell whether we have been successful in doing so? Is it a matter of imparting facts, of inculcating habits, of training in skills, of developing capacities, of forming the character, or something different from any of these?

Pretty clearly, it is not a matter of imparting facts. Of course a teacher can impart to his pupils a variety of facts about the practice of criticism – that it is vital to democracy, that it is essential to the development of science, and so on. He can tell them stories about Socrates or about Galileo. But imparting facts of this sort to children is not *sufficient* to make them critical, any more than talking to them about the importance of honesty in commercial relations or telling them stories about honest men is sufficient to make them honest. Being critical is not only logically but empirically dissociated from being in possession of certain facts about criticism.

Then is being critical a habit? This question does not admit of so straightforward an answer. For as we have seen, the word 'habit' is sometimes used in a very broad sense to refer to any type of regular behaviour acquired in the course of experience, whether it takes the form of regularly scratching one's head in moments of stress, or using a tool intelligently, or making good decisions. On this showing, to be regularly critical would be to have formed the habit of being critical. But 'habit', as we said, is also used in a more limited sense in which a habit is marked by the fact that, to quote William James again, 'in an habitual action, mere sensation is a sufficient guide'.[1] James tells the perhaps apocryphal story of an old soldier who was carrying his dinner home when a practical joker called out 'Attention!'. The soldier at once stood to attention, at the cost of dropping his dinner. We can similarly imagine someone who was so drilled that to any assertion he responded with 'I question that!', however inappropriate the response in relation to the assertion in question. Such a person might be said to have formed a habit of questioning, but he would certainly not have learnt to be critical. This case is, of course, an imaginary one, but there are real instances not so very dissimilar. A person can be drilled into uttering stock criticisms. He can be taught to say, whenever he sees a non-representational painting or hears jazz, 'That's decadent'. Or whenever he hears a certain type of philosophical view put forward 'That's nineteenth-century materialism', or 'That's old-fashioned rationalism'. Such a person has not been taught to be critical. Indeed, training in uttering stock criticisms is an excellent example of what we ordinarily call 'indoctrination' and set at the opposite pole from teaching to be critical.[2]

Should we say, then, that being critical is a *skill* to be taught, as skills are, by training as distinct from simple drill? There are certainly books which profess to teach critical thinking, just as there are books which profess to teach us how to drive. But suppose an undergraduate has read and mastered, let us say, Max Black's *Critical Thinking*. Suppose, that is, he can work out all the problems Black sets for his readers, and can answer any questions we care to ask him about the content of Black's book. He never for a moment doubts that everything Black says is correct; he is content to learn by heart what Black says and to follow in every detail Black's advice on doing exercises. His reverential attitude to whatever he reads, indeed, remains unchanged; it never even occurs to him to apply the skills he has learned to anything except Black's exercises. Has such a person learnt to be critical? The answer, I should say, must clearly be in the negative.

But perhaps this is because there is some other skill he has not learned. It is, of course, obvious that a person could answer any question we cared to ask him about a book called *Better Driving*, without being, after reading it, a better driver than he was before. We should have no hesitation, under these circumstances, in denying that he had learnt to improve his driving. Skill in driving is quite different from skill in reading books about driving. So the situation might be simply this: that although my imaginary – or not so imaginary – student of Black's *Critical Thinking* has learned how to read Black and to do Black's exercises, what he still lacks is skill in critical thinking. just as the man who has learned how to answer the questions set as exercises in a book on *Better Driving* may still lack skill in driving.

The two examples, however, are not analogous. For in so far as critical thinking is a skill, it consists in being able to solve problems of the sort Black sets his readers, whereas skill in driving does not consist in being able to answer the questions about driving which the author of *Better Driving* might ask his readers. One can answer the question 'What should you do when you are about to descend a steep hill?' with the answer 'Change to a lower gear' without being in the slightest degree a skilful driver. But one cannot be in a position to answer such questions as 'In what does the fallacy of the following argument consist?' without being in some measure skilled in criticism. If being critical simply consisted in possessing a skill, then it ought to be the case that to master Black's *Critical Thinking* would be to master, or gain some degree of mastery over, that skill. Our line of reasoning suggests, however, that one can master Black's book without having learnt to be critical.

This does not mean, of course, that the critical person has no need of logical skill. Training a person in the sort of skills in which Black tries to train his readers is an excellent thing to do; the schools do far too little of it. There is no reason why logic should not be taught extensively in schools and there are many good reasons why it should be. All I am suggesting is that the teacher who is content to teach such logical skills may still find to his surprise that his students turn out not to be at all critical, that they never use these skills in the conduct of their life or, if they try, do so in an uncritical fashion. For 'being critical' is more like the sort of thing we call a 'character-trait' than it is like being skilled in a performance. To call a person 'critical' is to characterise him, to describe his nature, in a sense in which to describe him, simply, as·'capable of analysing certain kinds of fallacy' is not to describe his nature. It is a natural answer to the question 'What kind of person is he?' to reply 'Very critical', when it would.not be a natural answer that the person in question is a skilful driver.

There is another way of bringing out the difference between being critical and being skilled in certain sorts of logical procedures. Skills, as Plato pointed out, are 'capabilities for opposites'. A doctor can use his skill to kill, as well as to cure. Similarly, an expert in the detection of fallacies can use his skill in order to conceal the fallacies in his own case, by drawing attention away from them, rather than in a disinterested attempt to arrive at the truth. It is one of Plato's reasons for objecting to the Sophists, as we saw, that they taught their pupils precisely this sort of skill.

In contrast, the critical spirit, in the sense in which an educator is interested in encouraging it, cannot be misused. No doubt those who possess it may sometimes be led, as a result of their exercise of criticism, to abandon views which are actually correct, as a just man can make a wrong decision, in virtue of being just, in a case where he would have made the right decision had he allowed partiality to sway him. (There are examples of this in Mr Allworthy's treatment of Tom Jones.) But this is quite different from the case where a judge uses the sort of skill he has acquired as a judge in order to pervert the

course of justice. The skills of a judge, let us say, in summing up, or
the skills of a critic, his capacity to detect concealed fallacies, can be
used or misused; justice or the critical spirit can be neither used nor
misused. And this is because neither being just nor being critical is a
skill.

If it is true that to be critical is a character trait, we can easily
understand why it is difficult for teachers to teach their pupils to be
critical. That sort of teaching which sets out to develop character-
traits relies to a considerable degree upon example and upon what is
often called 'the atmosphere of the school'. Admittedly, whatever the
character of school and teacher, an exceptional student – exceptional
in any respect, with no implication in this description of moral
superiority – may react against it. But, for example, a school in which
teachers never deviate from a fixed syllabus, in which masters and
students alike frown on every deviation from the conventional norm,
is unlikely to encourage its pupils to be critical, although its products
may be well-drilled and within limits, highly skilled – in, among
other things, logic.

The conditions of school-life being what they are, it is hard enough
for a teacher to set an example to his pupils in respect to such
qualities as courtesy, justice, consideration. But to set an example of
the critical spirit is still more difficult. In this instance difficulties
arise not only from personal defects of the teacher – out of his fear, for
example, that he may be unable to cope with a class in which the
critical spirit has been aroused – but even from the very conditions of
his employment.

Of course, in his everyday work as a teacher, the teacher will
inevitably be critical – critical of his pupils, of the answers they give
to his questions, of the work they present for his attention, of their
behaviour, of the principles by which they govern their conduct. If by
a 'critical person' we mean nothing more than a person who
regularly draws attention to defects in what confronts him, a teacher
cannot help being critical. And no doubt many of his pupils will in
some degree imitate him. They will take over his critical standards
and apply them to their own behaviour and to the behaviour of their
fellow pupils.

The authoritarian teacher, however, is content to draw attention to
the deviations of his pupils from fixed norms: their failure to work out
their sums by an approved method, to conform to the school rules, to
say the right things about Shakespeare, to adopt the accepted
techniques of folding a filter-paper. He may be in all these respects
highly critical of his pupils, he may devote himself zealously, even
fanatically, to criticising them at every point at which they deviate

from accepted norms and he may arouse a similar zeal, a similar fanaticism, in his pupils without being in the slightest degree a critical person, in that sense of the word which now concerns us. Authoritarian systems of education very commonly produce pupils who are extremely critical, but only of those who do not fully adhere to the accepted beliefs, the accepted rules, the accepted modes of action – only of those, in short, who are imaginative.

Critical ability of this sort is certainly a skill: the sort of skill possessed by an expert tennis-coach as compared with an expert tennis-player. Every expert possesses in some degree, as part of his expertness, the capacity to criticise his own performance and the performances of others, but in teachers this capacity is raised to the level of a skill. When we call a person 'highly critical' we are not infrequently suggesting that he is the kind of person – his enemies may call him 'querulous' or 'arrogant' or 'pedantic' or 'priggish' – who demands of everybody around him that they conform to what he likes to call 'high standards'. To a considerable degree that, in every society, is the stereotype of the teacher – although ideas about what constitutes 'high standards' vary, of course, from society to society. Nor is the stereotype completely unjustified. The competent teacher will rightly demand from his pupils a high standard of performance in the skills he is teaching: he will be hostile to shoddiness, laziness, contented mediocrity. But in teaching his pupils skills at a high standard, or in encouraging them to examine critically their own performances and the performances of their fellow-pupils, the teacher is not, I have suggested, automatically engendering in them a critical spirit, as distinct from the capacity to be critical of certain types of specialized performance. For to exhibit a critical spirit one must be alert to the possibility that the established norms themselves ought to be rejected, that the rules ought to be changed, the criteria used in judging performances modified. Or perhaps even that the mode of performance ought not to take place at all.

Fagin, for example, taught his young thieves to be critical of their own performances and those of their fellow pickpockets; an authoritarian society may, through its teachers, teach its young to recognise and to be expert at criticising heresy. But neither Fagin nor the authoritarian society is at all anxious to encourage in the young a critical attitude towards their own procedures – quite the contrary.

Teaching a child to be critical does, in contrast, involve encouraging him to look critically at the value of the performances in which he is taught to engage, as distinct from the level of achievement arrived at within such a performance. It is characteristic of societies in which criticism flourishes and develops that they abandon, under criticism, types of performance; they abandon, let us say, executions as distinct from seeking a higher level of skill in their executioners. A critical person, in this sense, must possess initiative, independence, courage, imagination – characteristics which may be completely absent in, let us say, the skilful critic of an executioner's skill.

To encourage the critical spirit, as distinct from professional competence as a critic of techniques, a teacher has to develop in his pupils an enthusiasm for the give-and-take of critical discussion. Sometimes he tries to do this by setting aside special occasions for formal debate. But debates are more likely to develop forensic skills than to encourage a genuinely critical spirit. A child will be encouraged to be critical only if he finds that both he and his teacher can be at any time called upon to defend what they say – to produce, in relation to it, the relevant kind of ground. This is very different from being called upon, on a set occasion, to produce a case in favour of one side in a debate.

The difficulty with encouraging critical discussion is that the teacher will almost certainly have many beliefs which he is not prepared to submit to criticism, and he will be enforcing many rules of which the same is true. These beliefs and these rules may be closely related to subjects which the pupils are particularly eager to discuss in critical terms – sex, for example, or religion and politics. If the teacher refuses to allow critical discussion on these questions, if he reacts to dissent with anger or shocked disapproval, he is unlikely to encourage a critical spirit in his pupils. If being critical consisted simply in the application of a skill then it could in principle be taught by teachers who never engaged in it except as a game or a defensive device, somewhat as a crack rifle shot who happened to be a pacifist might nevertheless be able to teach rifle-shooting to soldiers. But in fact being critical can be taught only by men who can themselves freely partake in critical discussion.

Secondly, even if the teacher is himself critical, there may be social pressure upon him not to admit that certain beliefs, certain practices, certain authorities, can properly be examined in a critical spirit. 'The values of rational, critical inquiry,' Alasdair MacIntyre has suggested, 'stand in the sharpest contrast to the prevailing social values.'[3] The word 'prevailing' may conceal an exaggeration. In no society, certainly, is rational critical inquiry the dominant social force; in every society, it meets with opposition. But there are differences between societies: our own society not only pays a certain lip-service to critical inquiry but in some measure values it. So the teacher who tries to encourage the critical spirit is not wholly isolated. But he will certainly find life less troublesome if he permits criticism only of what is generally admitted to be a proper subject for criticism – astrology but not Christianity, promiscuity but not monogamy.

A third difficulty arises from the fact that the teacher's training is very often not of a kind to encourage in him a willingness to participate in critical discussion. In some cases this is quite obvious. A Roman Catholic critic of the *collèges* of Quebec once wrote of the teachers in them in the following terms: 'In the ecclesiastical world, statements concerning learning and dogma from a higher authority are unquestioningly accepted as the most potent of arguments. Priests are not really trained to discuss ... They try to make their pupils into reflections of themselves. They find it difficult not to put a brake on independence or initiative.'[4] Indeed, in all authoritarian schools, secular or ecclesiastical or professional, the teacher counts himself successful when his pupils leave their school holding certain beliefs so firmly that no future experience could shake them; so committed to certain habits of behaviour that any modification of them will induce overwhelming feelings of guilt; so habitually deferential to authority that their unquestioning obedience can be counted upon. And not only, even if especially, in authoritarian societies the emphasis in teacher-training may be such that the teacher is encouraged to think of his main tasks as consisting in the maintenance of silence in the classroom, 'getting through' the lesson laid down for the day, adherence to a syllabus, the preparation of his pupils for routinised examinations. The ideal teacher as turned out by such systems has been described thus: 'They concentrate their efforts on preparing their pupils for examinations ...; they teach precisely the subjects named in the curriculum, guiding themselves by the textbooks in use and attempting to smooth the path for the children; they obey cheerfully the instructions issued by superintendent and principal, in so far as they can understand them.'[5] Such teachers are unlikely to encourage critical discussion among their pupils.

John Dewey's early educational writings were in large part directed against this conception of the teacher's task. The 'progressive schools', designed to give institutional expression to Dewey's educational ideas, took as their leading principle that neither teacher nor subject should be allowed to dominate the pupil. Dewey himself, as we have already seen, came to be alarmed at the consequences in so far as such an education destroyed 'organised subject-matter' and issued in 'dispersive, disintegrated centrifugal habits'. 'I am sure that you will appreciate what is meant,' to re-quote, 'when I say that many of the newer schools tend to make little or nothing of organised subject-matter of study; to proceed as if any form of direction and guidance by adults were an invasion of individual freedom, and as if the idea that education should be concerned with the present and future meant that acquaintance with the past has little or no role to play in education.'[6] Other critics have drawn attention to the fact that in such schools concealed manipulation by the teacher often replaces direct authority; the children end up by thinking that they always wanted to do what the teacher has got them to want to do – the ideal of the demagogue.[7] Explicit instructions are open to criticism, even in the most authoritarian of societies, by the more bold and adventurous spirits; secret manipulation is much harder to cope with.

But there is not the slightest reason why, rebelling against authoritarian schools which are wholly devoted to formal training of a sort which inhibits the critical spirit, we should advocate the setting up of schools in which instruction has no place. An educated man – as distinct from a merely 'cultivated' man – must be, let us agree, independent, critical, capable of facing problems. It will be obvious that the word 'education' has in this context its eulogistic sense. But these qualities, while necessary, are not sufficient; many uneducated nineteenth-century radical workmen possessed them in abundance. To be educated one must be able to participate in the great human traditions of imaginative thought – science, history, literature, philosophy, technology – and to participate in these traditions one must first be instructed, must learn a discipline, must be 'initiated', to use Richard Peters' language.[8] The critical spirit which a teacher is interested in developing is a capacity to be a critical participant within a tradition, even if the effect of his criticism is profoundly to modify the operations of that tradition.

Being critical, it will be plain, has a good deal in common with imaginativeness. Just as imaginativeness has to be distinguished from fancy, so criticism has to be distinguished from cavilling – even if, as also in respect to the distinction between fancy and imagination, it is only too easy to confuse them in a particular case, to dismiss as cavilling what is in fact a serious criticism. Cavilling consists in raising objections, making criticisms, in a manner which suggests that some very minor weakness, which would be easily remedied, is of major importance, constitutes a fatal flaw. Being initiated into a tradition is at the same time learning the difference between frivolous and serious criticisms. The caviller does not try to understand; he is intent only upon raising objections. He seizes upon an incautious concession, an obvious slip, without looking at the general purport of what is being said or done.

In spite of all these resemblances, criticism and imagination are often presumed to be antithetical, especially by artists. And it must certainly be granted that the teacher has a real problem, the kind of problem to which we have constantly adverted, in teaching the child to be critical without destroying his imaginativeness. It is at least a plausible theory that the Oxford tutorial system, with its severely critical atmosphere, has been in some measure destructive of the sort of imaginative genius which has flourished at Cambridge, whatever its virtues in training administrators and civil servants.[9]

Criticism, it might even be argued, is not something the teacher will wish to cultivate at all, except as that skill-criticism I previously described. It is essentially destructive, the objection might run, and it is no part of the teacher's task to encourage destructiveness. But the fact is that the continued existence of the great traditions of art, science, philosophy, history, as also the continued existence of democracy and of a reason-based morality, depend on the constant interplay between imagination and criticism.

That interplay may occur within a single mind. Indeed, any participant in the great traditions has to learn to be self-critical – critical, that is, of what he does. Otherwise his imagination will be dissipated into mere fancy. Similarly, as we saw, the critic needs a degree of imagination if his criticisms are not to be mere cavils, if he is to think out their force and their relevance. A wholly unimaginative critic will be a bad critic, fastening on inessentials.

Nevertheless, there are persons whose peculiar strength lies in criticism, there are other persons who are peculiarly imaginative. The person who is an especially gifted critic will often, let us grant, be destructive. But destructive, one hopes, of cant, pretence, hypocrisy, complacent conservatism and fanciful radicalism. A child is going to find himself surrounded during his entire life by persons who will attempt to defraud him, impose upon him; he is going to be surrounded by charlatans, cheats of every description, self-deluded prophets, hypocrites, mountebanks. If, as a result of his education in criticism, he can help to destroy them before they destroy human society, so much the better.

Our society needs its critics just as it needs its imaginative creators. Within the institutions of science, let us say, those scientists who are prepared rigorously to test the hypotheses which other scientists suggest play as vital a part as those more imaginative colleagues who formulate the hypotheses they criticise. Remember, too, that finding a method of testing is itself a task which can require imagination. No less is the critic essential for the health of art, philosophy, politics, morality. That is why there is no antithesis between initiating the young into the great traditions and teaching them to be critical – the great traditions are traditions of *criticism*, even if they are often not taught as such.

The importance of criticism thus granted, how can pupils be taught to be critical? The pedagogical problem which confronts the teacher who sets out to teach his pupils to be critical is very similar to his problem when he sets out to cultivate the imaginativeness of his pupils. Inevitably, instruction plays a large part in our school systems. In no other way can students be helped to participate in the great traditions. They have to learn a variety of dodges. They have to bring themselves abreast of the knowledge that has already been acquired. Only thus can they put themselves into a position fruitfully to criticise, usefully to suggest alternatives. To try to make of one's whole schooling a training in problem-solving, as the 'progressivists' hoped to do, is to produce students who will in fact be quite unprepared to cope with the principal problems within the great traditions. At what point, then, is there room for teaching the child to be critical?

One possible answer is that there is room for it only at a late stage in the schooling process and for a select group of pupils. This, so far as he permitted criticism at all, was Plato's answer. The majority of the citizens in an ideal state were to be instructed, taught to understand how to conform to rules, to apply broad principles to routine cases, but were not to be allowed to realise, even, that there are possible alternatives to those rules, that they can be subjected to criticism and replaced by different rules. Only a small élite was to come to a rational understanding of the rules, an understanding which would proceed by way of a criticism of established principles. For Socrates in contrast, if we are to believe Plato's *Apology*, the 'unexamined life is not worth living'; instruction should be left to the Sophists, the educator is by his very nature a disturber of the peace.[10]

Something like the Platonic assumption is not uncommonly accepted in our own communities. Only at universities, it is presumed, can students be taught to be critical. It is, indeed, by no means universally admitted that even at the university level students ought to be encouraged to think critically about the accepted beliefs and the accepted institutions of their communities; such critical reflection, it is sometimes suggested, should be restricted to 'mature minds'.[11] Furthermore, as the mass of instructible rules increases in volume, there is a growing tendency to postpone critical discussion, the confronting of genuine problems, to post-graduate levels, and, indeed, as post-graduate training becomes more and more professionalised, even beyond that level. (It is sometimes suggested that the Chinese never developed a tradition of critical thinking because, on account of the nature of their language, their teaching was so largely rote in kind, as characters were learnt one by one. A similar effect could come about in the Western world, as people spend more and more of their life in being instructed.) But many people would, however reluctantly, admit that independent, critical thinking is permissible in universities; at lower levels, they would nevertheless argue, it has no place.

For one thing, it is sometimes suggested, the majority of people *cannot* be educated, cannot participate in the work of facing, and solving, problems. Whether this suggestion is correct there is no way of deciding *a priori*. Very likely, indeed, there is no way of deciding it at all. Most of us could mention some field of activity in which we have learnt more or less effective procedures, without ever having advanced beyond that point. But whether, given better teaching, we could have done so is a matter in which we can speak with much less confidence.

In fact, our views on this matter tend to be determined by our social attitudes. Those who believe that it is right and proper for all but a small minority to accept uncritically the dictates of established authorities are very willing to believe that most human beings are incapable of doing anything else. The democrat is, in contrast, committed to believing that the majority of people are capable of participating at some level in discussions which lead to a change of rules, i.e. that they are capable of thinking critically about, as distinct from simply obeying, a rule. But he is not, of course, committed to believing that all men are equally capable of participating in every discussion which involves the criticism of existing rules or of accepted hypotheses.

This point is fundamental. It is related to the fact that critical thinking, like the imaginative thinking to which it is so closely related, is not a subject, in the sense in which chemistry or technical drawing or history are subjects. It can be fostered, or it can be discouraged, as part of the teaching of any subject – even if some subjects provide more opportunities for doing so, at least at an early stage, than do others. A student may exhibit it as a translator, but not as a mathematician; as a landscape gardener but not as a historian. There is always the possibility that in a new subject, or a new area of an old subject, a child will develop previously unsuspected critical capacities. It may be the case, too – although I do not know of any decisive evidence on this point – that an attitude of mind thus engendered toward, say, accepted techniques in carpentry will in some degree carry over to other modes of activity.

Plato certainly thought so; if the ordinary citizen is allowed in any respect to innovate – even in so harmless-seeming an activity as music – the whole structure of the State, on Plato's view, is in danger. Totalitarian states, operating on this same principle, are rigidly conservative in art, philosophy, moral habits; there is some reason to believe that the Soviet attempt to license technological, but no other, innovations is breaking down. It would be absurd to suggest that a man must either think critically about everything or about nothing. But it is not absurd to suggest that the critical attitude, once aroused, may extend beyond the particular group of problems which first provoked it. The educator's problem is to break down the tendency to suppose that what is established by authority must be either accepted *in toto* or else merely evaded – a tendency to which, very probably, the child's early training will have inclined him. Once the teacher has done that, once he has aroused a critical attitude to *any* authority, he has made a major step forward.

In any case, even if the teacher wholly fails in his attempt to encourage this or that child to be critical, it is a fatal policy to restrict the attempt to do so to the university level. If from early childhood a child is taught to do whatever he is told to do, if he is discouraged from asking questions, except in order to elicit information or receive instruction, he will completely flounder when he is suddenly called upon to make up his own mind, to face a situation where 'authorities' disagree. Observations made in Australia confirm what we would have expected: children from schools where the emphasis is on formal instruction find it extremely difficult to adjust to the more 'open' university conditions.[12]

How then can we reconcile the two requirements: the need for building up a body of knowledge, a set of habits, from which criticism can take its departure, and the need for introducing children from an early stage to the practice of critical discussion? The contrast, thus expressed, sounds absolute. But information can be imparted in an atmosphere in which the child is encouraged to question it, rather than discouraged from questioning it, in which he is not only permitted, but encouraged, to ask questions about its sources, its reliability. Subjects like history lend themselves particularly well to this sort of teaching. But science, too, need not be taught as a set of *obiter dicta*. It can be so taught as to emphasise that scientists often make mistakes.[13] Even habit-formation, as we saw, can have a rational basis; the question 'Why should I form that habit?' is one which can properly be asked. And the teaching of open capacities can certainly serve as a path towards critical thinking.

The skilful exercise of an open capacity, unlike the capacity to

recite a list of all the irregular verbs ending in '– oir', involves thinking
– if not the criticism of rules, at least the application of them to
circumstances which cannot be wholly predicted in advance. (This
sort of thinking we might call 'intelligence' without too much
disrespect to ordinary usage.) A French speaker never knows quite
what French sentence he might be called upon to utter, whereas the
child can know that the teacher will ask him to repeat words from a
predetermined list. Furthermore, it is often in the course of exercising
their skills that we discover the defects of accepted procedures. If the
skill has been properly taught, in an atmosphere in which criticism is
welcomed and the possibility of improving procedures emphasised,
this discovery will not give rise to a sense of helplessness or of anger
against the teacher and a simple rejection of his authority. Rather, it
will stimulate the attempt to find an alternative procedure.

So far, then, as a school emphasises, within the great traditions,
the practice of skills rather than rote learning, the use of intelligence
rather than the development of habits, it in some measure prepares
the way for critical thinking. A great deal depends on how a skill is
taught. The crucial principle seems to be: wherever possible and as
soon as possible, substitute problems for exercises. By a problem, it
will be remembered, I mean a situation where the student cannot at
once decide what rule to apply or how it applies, by an exercise a
situation in which this is at once obvious.

Thus, for example, a piece of English prose to translate into
French is a set of problems involving that imaginative insight checked
by facts characteristic of critical thinking; a set of sentences for
translation into French at the head of which the child is told that he
is to use in each case the imperfect subjunctive – assuming the
sentences otherwise contain no novelties – is an exercise. When a
child has to ask himself whether a given set of relationships constitute
a permutation or a combination, he is faced with a problem; when he
is asked to determine the number of possible permutations of a given
set, with an exercise. Whether for a particular child a question is an
exercise or a problem may, of course, be dependent on what he has
learnt. Questions which look as if they present problems – e.g. 'Why
does Hamlet attack Ophelia so fiercely?' – may turn out to be
nothing more than an exercise designed to test whether the student
can remember what he learnt in class; questions which would be
exercises to the mathematics teacher, knowing what he knows, can
be problems to the student.

Most of the time the teacher will be putting before his pupils a
problem to which in fact the answer is already known. His pupils
come to be practised in regular methods of tackling this class of

problem, in the intelligent application of accepted procedures. But the teacher should certainly place special emphasis, so far as he can, on problems to which the answer is not known, or is a matter of controversy – only in that way can he prepare his pupils for the future.

In practice, of course, a great many teachers deliberately avoid all such controversial issues. This is partly because they feel that they are not teaching if they make their pupils puzzled and then do not resolve their puzzlement for them; partly because so many of them, as representatives of authority, think it bad for their pupils to be unsettled – greatly underestimating the degree to which their experiences outside the school are in any case unsettling them. It is certainly *safer* and more comfortable to all concerned not to raise controversial issues. (It is surprising what a range of such issues there are, in any ordinary classroom.) The fact remains that unless pupils leave school puzzled they are unlikely to leave it as critical persons.

But at the same time a teacher will not want his pupils to be *merely* bewildered; he will hope to teach them in what way the questions which puzzle them ought to be discussed, what sort of evidence is relevant to their solution. Literature and history classes can be particularly valuable for the discussion of controversial issues. R.S. Peters has strongly argued that 'disciplines like history and literature are debased and distorted if they are used consciously to inculcate "critical thinking".'[14] What he has in mind, I think, is that the study of history and literature must not be thought of as a means to something else, e.g. to the acquisition of certain critical skills. Yet the fact remains that history and literature classes provide the teacher with opportunities for encouraging critical discussion of a wide variety of human activities, as well as of literature and history themselves. No one would wish to see all literature and history lessons turned into such discussions. It is a mistake nevertheless to divorce the study of history and literature from the critical understanding of human relationships.[15]

Quite ordinary children will be aware, too, that the plays of Shakespeare are in certain respects imperfect. Hearing from all quarters, and most conspicuously from their teachers, that Shakespeare was an overwhelming genius, they are likely to conclude either that genius is not for them, or that education is merely a racket, or, merely shrugging their shoulders, that this is one more thing to be learnt as a lesson and repeated in an examination. But there is not the slightest reason why pupils should not be allowed, or indeed encouraged, to do their worst in criticising Shakespeare, why they should not be allowed to defend the view that his plays are inferior to any well-made television play. Only through critical discussion of this sort can the pupil be brought to understand why Shakespeare is in fact a dramatic genius, as distinct from parroting the view that he is. If he ends up unconvinced, no harm has been done – he was not, anyhow, convinced in the beginning, he merely acquiesced – and he should have learnt a great deal on the way, not only about Shakespeare, but also about the critical discussion of literature in general. It can properly be demanded of him, of course, that at all points he supports his opinions with evidence from the plays.

But what about the earlier stages in schooling, the less intelligent child? From a very early stage he – or anyhow most children – can be taught what it is like to discuss a question critically.[16] Most of us can recall two types of teachers: for the one any criticism of his own views, his own decisions, a school rule or a textbook principle was a moral misdemeanour, to be greeted with wrath and disciplinary measures; for the second teacher such criticisms, unless circumstances were unusually unfavourable, were made the occasion for a rational explanation, with the frank admission, whenever this was the case, that a particular rule was purely arbitrary, not defensible in itself, although perhaps defensible as a rule in the game.[17] (Compare 'Why should I wear a tie?' with 'Why shouldn't I be allowed to come in late to class?'.) Any teacher, we suggested, has to instruct pupils to adopt rules which are arbitrary, at least in the context in which he teaches them. The fundamental difference between the educator and the indoctrinator is that the indoctrinator treats all rules as 'inherent in the nature of things' – as not even *conceivably* bad rules. What he takes to be fact, a principle, or presents as a person or work to be admired, is deified as beyond the reach of rational criticism. The educator, on the contrary, welcomes criticisms, and is prepared to admit that he does not always know the answers to them.

Critical discussion, at this level, of accepted rules can begin at a very early stage in the child's life; what happens later, as he begins to enter into the great traditions, is that the area of discussion widens and the difference between types of discussion more clearly emerges. Such critical discussion can be embarrassing to a teacher; he may himself not be convinced that a rule is a reasonable one or may never have asked himself how it can be justified. Anybody who sets out to teach his pupils to be critical must expect constantly to be embarrassed. He can also expect to be harassed, by his class, by his headmaster, by parents. If he gives up the idea of teaching his pupils to be critical and salves his conscience by training them in skills, this is not at all surprising. But he should at least be clear about what he is doing, and even more important, what he is *not* doing.

NOTES

[1] William James, *Principles of Psychology*, vol. 1, p. 115.

[2] I shall not face the question, in its full implications, what is to count as 'indoctrination'. That belongs to the philosophy of education. In an earlier version of this essay I linked indoctrination more closely with 'doctrines' than other writers have done. See Patricia Smart, 'The concept of indoctrination' in Glenn Langford and D.J. O'Connor (eds), *New Essays in the Philosophy of Education* (London 1973), pp. 33-46, for the literature on this topic.

[3] 'Against Utilitarianism' in T.H.B. Hollis (ed.), *Aims in Education* (Manchester 1964), p. 21.

[4] Roch Duval, 'The Roman Catholic *Collèges* of Quebec', in *The Year Book of Education* (London 1957), p. 274.

[5] G.Z.F. Bereday and J.A. Lauwerys, 'Philosophy and Education', in *The Year Book of Education* (London, 1957), p. 11. I should explain that in the text this is intended as a description of a conformist, not of an ideal, teacher. But in many quarters it would serve as a description of the ideal teacher.

[6] John Dewey, *Experience and Education*, p. 22.

[7] Kerlinger, Fred N., 'The implications of the permissiveness doctrine in American education' in *Educational Theory* (April 1960), pp. 120-7, reprinted in H.W. Burns and C.J. Brauner (eds.), *Philosophy of Education* (New York 1962), esp. pp. 384-5.

[8] Richard Peters, *Education as Initiation* (London 1963).

[9] On the problems set for the educator by the attempt to train the child to be critical without killing his imagination see J.W. Getzels, 'Creative thinking, problem-solving, and instruction' in *Theories of Learning and Instruction*, the *Sixty-third Yearbook of the National Society for the Study of Education, Part I* (Chicago 1964), pp. 251-4.

[10] See John Anderson, 'Socrates as an educator', in *Studies in Empirical Philosophy* (Sydney 1962), p. 206.

[11] See for example John Wild, 'Education and human society; a realistic view', in *Modern Philosophies and Education, Fiftyfourth Yearbook of the National Society for the Study of Education*, p. 44.

[12] See for example F.J. Schonell, E. Roe, I.G. Meddleton, *Promise and Performance* (Brisbane and London 1962), pp. 218-21.

[13] Garrett Hardin and Carl Bajema do this very effectively in their textbook, *Biology*.

[14] '"Mental health" as an educational aim', in *Aims in Education* (Manchester 1964), p. 88.

[15] 'It had never occurred to Sophia, nor to any of the other girls in the Latin class, to connect the words on the printed page with anything that ever really happened. Men marched, camps were struck, winter quarters were gone into; but to Sophia the Latin language did not concern men, camps, winter quarters and cavalry. It existed to provide Subjunctives and Past Participles and (oh golly!) Gerunds.' (Quoted in Rupert Wilkinson, *The Prefects*, Oxford 1964, p. 66, from Lionel Hale, *A Fleece of Lambs*, p. 38.)

[16] On the child's reaction to the fraudulent picture of life around him commonly presented in courses on 'social studies' see N. Frye (ed.), *Design for Learning*,

(Toronto 1962). Compare John Locke, *The Conduct of the Understanding*, §12.

[17] Compare R.M. Hare, 'Adolescents into adults', in *Aims in Education* (Manchester 1964). The difference between the two types of teacher is obvious in practice, although not easy to describe in words.

Chapter Ten

Teaching to Care and to be Careful

Summing up, in 1852, the moral qualities of the good schoolboy, Cardinal Newman listed them thus: 'diligence, assiduity, regularity, despatch, persevering application.' Ten years later, Lord Stanley described what he called a 'well managed school' in very similar terms. It should inculcate in its pupils, he said, 'habits of order, discipline and neatness'. Many schoolmasters would have agreed with Newman and Stanley; the ideals of carefulness, indeed, still dominated our primary schools at least until the Second World War. The careful child, spelling correctly, getting his sums right, drawing careful maps, carefully delineating, with pastels and brown paper, the shapes of boxes and bananas, with tidy writing and tidy hair, need not fear for success.

In the secondary school, the situation was not very different. There the pupil encountered what are significantly called 'disciplines'; he learnt to submit to them, under the guidance of a 'master'. He translated oddly inconsequential sentences from one language to another, carefully following fixed rules; he carefully set out mathematical proofs; he carefully engaged in what was called 'practical work' – learning carefully to fold filter-papers, to balance weights, to titrate solutions, or to dissect frogs. Carefully he analysed the grammatical structure of the more tractable sentences, carefully he pored over Shakespeare, line by line, phrase by phrase, word by word. And if he did all this in the approved manner, no one subjected him to censure.

The university was a different, a freer world. Or so Newman thought, and so the young man and the young woman were told when they entered its walls. But they did not always find it to be so very different. Once more, carefulness could carry them a long way: carefulness in reproducing arguments, carefulness in reading historical sources and summarising what they contained, carefulness, even if now at a higher level of competence, in calculating, in translating, in writing, in reading, in laboratory work.

The picture I have painted is, quite deliberately, a somewhat dreary one. And it exaggerates the situation; not always did pupils find that carefulness was enough. Sometimes they had to use their imagination, their critical powers; the merely careful student might get second-class honours, but rarely a first. Nevertheless the general picture is not, in outline, wholly inaccurate. To recall our school days, and some of our days at university, fills many of us with images of intense boredom, recollections of meaningless exercises, whether literary, linguistic or scientific, designed to make us careful in activities which we found completely pointless. (That is not a merely personal reaction; one encounters it in the autobiographies of philosophers so different in training and interests as Sir Karl Popper and G.E. Moore.) Yet at the same time many of us are beginning to look back on such an education with unexpected nostalgia, surrounded as we now are in our everyday relationships by carelessness, shoddiness, inaccuracy, ineptness.

But before permitting that nostalgia a wider freedom, let me for a time continue the case against the older methods. The traditional teacher, the indictment can properly continue, not only emphasised carefulness, he emphasised the wrong sort of carefulness, *extrinsic* as distinct from *intrinsic* carefulness, the sort of carefulness that is, relatively speaking, ornamental rather than the sort that is essential to a form of activity. Let me take an example. There once used to be teachers of English composition who were mainly concerned that their pupils should draw neat red lines at the appropriate distance from the edge of the page and that the compositions they submitted should contain no cancellations. The pupil who wrote feebly went unrebuked, the pupil who crossed out a word to substitute a better word was the victim of his teacher's wrath. Such a teacher completely failed to appreciate – perhaps because he thought of himself as training ledger-keepers – what sort of carefulness was his proper concern. Neatly ruled lines, tidy pages, are extrinsic forms of carefulness in relation to the task of writing good English. The choice of the appropriate word, in contrast, is an intrinsic form of carefulness. The pupil who crossed out a word to substitute a better one was the *careful* student, the pupil who let the feebler word remain was the *careless* student. But that is not the way the more inflexible sort of teacher saw the situation.

Just because he emphasised the wrong sort of carefulness, this sort of teacher, one can also correctly argue, did not set before his pupils the right sort of problem. He chose 'problems' which presented the pupil with opportunities for exercising a certain sort of carefulness, rather than problems which stimulated the pupil's imagination, which encouraged him to think for himself – as distinct from carefully applying rules in a routine fashion. So the pupil translated into and from foreign languages sentences which were chosen to illustrate grammatical points, not because they were at all the sort of thing he would ever wish to write or say; he had to conduct scientific 'experiments' which had no bearing on the scientific theories to which he was at the same time being introduced but were used as a training in the careful use of apparatus. What purported to be 'problems', in short, were actually exercises in the application of rules.

Even at the university, the case for the prosecution can continue, the same pattern continued – to an ever greater extent, indeed, in the post-war years as the traditional disciplines acquired novel techniques. In almost every subject, technical advances had the effect that new ways of being careful emerged, new forms of meticulousness, often mathematical or quasi-mathematical – or at the very least pseudo-mathematical. And the university student was encouraged not only to take up, but to confine himself to, problems which could satisfactorily be tackled with the new meticulousness. The effect was that areas of great concern to human beings were cast into outer darkness as not lending themselves to the new modes of analysis. Technical progress was achieved at the cost of an ever-increasing triviality.

At the same time, so the prosecution even more indignantly proceeds, no one ever officially admitted that schools and universities were interested in nothing except turning out careful technicians. They professed higher, nobler aims: to initiate pupils, let us say, into the great traditions of civilisation, to make accessible to them, through the medium of foreign languages, the masterpieces of other lands and other times. But what in fact happened? After years of studying foreign languages, the student could pass with difficulty a very simple examination, but he could neither read nor write with any fluency the language over which he sedulously toiled; he could fold filter-papers but had not the slightest idea of the role which experiment played in science; he could explain the meaning of lines in a 'set' Shakespearian play but, except on a school expedition which not uncommonly turned into a school riot, would not voluntarily attend the performance of a Shakespearian play and showed not the slightest interest in reading any of the plays which he had not been officially set. In short, he did not learn to *care about* science, or literature, or mathematics, or art, or foreign cultures; all he learnt to do was to be careful, to a degree and in a way which actually inhibited him from using what little he had learnt. He was terrified at the idea of speaking French, so conscious was he of pitfalls in pronunciation and grammar. The effect of his language courses were not to give him confidence but to sap his confidence. And as for seriously reading Shakespeare, or indeed any great work of literature, without a teacher's guiding hand, that would have struck him as audacious in the extreme.

Finally, the prosecution concludes, the pupil's imagination and creativity had been destroyed once and for all by the continuous application the school and University demanded of him. Everything conspired to turn him into a 'convergent' rather than a 'divergent' thinker: someone whose thinking would run, always, along conventional lines, who would neither be alert to, nor help to open up, new possibilities, who lacked any sort of imaginativeness.

One begins to understand how Herman Hesse could write as he did in *The Prodigy*: 'It is the school's job to break in the natural man, subdue and greatly reduce him; in accordance with principles sanctioned by authority, it is its task to make him a useful member of the community and awake in him those qualities, the complete development of which is brought to a triumphant conclusion by the well-calculated discipline of the barrack square.'[1] And this, it is now sometimes added, is no accident, is indeed part of a conscious conspiracy. While pretending to be a place where the child would be brought to realise his own potentialities, where he would be liberalised, humanised, the school was actually designed to inculcate in him the rules and regulations of a bourgeois society, with its characteristic emphasis on neatness, regularity, and order.

So much for the indictment. Some articles in it I cannot but accept, as I have already made clear. That there is an extraordinary discrepancy between the large claims that were made for the traditional carefulness-oriented education and what it actually achieved I should not at all wish to deny. It is by no means surprising that so many dissentient voices should now tell us that the educational Emperor wore no clothes, that even 'de-schooling' should have its advocates. In many respects, the traditional carefulness-centred schooling was a farce for the very best students, and a tragedy for the poorest students. A farce for the best students to the extent to which they saw through it; they did what they had to do, and meanwhile educated themselves by reading, by talking, or by seizing upon those rare teachers who themselves despised the system and gave their boys – less often, unfortunately, their girls – a chance to break loose from it, for at least a few periods a week. It was a tragedy for the weakest students, for they left school firmly convinced that they had been introduced to culture, and not unnaturally concluded that they wanted as little as possible to do with so boring a set of meaningless exercises.

For a considerable body of students, admittedly, it was neither farce nor tragedy; they took their education as it came and got some satisfaction out of regular rules, routine tasks, even rejoiced in them, just as they now rejoice in the professionalised graduate school.[2] The system defined 'accomplishment' very clearly and laid down a well-marked route to it. It enabled not very imaginative pupils, with a reasonable degree of diligence, to do well. It was in many ways a good preparation for the mode of life which many children would live after they left school: as a preparation for certain branches of the civil service, of business, of the army, it was excellent. Not because the details of what was taught were in any way called upon in their adult life, but because the school work engendered a particular type of moral atmosphere, the moral atmosphere Newman and Lord Stanley had so warmly advocated. There is a real danger that educational reformers will leave this class of pupil, whom they tend to despise, uncared for and in the process destroy a mode of life, a type of person, for which there is plenty of room in our own or any other society. Conscientiousness and carefulness may not be the most fascinating of virtues, but virtues they are. And virtues which have at least an ancillary role to play in any worth-while activity. Indeed, if our schools and universities could really turn out men and women who were skilled in the fundamentally important forms of carefulness, if their graduates were able to write clearly, unambiguously, concisely, to read with accuracy, to argue cogently, to calculate accurately, to work carefully with their hands, they would be making a not inconsiderable contribution to the continued existence of civilisation. The bourgeois virtues are genuinely virtues, in any society, for all that their presence does not suffice to guarantee that a life, or a society, will be a good one.

At this point, fashionable cant about 'élitism' is at its most damaging. There has always been a tendency to suppose there is something snobbish about being able to speak clearly. Now there is a growing tendency for that same fearful accusation to be applied also to clear writing, careful reading and – what fills journalists with particular horror – the careful acknowledgment of one's sources. Each of these forms of behaviour can, admittedly, have attached to it an absurd sort of snobbishness. The 'right accent', as we have already suggested, is by no means always the clearest accent; there is an affected kind of meticulous writing which is quite as trying in its own way as the blowsy rhetoric, the insistent over-emphasis, the musky obscurity, of the nineteen-sixties underground press. Footnotes are often multiplied beyond necessity. All this granted, the virtues of carefulness and clarity remain undiminished. They are peculiarly essential in a democratic system, with its emphasis on settling arguments by communication.

But to teach pupils to be careful, if carefulness is considered merely as a skill, is not, for all that, enough. In the first place, as we have said about capacities in general, the point is not merely to teach a pupil how to do something, but to persuade him that it is worth doing, worth persisting with. He must learn, that is, to *care about* carefulness as distinct from knowing how to be careful. And in the second place, there are many other things that a teacher will wish his pupils to care about; caring about carefulness, while something, is not enough. The merely careful help to keep civilisation going but they do nothing to advance it; indeed, they may cause it finally to decline, if they do not themselves realise that carefulness is not enough.

Let us begin, nevertheless, from the first point, that pupils must learn to care about carefulness, not merely how to be careful. The good teacher of the traditional sort knew this. He hoped to develop in his pupils not only the capacity for proceeding carefully, but a caring about, a passion for, accurate statement, careful reading, sound arguments. He set out to ensure, in other words, that the pupils would care about carefulness.

Many students think of the meticulous methods they learn at school or university merely as a form of toil, something they have to acquire in order to pass examinations; for others they are nothing more than games at which they are good. Neither sort of student can be trusted to continue to value clarity, careful reasoning, scrupulous reading, throughout his life. The first cannot be so trusted because he takes no pleasure in the forms of carefulness he has acquired and will abandon them if he possibly can; the second because if an opportunity arises for constructing plausible but fallacious arguments, or deliberately misreading while pretending to read accurately, or marshalling what pretends to be evidence but really isn't, these, too, he can learn to enjoy as a form of game, as in the more unscrupulous forms of propaganda or advertising. Only those who have learnt to *love* accuracy and precision and clarity, as distinct from merely being good at them – whether as a form of toil or as a game – can be trusted to persist in the humane forms of carefulness when, as in our community, there is strong pressure upon them not to do so, when accuracy and clarity are mocked at as pedantry.

Indeed, it is a more serious objection to the older education that it so often failed to produce pupils who cared about carefulness than that it concentrated so much of its attention on training in being careful. To teach careful writing, for example, involves close and patient work, teaching which makes exceptional demands on the teacher, particularly as year after year rolls on, and new generations arrive in the school making the same familiar mistakes. (Perhaps the most important single fact about teaching is that teachers, at every level, get bored.) In the world outside the classroom, to make matters worse, the pupil daily hears approved the sophistry and inaccuracy, the loose reasoning, the impressionistic judgments from which his teacher tried to wean him.

The contemporary situation is so far worse than the situation in pre-war years in that, even amongst educators, there is nowadays a wide-spread revolt against carefulness and the kind of apprenticeship it entails. Some teachers positively pride themselves on not teaching their pupils to write or think carefully. In an age in which every tyro likes to think of himself as having the privileges of a genius, carefulness is despised as a skill which, so it is said, 'anyone' can pick up. 'It's *stupid*,' the futurist Marinetti once wrote in this spirit, 'to allow one's talent to be burdened with the weight of a technique that anyone (even imbeciles) *can acquire by study, practice and patience.*' We should laugh to scorn a scientist who wrote in this way, who told us that his scientific talent was 'burdened' by the experimental and mathematical techniques he had to acquire; being a scientist, we are well aware, necessarily involves learning these techniques. In the humanities, such nonsense unfortunately finds receptive readers, particularly among those who have become tired of the intellectual emptiness, the mere tidiness, of so much scholarly work.

Obviously, however, it is not even true – so far as this is of any consequence – that 'anyone' can think, read and write carefully. These skills are hard to acquire and even more difficult to retain. As for the view that such skills constitute a 'burden' on a person's talents, this can appeal only to those Romantics for whom all that matters is the 'free expression' of the personality, who see in any kind of care-taking apprenticeship an unwarrantable interference with intellectual and artistic liberty. For the most part, such Romantics abominate science; to my argument that this attitude is nonsensical within science they would reply: 'So much the worse for science.' They prefer mysticism, they prefer to believe that, as one of the mystics has written, 'man was made to discover the truth without labour'.

There are, admittedly, risks in communicating a passion for carefulness and this is what lends the case for the prosecution part of its power – the risk that the teacher will produce, in a rather extended sense of the word, pedants. There are two extremes between which the humanist, in particular, has to steer his way –

pedantry and woolliness. Woolliness disregards carefulness in the supposed interests of imagination. So, in philosophy, wild generalisations replace close reasoning; in literary criticism, emotional effusiveness replaces a close attention to the text; in history, reflexions on human destiny replace an appeal to evidence, documentary or archaeological. The pedant shudders at the woolly type of humanist and emphasises, in contrast, the virtues of rigour, clarity, accuracy, even when, and this is what makes him a pedant, what he is doing is simply not worth being rigorous, or clear, or accurate, about. In philosophy, he will praise the formal structure of an argument from trivial premises to a trivial conclusion; in literature, the meticulousness with which a worthless text has been edited; in history, the documentation of a wholly unimportant thesis. Furthermore, as we have already suggested, he often looks for carefulness in the wrong places. He is more offended by a minor infraction of the conventions of English grammar than by vagueness, by a departure from accepted rules of bibliographical reference than by a failure to make intelligent use of evidence, by an unformalised philosophical argument than by one which does not really bear upon the philosophical problem to which it is ostensibly related.

At this point we need, then, the distinction we drew earlier between intrinsic and extrinsic carefulness; it is *intrinsic* carefulness which interests us. Every valuable form of human activity depends on the exercise of a certain degree and kind of carefulness, whether it be courage as distinct from foolhardiness, love as distinct from casual sexuality, science, art, literature, philosophy, scholarship, industry or statesmanship. So although, as I have already suggested and shall be further explaining later, caring about carefulness is not enough, even although other forms of caring about, loving, are of fundamental importance, the fact remains that these other forms of loving are all ways of being careful.

But carefulness, the reply will no doubt come, destroys spontaneity, imaginativeness, self-expression, and thereby makes impossible the practice of these other loves. That is nonsense – if, at least, the carefulness in question is *intrinsic* carefulness. One can partly understand the rejection of carefulness as a reaction against the pedantry which sometimes disfigures the humanities. One can understand the emphasis on self-expression, too, as a reaction against that training in hypocrisy which encouraged young men and women to repeat conventional judgments without looking, or thinking, or feeling for themselves, defining in text-book phrases the greatness of poets who in fact bored them beyond endurance. But the fact remains, as I have already argued, that even to express oneself, one must first learn to *express*; to learn to express entails an apprenticeship in being careful. Furthermore, the value of the self-expression will depend on the quality of that expression. Teachers who are content to tell their pupils: 'Only react' or 'Be yourself' are abandoning their task as educators. In history, in philosophy, in literary criticism, as much as in science, we have to learn to forget ourselves; we have to learn to participate in a disciplined, cooperative form of life, which is properly harsh in its judgments on those who obviously love themselves rather than the activity in which they are participating.

As for the belief that learning to be careful is fatal to the imagination, that rests on a misunderstanding of the nature of imagination. No doubt it is fatal to disordered fantasies, which the careful will rightly subject to critical scrutiny. But it is not fatal to *being imaginative*, to imaginative thinking, action or judgment. An historian, as we have already seen, does not demonstrate his imaginativeness by his carelessness in his use of sources, or a philosopher by the carelessness of his reasoning, any more than a draftsman's imagination is made clear by the shoddiness of his execution. Quite the contrary. Their imaginativeness comes out in their capacity to draw attention to new connections, to discover unfamiliar approaches, new methods of working, new types of argument, new ways of being careful.

It is vital at this point to make a distinction between carefulness and neurotic anxiety. To be imaginative, to move away from routine modes of thinking, is to take a risk. The pedant refuses to take this step, and resents those who do so. His reputation rests on his control over established modes of procedure; the last thing he wants to see are new procedures, new approaches. But if one cannot make discoveries simply by taking care, the fact still remains that making discoveries entails exhibiting particular kinds of care. The daring of Columbus is distinguished from the foolhardiness of the week-end harbour sailor venturing into the Atlantic just because it is based on his skill as a navigator.

What one does have to admit, no doubt, is that at a particular stage in a particular person's development, a teacher can by too great an insistence upon carefulness destroy imaginativeness, spontaneity, joy, the zest for discovery. One of the central problems for the teacher, as we have many times suggested, is to teach his pupils to be careful without destroying spontaneity. When a subject, or a new form of activity, is first introduced to a pupil this, most often, is not a serious problem. The child will at first treat the subject as a game, as having rules like a game but rules which, far from inhibiting, actually give a meaning to enjoyable accomplishment. So in learning a new language, for example, the child will at first derive enjoyment from the fact that he can do something he could not do before, from a sense of mastery, as he might in learning any new game. The problem is with the loss of momentum which occurs when, as teaching proceeds, the child finds that the rules he at first has to obey, the restrictions to which he has at first to submit, are only a very small part of the story. More complicated rules are constantly thrust at him. Whereas at first he learnt fairly rapidly the method of constructing the relatively simple sentence types to which he was introduced, he now finds accomplishment difficult and enjoyment vanishing in anxiety about rules. Something very similar can happen in learning mathematics, or science, or history, in learning to write one's own language, or to read. If not rules, then information, vocabulary, practical precautions, habits, can come to function in the same way as obstacles to enjoyment.

The child may react to this situation in a number of different ways. First, he may simply give up, become a drop-out mentally, if not physically. He has lost all enjoyment in what he is doing, the burden of care is too great, and he sees no reason for continuing. Or, as a second mode of reaction, his school subjects (or some of them) may come to be, for him, purely and simply a form of toil, that is, work without enjoyment but toil he is prepared to undergo because he thinks of it as being essential for some external end, whether it be satisfying the demands of his parents, avoiding trouble at school, passing an examination, or taking up a profitable career. In itself, however, the subject he is learning is in his eyes a meaningless, artificial, pointless, arbitrary collection of facts and techniques to be learnt, rules to be obeyed. So he learns, let us say, to solve simultaneous equations, to take care in doing so but with no enjoyment and with no permanent intellectual effect. While he is at school he is not a drop-out, for reasons of prudence, but he drops out of any form of intellectual and artistic activity, with enormous relief, as soon as he is free from the schoolroom.

As a third possibility, he may continue to participate in the subject as a game. He is intelligent enough to take the new rules in his stride, he enjoys the challenge they present to him; he likes the feeling he is 'winning' in his relation to them, the praise which his successes bring to him, the feeling of superiority over his fellow-students. But he has no particular interest in what he is doing for its own sake, and no devotion to it. If he has to decide whether to drop a subject the only question for him will be how good he is at it, whether he will gain more of the satisfactions of success which are all-important to him in that, or in some other, subject. The *nature* of the subject is of no intrinsic importance to him.

The final possibility, however, is that the game turns into a form of love. The child comes to *love* the subject. I am not using the word 'love' in its vulgar sense in which it is equivalent to 'like very much' ('I *simply love* chocolate creams'). In that sense a person for whom a subject is a game may love it. The lover comes to care for the subject in the sense that its absence from his life would bring with it a genuine sense of loss. He will fight for its continuance as a subject, he cares about its development, he cherishes it. And now when he is careful it is no longer as a form of toil or because the need for care presents a challenge to him but because he loves what he is doing. *Care within* what he is doing is one aspect of his *care for* what he is doing; just as a parent's care in relation to his children or a potter's in relation to his pots is one aspect of his caring for them and is otherwise only a form of toil.

Love for a subject is logically independent of being good at it. Many people are good at a subject merely through assiduity, toil, or as they are good at games. On the other side, a person may care deeply for a subject without being particularly good at it, just as a man may love a woman and yet be clumsy and ineffectual in his relationships to her, much more clumsy and ineffectual than those for whom relationships to women are nothing but a game. (This, of course, is a constant theme of novels, the clumsy lover contrasted with the skilful seducer.) But the two run together in the sense that if we care for or about what we are doing then care for us is no longer a form of mere toil, or a mere game. When we work at it our work involves both care and enjoyment, it is a labour of love. If we care for subjects or for persons we will not be *care-less* in our relationships to them, even if, as I have admitted, we may be clumsy.

A teacher may well feel that the vital thing is to avoid drop-outs. This is a sufficiently difficult task and it would be unduly harsh to condemn teachers who devote all their attention to it. If a child works hard, is careful in his work, the teacher will rarely feel that he can afford what looks like the luxury of asking whether this is out of love or as a form of toil. Indeed, in the Christian tradition, which is still in some measure influential in our lives, enjoyment has often been regarded with suspicion as has any form of love except the love of God – not uncommonly identified with the fear of God. It was therefore taken to be the teacher's task to encourage in the child in relation to his worldly activities a sense of duty and habits of working at any task without seeking any enjoyment in it. To be successful, by means of assiduity, at what one was doing was at once a mark of

God's favour and a recognition of one's own acceptance of one's station, one's place in the world. To work for enjoyment was to make a deal with the devil.

Nowadays a teacher, without fear of theological reactions, can confess himself somewhat bored with a class which, although it is hardworking, displays no real interest in a subject and works only at those aspects of it which are forced upon it by syllabus and examination; for whom, that is, school work is simply toil. But he will still contrast such a class favourably with one which is not prepared to work at all.

As for such children as treat their studies as a game, and classes in which this spirit prevails, the teacher is likely to be delighted by them. Quick, lively, intelligent, emulative, they can be exceptionally easy to teach. Pascal feared such an attitude to learning and saw in it the seeds of corruption – it was one of his objections to Jesuit educators that they encouraged emulation – but it is easy to dismiss Pascal as absurdly puritanical. Children who treat their studies as games will often go on to marked success in later life, perhaps within, perhaps outside, the academic area. Philology or science, history or mathematics, is to them a game at which they are good. But if opportunities offer elsewhere, in administration, let us say, they will change their field without a qualm. Nor does it take any very careful scrutiny of their work to see that it lacks a certain kind of seriousness and devotion, as distinct from cleverness and dialectical skill. (This is the sort of thing Wittgenstein particularly hated.)

In the long run, therefore, it is those who love who matter most. I do not mean that it is useless for a teacher to send out into the world children who will work diligently at whatever task faces them – although there is always a risk that such students will be as diligent in charge of extermination camps as in charge of factories – or children who will apply a lively intelligence, even though only so long as it secures them personal victories, to the problems which confront them. The fact remains that without lovers civilisation will slowly die.

In thus contrasting love with toil and games, I do not mean at all to suggest that there can be love where there is neither a willingness to work nor the exercise of intelligence – in short 'care' in the 'take care' sense. The view that there can be is, of course, a common one; it has been characteristic of mystics throughout the ages that they have looked for a form of love which would be entirely free of care, involving neither work nor intelligence, the simple illumination of the mind by, or its absorption, into, the One. To love, I am suggesting on the contrary, is to take trouble over, to care about and for, to cultivate and cherish. A love without care is not love at all. It is a form of immediate, direct, sensual enjoyment – what we might call pure play, just as love without enjoyment is pure toil. A love of art, of literature, of science, of nature, of persons, of machines, does not consist in a sort of ecstatic swooning: it involves understanding, imaginative thinking, consideration, courage, a willingness to work and to exercise one's intelligence.

But what exactly ought the child to be taught to love? The question what kinds of love are desirable is one which divides men – perhaps it is the most fundamental division between them – and profoundly affects what they are prepared to count as education, in the eulogistic sense of that word. So there are those, as we said, for whom there is only one love of any consequence, what they describe as the love of God; and the whole of a child's training ought to be directed towards ensuring that he loves nothing else for its own sake. For others the crucial thing is that a child should love his country – which in practice means the political system in which he has been brought up; he is to love nothing else except as a means to the maintenance of that system. 'I was born,' children used to be taught to say every morning in Germany, 'to die for my country.' Both the theologian and, let us say, the communist realise that if the child loves anything else for its own sake, there is always the risk that this is the love which will conquer if a conflict arises – a conflict, for example, between his love of science and his devotion to the State or the Church. So Simone Weil wrote thus: 'School children and students who love God should never say: "For my part, I like mathematics"; "I like French"; "I like Greek". They should learn to like *all* their subjects because all of them develop that faculty of attention which, directed towards God, is the very substance of prayer.'³ To love a subject, singling it out as love does, is, on this view, a threat to the love of God.

It is certainly not to be presumed that all loves are good; the ultimate dispute is about what kinds of love are good. There has come to be, however, some measure of agreement about the kinds of love which are characteristic of an educated man even among those who do not like educated men or who believe that these loves ought to be cultivated only as subsidiary interests, as means to the love of God, or the love of community or humanity. These are the loves the cultivation of which is the 'proper excellence' of the school. They used to be summed up in a language which now has an old-fashioned ring – certainly it has often been used in a merely sentimental fashion – as the love of truth and the love of beauty. They are the kinds of love which are manifest in a devotion to science, to art, to literature, to history, to philosophy, to craftsmanship. We expect an educated man at least to understand these passions, to see how men can dedicate themselves to these forms of activity, even if it is not humanly possible fully to devote oneself to more than one or two of them as a participant. There are not only kinds but degrees of love: a person can have a passion for philosophy and, at the same time, a sort of loving friendship for art and science.

If we raise the question exactly how a teacher is to arouse in his pupils a passion for his subject as distinct from a mere willingness to work at it – difficult enough it itself – the answer is by no means a simple one. It is here perhaps that the personality of the teacher is at its most important, the teacher's own passion, or at least affection, for his subject communicating itself to his pupils. That is one of the difficulties with the attempt to set up a universal education system; many, perhaps most, of the teachers will think of their work simply as a form of toil or at best a kind of game; it is unlikely that more than a few of them will have a passion for the subject they are teaching. (The most important question to be asked about a teacher is not: 'Has he been trained?' but 'Does he love the subjects he will be teaching?'.) I suggested earlier that the teacher's role is anything but passive – he is, among other things, a begetter of passion.

In a child's mind a love for the teacher and a love for the subject may run together; he may learn to love the subject through loving the teacher. It can happen indeed, that he only *thinks* that he loves the subject, that his real and sole love is for the teacher, as will come out by his lack of interest in other people's contributions, in other men's books and ideas. A good teacher will try to avoid this outcome by getting his pupils to read and work independently so that the subject exists for them as something other than a mode of activity of their teacher. But there are problems here of quite a serious kind, not unrelated to 'transference' problems in psychoanalysis. What are often thought to be good teachers may, in fact, make their pupils so dependent on them that their interest in the subject disappears as soon as they lose contact with the teacher or continues only as a kind of reminiscence of what they learned from him, not as an independent love.

Certainly there is no pedagogical method by which a teacher can ensure that his pupils will develop a passion for the subject he teaches. Perhaps, indeed, in the actual conditions of our schools, he will be achieving more than most of his colleagues if his pupils leave his hands not positively hating, and seeking to destroy, the forms of activity into which he has tried to initiate them; if they are not, that is, anti-intellectuals of the kind which at present some educational systems produce in vast numbers. If our education system turns out men and women who are indifferent to or positively hostile towards art, science, literature, philosophy, history, that is the strongest possible indictment of it.

These attitudes can be engendered in a variety of ways. As a pupil can learn to love a subject through loving his teacher so he can come to hate a subject through hating his teacher. But also, if a subject is presented to him simply as a form of toil, or only as an opportunity for children brighter than himself to engage in a kind of game, he is unlikely to come to think of it as something which should engage his devotion. He may become hostile to it because he fails to understand it, to see its point, or because it is taught unimaginatively. And it must all the time be remembered, of course, that in treating intellectual loves as important, the teacher is not dealing with children who are *tabulae rasae* but with children whose own parents may be hostile to the intellectual life, and who are living in a society in which such loves count for nothing. In those pupils in whom the teacher stirs up a passion for his subject he finds his highest justification; but the more modest aim of turning out pupils who have at least a mild affection for, a friendship for, as distinct from a hostility towards, the main forms of intellectual activity is by no means to be despised.

There is one final question I should raise. Discussing these issues at seminars and with individuals, I have found myself condemned as an indoctrinator. It is all very well, the argument runs, for a teacher to help a child who already loves literature to learn more about it, but he should restrain himself from any attempt to get his children to love literature; for if he does this he is imposing himself on his pupils. He must confine himself to teaching the facts.

But what importance do these facts then have? They are important only insofar as literature is important. To try to persuade pupils to learn these facts while being at the same time careful, in case one indoctrinates, not to try to encourage them to love literature, to conceal even, one's own love of literature, makes, in my judgment, no sense at all; it turns English-teaching into a meaningless exercise. And where else, if not at school, is the child to acquire the intellectual loves?

NOTES

[1] Herman Hesse, *The Prodigy* (1905), trans. W.J. Strachan (Harmondsworth 1973), p. 43.
[2] Compare John Passmore, 'The philosophy of graduate education', in W. Frankena (ed.), *The Philosophy of Graduate Education* (Ann Arbor 1980).
[3] Simone Weil, *Waiting for God* (London 1951), p. 51.

Chapter Eleven

Teaching to Understand

This chapter is rather different in style from any other in the book: it is more schematic. This is not because its topic is unimportant. Quite the contrary. It is so important that I have reverted to it again and again. So now, in large part, I can be content to summarise what I have previously argued, to bring it together in a systematic form. True enough, there are problems about understanding which I have not touched upon and shall not be touching upon. Some of them lie, furthermore, at the centre of contemporary professional philosophy – problems about meaning, sense, interpretation. I shall refer to some of them in passing, but only in passing. For the most part, or so I hope, the teacher can set them aside as not his concern.

When does a pupil not understand? At the most general level, when he misunderstands, fails to understand, half-understands, or sees no need to understand. Misunderstanding, he wrongly believes that he understands; failing to understand, he has tried, but unsuccessfully, to understand and is aware of that fact; half-understanding, he has grasped some relevant features of what he is called upon to understand, but not others; not seeking to understand, he takes for granted what confronts him, thinks of it as 'perfectly natural'. Correspondingly, the teacher can promote understanding by destroying misunderstandings, by breaking down the barriers which prevent the child from understanding, by trying to extend the range of his understanding, by making him puzzled and then bringing him to understand.

If we go on to ask what *kinds* of thing a pupil might fail to understand, can misunderstand, can half-understand, can see no need to understand, the answer has to be a complicated one. Theories, persons, works of art, sentences, instructions, intentions, purposes, feelings, institutions, how something works, how to do something – these will illustrate the range. Let us begin from sentences, for since teaching is a form of communication, most often verbal, this kind of not understanding is of great importance to it.

Why might a pupil not understand a sentence? In extreme

instances, because the teacher, or the author the pupil is reading, is using a language which is not the pupil's language or which only partly coincides with that language. In schoolrooms over the last fifty years, in some countries for a much longer time, this has been a very common phenomenon. (Setting aside the obvious case of the foreign-language classroom.) The refugee, the migrant, have come to be familiar faces in a great many classrooms. 'Internal' migration from country to city, even the widening of educational opportunities, can give rise to a similar situation, if in a less acute and therefore less obvious form. Schooling systems, with some notable exceptions, have not been very responsive to the needs of the 'foreigner'. Many children have found themselves in a linguistic situation so difficult, so alien to them, that their chance of learning effectively has been negligible. It is sufficiently clear, however, what under these circumstances is needed – special classes designed to bring pupils up to that level of competence in the teacher's language which will enable them to follow him, to understand what he is saying. The problems in doing this are financial and administrative, rather than pedagogical.

Even if, however, a pupil recognises a teacher's language as his own language, he may still fail to understand a sentence for linguistic reasons: it may contain words, or idioms, or syntactical constructions, which are unfamiliar to him. In general, no doubt, syntax is not a problem except for the migrant child, at least at the level of comprehension as distinct from composition. Asked to read a text from an earlier period, however, any child may be puzzled. It used to be said that English prose began with Dryden, with the implication that after that time no problems were to be expected with comprehension. Now, however, university students who have been brought up on the single-clause sentences so characteristic of contemporary writing and who encounter at school neither the Authorised Version of the Bible nor the eighteenth-century essayists may find it extremely difficult, for syntactical reasons, to read Locke, or Berkeley, or Hume. This is so, even though these writers were, until recently, acclaimed as masters of a clear English style. At quite a late stage in their education, then, a teacher may have to help his pupils, if they are to have any hope of understanding, to master problems of a syntactical kind. And he may not recognise what the problem is.

As for the difficulties which arise from a defective vocabulary, the child, or any of us, can, of course, fail to understand a sentence because it contains an unfamiliar general word. Extending the child's vocabulary by whatever means are most effective, helping him to use

a dictionary, making him familiar with the broad range of
dictionaries, technical as well as general, is one important way of
promoting understanding. Every new word the child masters helps
him to understand not only some particular sentence but a wide
range of sentences. Few forms of 'learning for the future' are so
valuable.

Next, and now we begin to approach a more controversial area, a
child may fail to understand a sentence because it contains a proper
name which is unfamiliar to him. He cannot understand the sentence
'If it were not for Einstein, we should not have had the atom-bomb'
unless he knows who Einstein was. He may well, indeed,
misunderstand that sentence, supposing Einstein to be the name of a
politician or an engineer. This is only one illustration of the fact that
in order to understand a sentence, a pupil will often need
information. He cannot expect to discover who Einstein is by looking
up the *Oxford English Dictionary* as he can, in that way, find out what a
word means. True enough, some works which describe themselves as
dictionaries *do* give this sort of information, especially in the United
States, and we can easily imagine a philosophical defence of this
practice, to the effect that 'Einstein' is as much a part of our
vocabulary as is 'physics', 'Freud' as is 'psycho-analysis'. That is
why I said that this is a controversial case. But we do not normally
count learning who Einstein is as one way of enlarging our
vocabulary. (If a Frenchman were to say that he 'knew a lot of
English words' and then it turned out that these were all proper
names, we could rightly accuse him of misleading us.) It counts,
rather, as the acquisition of 'historical' information, information
which we may need, however, in order to understand a certain class
of sentences.

Consider a rather different case. Very often, in order to understand
a sentence we have to work out to what person, or thing, or event a
pronoun refers. There may well be sentences in this book in which,
from the standpoint of syntax, the word 'he' could refer either to
teacher or pupil. I do not think that any such sentence will generate
misunderstandings. But this is because the reader already has at his
disposal a certain 'information-frame'. Acquainted with the teacher-
pupil situation, he knows that in the sentence 'When a teacher tells a
pupil who Einstein is, he gains in understanding' the 'he' refers to the
pupil. If, similarly, he reads 'As the Ambassador approached the
President, he bowed deeply', the reader knows that it is the
Ambassador, not the President, who bows. The child may not know
this; he may be puzzled, as a computer may be brought to a
standstill, by any of a number of 'indexical' words, just because he

lacks the appropriate information-frame. To teach the child about social situations, social relationships, is at the same time to teach him to understand such sentences.

Suppose, again, a North American child reads the sentence in an Australian adventure-story: 'It was mid-January, and the sun beat down mercilessly on their heads.' He has no problem with the vocabulary; the concept of a 'merciless sun' is not strange to him. But he still does not understand. 'A merciless sun in *mid-January*'? He may, of course, misunderstand, answering that question for himself, contentedly assuming that in Australia it is always hot, even in mid-winter. But the structure of the sentence ought to suggest to him that this is not the explanation. To understand, he needs information, the information that in Australia mid-January comes in mid-summer or, more generally, that this happens throughout the southern hemisphere. Otherwise, he may suppose the sentence to be a joke, to be ironical or to contain a misprint.

It is sometimes supposed that giving information and promoting understanding are utterly opposed to one another: 'Understanding, not facts' is a familiar slogan. But, as we saw, unless the child understands what he is being told, the teacher is not imparting information, he is simply establishing verbal habits. So it is only in virtue of the child's having already acquired certain kinds of understanding that the teacher can impart facts. And, secondly, information, as in the cases just cited, may be exactly what the child needs in order to understand. With a view to future understanding, or so I have already suggested, the teacher needs particularly to concentrate on information which is likely to be usable as an aid to understanding in a wide range of situations. Nevertheless, as we also granted, he will often be called upon to impart quite particularised information in order to help the child to understand specific sentences – information, sometimes, of a 'historical' kind, sometimes of a 'theoretical' kind, to refer back to our earlier distinction. (When the information the child needs is of a theoretical sort, we often say of him that he 'hasn't grasped the concept' rather than that he 'lacks information'.)

To sum up, then, when a child does not understand a sentence, a teacher will sometimes have to help him to cope with a puzzling syntactical construction – or perhaps a literary device, like irony, or metaphor, or metonymy. On other occasions he will have to enlarge the child's vocabulary. We can think of all these means of teaching to understand as linguistic instruction. On other occasions, the teacher will need, rather, to give the child information about the world around him, about the life and work of a particular person, about a social relationship, about an event, or about one of those very general relationships to which theories point.

Let me turn now to a second class of cases, when a child understands what a sentence says, but not why what it says should be so. We tell him that mid-January is mid-summer in Australia and he still asks 'Why is that so?' or 'How does that happen?' He is no longer puzzled about the meaning of the sentence 'It was mid-January, and the sun beat down mercilessly on their heads'. But he still wants to know *why* it is hot in mid-January in Australia. Or he might ask, in a similar spirit, why the light goes on when he presses down a switch. What he is looking for is a general principle from which the occurrence's taking that form will follow. And he can be answered in the first case in terms of the rotation of the earth, in the second case in terms of electrical circuits, achieving thereby a degree of understanding which will, of course, vary with his age, the concepts and vocabulary he has already mastered, the information at his disposal.

Bringing a particular event under a known principle is often supposed to be the distinctive characterising feature of all understanding. 'Understanding occurs,' we are told by an educational psychologist, 'when the thing to be understood is seen as a particular instance of what is already known.'[1] This is the converse of the familiar view that explaining consists in offering such a general principle.[2] The sort of cases we have already considered will suffice to make it plain that, as a general account of coming to understand, this will not do. When, for example, a child learns that 'troglodytic' means 'cave-dwelling', thus enlarging his vocabulary, he is not learning that the word 'troglodytic' is a particular instance of the word 'cave-dwelling'. Neither are the principles of electrical theory 'more familiar' than the experience of turning on a switch and seeing the light come on. Nevertheless, the sort of understanding which consists in bringing something under a familiar principle is an important one, characteristic even of a great deal of science. (The discovery, for example, that the heart is a sort of pump.) The etymology of 'understand' itself suggests that 'understanding' is a matter of seeing one thing as coming under another – although neither the French 'comprendre' nor the Latin 'intellegere' carry this suggestion.

So the teacher is justified in believing that he can promote understanding by teaching the child general principles, as he most conspicuously does in science, but also attempts in the teaching of, let us say, grammar. (We can think of a rule, for our present purposes, as a particular type of principle, for all that in other contexts it is desirable, in my judgment, sharply to distinguish between them.) But it is equally important for him to recognise, as Wittgenstein liked to insist, that a principle does not carry the conditions of its application with it. As the French 'comprendre' etymologically suggests, understanding is always a matter of 'taking things together' or as the Latin 'intellegere' suggests of 'choosing between' what does and what does not come under a particular principle. That is why a good teacher will always try to vary as much as he can the exercises and problems he sets his pupils; he tries to ensure that they understand the principle by testing whether they can work with it in a wide variety of circumstances. A teacher cannot *guarantee*, whatever he does, that the child fully understands. But the teacher has learnt to live without guarantees; he can only do his best. What he needs always to remember, however, is that to learn a principle off by heart as a verbal formula is one thing, to understand it is quite another.[3]

Even if, furthermore, bringing under a principle is one way of helping a child to understand why something happens as it does, it is far from being the only way. Sometimes the teacher will need, rather, to construct a narrative. There may be no reason why an occurrence is as it is except that it had a past history of a certain kind. Suppose the pupil is puzzled why the United States, uniquely among industrial democracies, does not possess a Labour Party. He can be brought to understand why this is so by being told a story, a story which will perhaps make use of rough-and-ready general-isations but will not be *deducible* from such principles. There is no law, or set of laws, from which it follows that the United States does not have a Labour Party. 'History' is the principal source of such understanding – 'history', of course, in a broad sense. If a child wants to know why dinosaurs died out or why Shakespeare wrote in blank verse, this is the sort of help he will need. Information, then, information in the narrowest 'historical' sense, is important not only to enable the child to understand a sentence but to help him to understand why something happens. Even when there is a principle in the background its role may be very limited. If a child asks 'Why does a giraffe have a long neck?' and is simply told 'as a result of the operation of natural selection', this, in most contexts, is scarcely illuminating.

As a third possibility, a child may be interested neither in what principles govern an occurrence nor in how it came about historically but rather in what its point is. Post-mediaeval science has rejected this question in relation to a great many occurrences. We no longer ask 'What is the point of rainbows?' or 'What is the point of the earth going around the sun?' But in other cases, it is still a perfectly proper question – even, interpreted in a certain way, in relation to the giraffe's long neck. It is certainly proper in relation to the whole apparatus of schooling, the studying of particular subjects, examinations and so on. A pupil may ask, in this spirit, 'Why should I study mathematics?' What he then wants to be shown is either that mathematics has a value in itself or that it is a means to some end he accepts as being worthwhile.

Confronted with such fundamental questions, the teacher is often in a quandary. He himself, at least in some measure, has come to be accomplished in a subject; he has learnt to take the importance of the subject for granted. He is not accustomed to being asked, or to asking himself, what its point is. I suggested earlier that part of the responsibility of his teacher-training course is to get him to consider questions of this sort; indeed, I have elsewhere argued, this is also the responsibility of graduate schools insofar as they are engaged in training future college teachers.[4] (In the nineteen-sixties many university teachers were completely nonplussed when they were asked to justify what they were doing.)

There is a strong temptation, as we saw, for the teacher to reply to such questions in a manner which would not stand up to critical examination – as when Latin-teaching was defended in terms of its developing in the child habits of exactness or when mathematics-teaching was defended as teaching children to be logical. The situation is at its worst when, as happens more often than one likes to think, the teacher is teaching a subject, or a part of a subject, about the value of which he is more than doubtful, at least in relation to a particular child or a particular class. Then the teacher, too, does not understand why the pupil should do what the teacher is calling upon him to do. Yet to tell the child that what he is doing is pointless is scarcely to encourage the child to continue to learn – as is the teacher's responsibility. Some teachers fall back, in these circumstances, on a complicity with their pupils: a joint cynicism at the expense of the people 'up there' who insist on these things being taught and who have to be placated. Learning then becomes a ritual. This is perhaps one degree better than pretending that what the child is doing has an educative value which it simply does not have. But that is the most that can be said in its favour.

Fortunately, the situation is not always as bad as this. There may be good reasons for the pupil learning what he is called upon to learn; the teacher sometimes knows these reasons; the pupil can be brought to understand them – even if at other times the teacher can only 'soldier on' in the hope that the point will gradually dawn on his pupils. The child may, for example, not understand why, when he likes and has mastered algebraic methods, he should be called upon to solve equations graphically. In this instance, explanations *can* be offered, if they seldom used to be, which both teacher and child can understand.

Fortunately, when pupils ask about the point of occurrences, it is not always a question about what goes on in the schoolroom. They may ask, rather, 'What is the point of voting?', or 'What is the point of going to sleep?', or 'What is the point of non-representative art?' – calling then on the teacher's resources of political theory or biology or art theory. 'I don't understand the point of ...' is indeed a very common form of not understanding. And often enough, as in the above instances, the answer is far from being obvious.

Sometimes the teacher can bring the pupil to understand the point of an activity by showing that it plays an essential part in some activity about the value of which the pupil has no doubt. For many Idealists, this is the only sort of explanation which can properly be counted as such; to understand, they would say, is to see how something functions as part of a wider system. But we can agree that this is one way of understanding without granting it to be the only way. A teacher can answer the question 'Why does the blood circulate?' by replying in terms of the manner in which the circulation of the blood helps the body to stay alive. But he can also, in response to a different sort of puzzlement, reply that it is pushed round the body by the heart. The teacher has to determine what the pupil wants to know, exactly what question he has in mind, before he can promote his understanding. Often enough, of course, he will find this out by answering what he takes to be the question and getting the response 'I know that already. But ...'. The less confident child, however, may pretend to be satisfied.

In some circumstances, indeed, the child will have to be told that his question what is the point of this or that is one which cannot be answered. That is true, as I have already said, of such questions as 'What is the point of the earth going around the sun?' It is true also of such questions as, in the course of learning French, 'What is the point of "table" being feminine?'. It is true, even, of the question 'What is the point of becoming an educated person?'. A child has to come to see that, in the sense in which he is looking for a point, not everything has a point. Other forms of understanding, but not this particular one, can be called upon.

There is another sort of understanding which is obviously important – coming to understand how to do something. This, too, is sometimes taken, as by Gilbert Ryle, to be the essence of understanding. 'Roughly,' Ryle writes, 'execution and understanding are merely different exercises of knowledge of the tricks of the same trade.'[5] Understanding how to play chess, for example, is knowing those tricks of the trade which enable one to play chess. We can tell, Ryle is arguing, whether a person understands, or misunderstands, the rules of chess, understands or misunderstands a particular gambit, by watching him play or listening to him talking about a game he has watched. And this he takes to be typical of understanding in general.

Ryle is particularly concerned to reject another, mentalistic, view about understanding, according to which to understand is to experience some sort of internal mental click. The main objection to that view – as no less, indeed, to the non-mentalistic view that understanding consists in 'having one's face light up' – is that, whatever we take this click to be, it can occur just as readily when a child misunderstands as when he understands. If this were not so, he could tell by introspection – which would save a lot of hard work – whether or not he had understood. At most the *absence* of such a click, such a lighting-up, is a sign that the child has failed to understand; its presence does not constitute understanding.

But, rejecting any such view, we are not bound to conclude that to understand means to have learnt how to do something. Suppose a child says 'I don't understand chess'. Then, indeed, he might mean 'I don't understand how to play chess', and he will come to understand by learning to play it. But he could also mean 'I don't see the point of chess', and having learnt to play chess, he may still find it a pointless pursuit. If he says 'I don't understand why Hitler invaded Russia' the only thing he wants to do is to understand; his lack of understanding does not consist in his not being able to perform some other action, corresponding to playing chess. We can ask him to spell out the *kind* of understanding he lacks. 'Do you mean,' we might ask, 'that you can't understand why he didn't invade England first?' But there is not some skill, some technique, the lack of which prevents him from understanding. When we say of an adolescent, to take a different sort of case, that he 'only half-understands' *Romeo and Juliet*, what he needs in order fully to understand is to fall in love, not to acquire a new technique.

On the other side, does mastering a technique always amount to understanding? It is certainly quite natural to say that if a person can do something then he understands how to do that thing. But consider the following case. Our refrigerator refuses to work and a visitor tells us: 'Let me see what I can do. I understand that sort of refrigerator.' And then he opens and shuts the door rapidly three times in succession. At once the refrigerator starts into life. We ask him:

'What does opening and shutting the door do?' And he replies: 'I haven't the slightest idea; I only found out by accident that it is the best thing to do, but it works.' (He might have kicked it instead.) Had he then the right to say, as he did, 'I understand that sort of machine?'

We are, I think, rather torn on this point. Generally speaking if someone says 'I understand that sort of refrigerator' we expect him to be able to tell us something about the mechanism and how it makes the interior of the refrigerator cool. We expect him, that is, to be able to tell us how it works as distinct from telling us how to make it work. He himself might well say: 'I don't *understand* how refrigerators work but I have been told that if it doesn't work, it helps to open and shut the door three times.' If we can always count being able to do something as understanding how to act, then the sort of distinction on which we relied in our discussion of habit would not have any force; it would not make any sense to say: 'He has learnt how to do that but has no understanding of what he is doing.' The child who is drilled to undertake a chemical analysis in a certain regular order understands, on this view, how to undertake such a chemical analysis; he has 'mastered a technique'. And yet these are precisely the cases when we might wish to say that the child has been drilled but does not understand what he is doing.

Chess-playing, as so often, is a misleading example just because it is impossible to imagine someone regularly making the right moves but not understanding what he is doing. (Impossible to imagine, at least, except in fancy.) But consider our dealings with a television set. We are able, let us presume, to turn the various knobs in order to make the picture appear or the sound come on, to change channels or to correct certain faults. If we were asked whether we understood how to work the set, we should reply 'Yes'. Contrast our comment in a hotel room when we turn knobs, press buttons, and the wrong sort of thing happens: 'I don't understand this set.' Yet, in a somewhat different context, if we were asked whether we understood how a television set works we should reply in the negative.

Instead, then, of trying to lay it down in what 'real' understanding consists, let us call knowing how to work something – that knowledge of the television set which we can properly claim to possess – 'practical' understanding, and knowing how something works, why what happens when we press buttons happens – the knowledge we lack – 'theoretical' understanding. A child has a practical understanding of calculators if he knows how to use a calculator to do exercises or solve problems. But he has a theoretical understanding only if he understands why the calculator is constructed as it is. When we say that a pupil can master a routine, grasp a technique, 'without real understanding', we mean that he does not have a *theoretical* understanding. Theoretical understanding involves not only a mastery of technique, in the sense of a capacity to do something effectively, but an ability to see what we are doing as an instance of some general principle.

When a person learns how to do something 'on the job', he generally has a practical, not a theoretical, understanding of what he is doing. (I am using the expression 'on the job' very broadly: a child who learns the language of a country by living in that country learns it 'on the job'.) The special function of schools and universities, however, is to offer *theoretical* understanding. This can sometimes distort teaching.

The teaching of language is a case in point. I have heard language teachers say: 'We are not a Berlitz school.' And they meant: 'It is not simply our object to get children to speak or read a language: we hope to teach them the rules which govern the language.' They remained unperturbed, or not sufficiently perturbed, when after years of learning the language the vast majority of pupils had no mastery over it, still failed to 'understand French'. Grammar, philosophy, linguistics are, of course, important theoretical fields, not to be despised. But, as we have previously had occasion to insist, teaching a child to understand French grammar is one thing, teaching him to understand French quite another. They are too often identified — in the name of an 'intellectualist' criterion of understanding to which the Ryle-Wittgenstein view is a useful corrective.

Then why did I say that the special province of the schools, as distinct from 'on-the-job' training, is to give *theoretical* understanding? Because, I should say, that is their 'proper excellence', in a Platonic sense, what they are best at doing, what will not be done unless they do it. It is no part of the ordinary school's task to prepare children for particular employments, if by 'preparation for employment' we mean so preparing a pupil that he will no longer need any sort of 'on the job' training. It is, however, the school's task to give the child that sort of understanding which will enable him more readily to adjust to the great changes which are bound to take place in his lifetime. And theoretical understanding is one important way of doing this. A purely practical understanding, in a good many areas, confines a pupil to what he has specifically learnt. In an unchanging society this need not greatly matter; in our society it matters a great deal. A person who understands electronics, as distinct from merely knowing what to do when a set breaks down, is prepared to work not only with television sets but with a great variety of other electronic devices. He is not, of course, *fully* prepared to understand each and every such device. There is always something new to be learnt, how to apply electronic theory in relation to a new set of problems. But he does not have to begin again from scratch.

Consider a motor mechanic who has learnt to repair only a particular kind of car. Some automobile manufacturers prefer this. The mechanic will have an intimate practical understanding of that car; he will not be able to leave their employment to work on other cars. (Of course, there will be *some* transfer, but only to relatively similar cars.) If a new model is introduced, the mechanic is 're-tooled', along with the rest of the equipment. But what is a virtue from the standpoint of the employer is a defect from the standpoint of employee. His capacity to change his occupation is greatly reduced. Theoretical understanding offers mobility, the capacity to change, to cope with unexpected situations. So far it is linked with freedom.

But we should not suppose that theoretical understanding is *always* what is called for. There are forms of practical understanding so fundamental that everyone needs to possess them. Literacy, numeracy, are obvious examples. Theoretical understanding is always 'open', much practical understanding is 'closed'. But, as I have already argued, a closed capacity can be so wide in its application that no school can afford to neglect it. Schools have to pay special attention to theory, because that is something a child is unlikely to acquire anywhere else – which is not to say that he will not need, in later life, to go back to school. However, they must avoid either inadequately training the child in fundamental forms of practical understanding or inflating practical understanding into pseudo-theoretical pseudo-understanding in order to make it sound respectable, in a manner only too typical of some forms of technical training. If they can relate practical understanding to *genuine* theoretical principles, as the best technological schools and universities do, this, to be sure, is a consummation devoutly to be wished. But a willingness to grant, first, that practical understanding is, in many circumstances, all that is either possible or necessary and, secondly, that many forms of practical understanding are best learnt 'on the job' rather than in educational institutions could at once preserve the schools from the inroads of a narrow utilitarianism and act as a prophylactic against pseudo-theory.

I have still not considered the case where a child does not understand because he has never tried to understand. If Dewey is right, if the teacher should always begin from the pupil's own problems, then presumably the pupil should be left in his happy state of non-puzzlement. But I suggested earlier that a teacher will often need to get his pupils puzzled in order to teach them. This is very obvious in teaching philosophy: the teacher has to raise questions about 'understanding' with pupils who have never seen any difficulty in the concept, he has to get them puzzled about the character of their freedom or why they take some actions to be right and others wrong. This is what Socrates did in his questioning of the citizens of Athens. Teaching the child to imagine 'real alternatives' is one way of getting him to ask himself why one of these alternatives is realised in a particular case, e.g. why male-female relationships take the form they do in his society. In general, the unpuzzled child is a child who will understand very little. And there may be nothing in his environment, outside the schoolroom, to encourage him to be puzzled. Making him puzzled is the first, essential, step towards helping him to understand.

Without having by any means exhausted the topic we have now distinguished a number of different ways of coming to understand. Philosophers have often tried to persuade us that only one of these forms of understanding provides us with a 'real' or 'ultimate' understanding of a situation. For Plato in the *Phaedo*, to understand something is to see its point; for German idealism to know what part it plays in the system; for some varieties of positivism to bring its behaviour under a law. More recently understanding has been identified with being able to bring under a rule or with mastering a technique. It is a mistake, I am suggesting, to think in this monistic way. There are many different ways of understanding, overlapping but not reducible to one another and, correspondingly, many different ways of teaching to understand. What they have in common is that they all help a pupil to go ahead, they provide him with a way of solving his problems, actual or potential. But this is a very general observation which gives the teacher little indication of what he has to do.

Suppose, for example, a science teacher is told that his job is to get his pupils to understand science. A great many possibilities still remain open. It may be his task to bring out the point of science as a form of human activity, to teach his pupils the major concepts and laws of science, to teach them how to perform experiments, to teach them the rules by which science is governed or allegedly governed, whether in the form of a scientific morality or a scientific method. Controversies about science teaching are often disputes about whether, for example, a pupil *really* understands science who does not know what role it has played in human society. On the view we have been taking it becomes clearer that understanding science can assume any of a number of different forms and that no one of them constitutes 'really' understanding science.

More generally, when a pupil says 'I don't understand' – or shows in his work or in what he says that he does not understand – he may be puzzled for any of a number of quite distinct reasons. The context will generally make it clear what he is looking for. If he says 'I don't understand' when his teacher instructs him to 'give the answer correct to three decimal places', then the teacher would normally be correct in assuming that his pupil lacks a technique; if he says 'I don't understand' when the teacher tells him that Hitler was paranoid, the teacher might try out 'Hitler suffered from a persecution-complex and delusions of grandeur' or he might have to end up teaching his pupil a little psychology. If the pupil complains 'I don't understand why we have to do it in that way', then he wants to know the point of acting thus; if he says 'I don't understand why England still has a Royal Family', his teacher may have to tell him a long historical story. The teacher helps him to understand how to do things by developing his capacities; he helps him to understand why things happen as they do by offering him information, theoretical and historical, by cultivating his imagination and his critical abilities; he helps him to understand sentences in all of these ways and by extending his mastery over language.

Sometimes, however, it can be very hard to know precisely what is puzzling; a pupil may feel at a loss, without being at all clear about the sort of elucidation which would satisfy him – just as any of us may feel at a loss when we are confronted with certain kinds of contemporary music or contemporary painting: we don't, as we say, 'know what to make of it'. Finding out what exactly is puzzling a child, how to remove that puzzlement, can be a task of great pedagogical difficulty, calling upon resources which the teacher simply does not have. (I am not at all sure myself what constitutes 'understanding a piece of music').

Every teacher is aware, too, that there are things which, at a certain stage, he cannot bring his pupils to understand. They do not know enough. Since Piaget's investigations, he may also recognise that there are *types* of understanding which he cannot expect from children at a certain stage of their development; they may not yet have learnt the idea of a rule, or the point of a law. In the end everything depends on the child's own exploration of the world, his familiarising himself with it under the guidance and training, as distinct from the formal instruction, of his parents.* So the child

* Compare the emphasis on 'common understanding' by R.K. Elliott in his contribution to S.C. Brown (ed.), *Philosophers Discuss Education* (London 1975). But I should not be prepared to accept what seems to be his view, that 'common

learns what a rule is through his encounters, successful and unsuccessful, with the human beings around him. Only then can he be brought to understand by being told: 'That happens because it is the rule.'

The precise nature of this initial familiarisation is another matter of debate. If Chomsky is right then the child learns to use and to understand a language only because he has already a knowledge of language; he knows what he has not learnt. This doctrine is far from being universally accepted. On anybody's view of the matter, however, except the most outré inheritors of the Lockean tradition, the child is born with expectations, wants and ways of coping with and reacting to the world. He learns what the world is like by way of his achievements, his disappointments. He comes to grasp the fact that actions have consequences, that sequences are regular, that conduct is rule-governed. Upon that initial grasping the teacher can build when he sets out deliberately to help the child to understand. The teacher has to think of himself not, in Locke's manner, as someone who moulds a piece of wax or writes upon a blank sheet, but rather as someone who interacts with a child who is already, of his own account, exploring the world, including the other people around him. The teacher, for good or ill, can make his own peculiar mark on the child – that is all, but more than enough.

---

understanding' is often enough. 'Common understanding' generates myths, confusions, prejudices, of a sort which only education in disciplines can hope systematically to correct. The teacher has to work with, and upon, 'common understanding'. He should not underestimate its importance and its value. But formal education is necessary precisely because 'common understanding' does not, in the end, suffice.

NOTES

[1] J.M. Thyne, *The Psychology of Learning and Techniques of Teaching* (London 1963), p. 128.

[2] Indeed, much of what I am now saying can be read as the converse of my 'Explanation in everyday life, in science and in history' reprinted in G.H. Nadel (ed.), *Studies in the Philosophy of History* (New York 1965), from *History and Theory* 11, 2, pp. 105-23.

[3] For ways of trying to ensure that the child understands mathematics see J.D. Fearnley, 'Mathematics', in Keith Dixon (ed.), *Philosophy of Education and the Curriculum* (Oxford 1972), pp. 7-27.

[4] John Passmore, 'The philosophy of graduate education', in W. Frankena (ed.), *The Philosophy of Graduate Education* (Ann Arbor 1980).

[5] Gilbert Ryle, *The Concept of Mind*, p. 55.

PART III

Some Applications

Chapter Twelve
The Anatomy of English Teaching

Of all school courses, English has tended to be the most chaotic, the most fragmented in its objectives. '*Macbeth*,' as an American Commission has put the point, 'vies with the writing of thank-you notes for time in the curriculum, and lessons on telephoning with instructions on the processes of argument.'[1] In some school-systems, reading and spelling count as 'English', in others they do not; when reading is a separate subject, literature is sometimes linked with reading, sometimes taken to be the central core of English. I propose to consider the subject in its widest span, as including any formal instruction in the understanding and use of the English language and any introduction to the literature written in that language. So reading, spelling, literary appreciation will all form part of 'English'. If I have chosen to give special attention to English teaching this is just because the English teacher has so exceptionally complex a set of tasks, illustrating with special vividness the kinds of pedagogical problem I have been discussing.

What long-term changes do English teachers hope to produce in their pupils? In speaking of 'long-term changes' I am distinguishing the teacher from the crammer; the crammer is not in the least concerned with long-term changes. He knows what he is doing and he has an easy, objective, way of judging whether he is successful. He sets out to get his pupils through an examination. If he succeeds in getting them through he is a good crammer, if they fail he is a bad crammer. What happens to his pupils in later life is of no concern to him.

If, for example, his pupils pass the questions on Shakespeare in their examination, it is a matter of indifference to the crammer whether they leave school detesting literature. The teacher cannot feel the same indifference. It is, indeed, very hard for him to judge his capacity as a teacher, just because his success or failure resides in his long-term influence on his pupils and cannot be judged by their immediate success, or even their immediate enthusiasm. Whatever enthusiasm they display for literature in his classroom, or while he is actually teaching them, he has failed, as we have already suggested, if only his personal influence over his class sustains their interest, if they love him rather than literature.[2]

The most obvious thing a teacher can do, and the thing many teachers feel happiest in doing, is to impart information. The English teacher not uncommonly acts as the 'general knowledge master'. It then falls to his lot to pass on to his pupils the sort of information they do not acquire from any other specific subject. In some English courses, this aspect of his work is formalised. A text-book published in 1947 – not merely freakish if one may judge from the fact that it was still in print in 1977[3] – invited pupils as part of an end-of-term test, to expand the initials Ph.D., B.O.A.C., and L.P.T.B.; to explain who Orpheus and Neptune were and for what such persons as Beethoven, Agatha Christie, Helen Keller and Spartacus were famous; to give the Christian name of Nightingale, Pasteur, Cavell and Crosby, and to explain what each of the following is: catarrh, court-martial, the Balkans, sombrero, psychologist, cochineal, reparations and credit-titles – a list of truly formidable heterogeneity. It is in virtue of such questions, so far as I can make out, that the author of this text-book would wish to justify his claim, in a book otherwise largely devoted to questions on the English language, that he has 'tried gently to turn his pupils' minds to an increasing number of cultural matters'.

The text-book I have been discussing was designed for secondary-modern schools in Great Britain; in America the emphasis in English courses has been on 'social science' rather than on 'general information'. Thus, for example, the *Report on The English Language Arts in the Secondary School* prepared by the Commission on the English Curriculum of the National Council of Teachers of English laid it down that 'understanding life and thought in the United States and in foreign countries is the goal towards which courses in American, English and World literature are directed'.[4]

Now the imparting of general information is not in itself objectionable – I have suggested indeed that the teaching of such information is an important responsibility of the schools – and it is obviously true that we can learn from literature something about the life and thought of other countries. But it is quite another matter to make either general information or social science the central point of concern in English courses. The attempt to treat such forms of information as central surely arises out of despair, the attempt to find something to do in English courses, rather than out of a conviction that this is the most important activity the English teacher can possibly engage in. For the Greeks, no doubt, the poets were a principal source of information, but now we read books on agriculture, not the poetry of Hesiod, in order to learn how to farm. We do not turn to Homer, as Xenophon's *Symposium* (4.6) urges his readers to do, in order to learn how to drive a chariot, or how to use onions to make our drinks more tasty. If we are in search of accurate information about foreign lands and ways of life, or about anything else, we shall do best to turn to non-fiction rather than to fiction, to history, to geography, to science rather than to English.

The followers of Herbart had urged that literature be used as an approach to the study of society. But John Dewey's objection is unanswerable. If, for example, the life and culture of the Red Indians is worth studying for its own sake, why approach it circuitously by way of a study of Longfellow's *Hiawatha* rather than directly and immediately? 'If it has such a value, this should be made to stand out in its own account, instead of being lost in the very refinement and beauty of a purely literary presentation.'[5] To say this is not to deny that the child can and does learn from literature. 'We expect a literary education,' writes Graham Hough, 'to expand their [i.e. the pupils'] range of human awareness and sympathy; to enlarge their imagination beyond the limits of their own class and country; to show them that our problems and obsessions are part of a larger pattern of human experience.'[6] Through literature – although not through literature solely – the pupil can learn that he does not stand alone; that his secret worries, his hidden passions, his furtive curiosities, are not unique to him. He can come to understand modes of life, kinds of person, types of social situation, which would otherwise be wholly alien and incomprehensible. He can do all these things, in virtue of the fact that literature functions in some degree as vicarious experience, it presents him with 'real possibilities' which he has not experienced or actualised.

But what is in such instances important is not the acquisition of information but the modification of feelings, the reduction of guilt, the enlargement of sympathy, the growth of tolerance. If as a result of reading *Tom Sawyer*, let us say, a child does no more than acquire such information as that in some parts of the nineteenth-century America it was customary to paint fences with whitewash, one might as well take him off reading novels. The information derivable from works of literature is neither sufficiently reliable nor sufficiently systematic nor sufficiently up-to-date to justify, if the acquisition of information is one's principal object, the reading of literature rather than the reading of encyclopedias.

Then what of habits? What habits can the English teacher hope to inculcate? Although English is normally thought of as being a nonvocational subject, in fact it has often been closely tied to, and has set out to prepare its pupils for, a particular set of occupations, which can compendiously be described as 'office work', demanding, in large part, the performance of habitual actions. So English teachers used to spend a considerable amount of their time, in some class rooms, establishing such habits as beginning and ending letters in a conventional form. An ideal pupil for English teachers of this persuasion, as we have already suggested, will be one who hands in essays in clear handwriting, with accurate spelling and a properly underlined heading, which are entirely free from any sign of ink-blot or correction. If the essay consists of conventional commonplaces, this will not in the least disturb such a teacher; the inculcation of clerkly habits represents the limits of his aspirations.

But these are not the only habits the English teacher commonly sets out to form. He often feels a special responsibility for ensuring 'good habits of enunciation'; whether in the sense of teaching his pupils habitually to speak clearly or to speak with a particular accent the possession of which he takes to be desirable. He may even – this certainly happens in the United States, but not only there – think of those habits we call 'etiquette' or 'good manners' as falling within his sphere.

What are we to say about these responsibilities? So far as letter writing and the like are concerned, they do form part of English usage. But to make too much of a fuss about them, especially at a time when conventions are rapidly changing and the formal letter notably declining in importance, would certainly be absurd. As for etiquette and manners, they are best taught informally, as part of the practice of the school.

There can be more argument about habits of enunciation. These have been brought into disrepute by their association, especially in England, with class distinctions. The emphasis, often enough, has not been on *clear* enunciation – indeed, 'upper class' English is often exceptionally gabbled and unclear as compared with North-Eastern American – but on acquiring 'the right accent' as an element in vocational training. But a genuinely clear enunciation, of whatever form of English, has a real value in communication and it can properly fall within the English teacher's function to try to establish it as a habit.

Habits, of course, are based on capacities. But I have chosen to discuss them first, because the capacities the English teacher seeks to develop are so complex and difficult; it is useful to get out of the way first the relatively small number of habits which it falls to his lot to establish. It will be useful to divide such capacities into two groups, which I shall call *professional* and *general*. By 'professional capacities' I mean the capacities in which the scholar exhibits a high degree of skill and which constitute his expertise: grammatical analysis, etymology, prosody, the analysis of literary devices, the tracing of influences, the interpretation of complex poetic texts, translating from Anglo-Saxon into modern English. None of these capacities is employed by the ordinary citizen in his everyday life, but, quite properly, competence in them may get a man an honours degree or even a professorship.

By 'general capacities', I mean such capacities as the capacity to write, read, listen and speak. Writing, listening and speaking are not the peculiar prerogative of scholars; indeed, scholars are sometimes notably defective in their exercise. To be an exceptionally good writer or an exceptionally good speaker, in any sense of these phrases, it is neither necessary nor sufficient to be an exceptionally good scholar, although the scholar does need to be an exceptionally good reader.

It is only human to be proud of possessing the capacities which distinguish us from others and it is natural for a teacher to try to pass on that kind of professional capacity to his pupils. The very fact that English is so amorphous a subject, so uncertain of its aims and its boundaries, led at first to a quite special emphasis on expertise. So English justified itself as a new subject at Oxford – where it was not taught until late in the nineteenth century – by concentrating upon the professional skills of philology or literary history. In the schools, similarly, children were taught in their English classes grammatical analysis of a very detailed kind, instructed in elaborate prosodic distinctions and in the recognition of intricate figures of speech; by way of the study of a Shakespearian play they were introduced to the conclusions, although much more rarely to the method of argument, of textual critics and historical scholars.[7] All of this was done to demonstrate that English was not merely a 'soft option' to classics and mathematics.

The teaching of such professional capacities to schoolchildren was not uncommonly supported on the ground that this is the best way of improving their general capacity to communicate. But everyday experience suggests that this is not so; books written by grammarians are not, to put the matter mildly, notably superior in sentence-construction to books written by a great many authors who, by some accident of schooling, have never heard of a fused participle. 'Plato,' as P.B. Ballard has remarked, 'never saw a Greek grammar and Shakespeare never an English one.'[8] The investigations of educational psychologists bear out this everyday experience; children who have been taught grammar by formal parsing and analysis are not better at writing or reading than children who are ignorant of grammatical terminology.[9] Nor, it appears, are they better at learning foreign languages, although the foreign language teacher often thinks they are, mainly because they are better at naming the parts of speech. Similarly there is no direct relationship between caring about poetry and being expert in prosody, or between appreciating dramatic structure and being expert about the relationships between folio and quarto versions of Shakespearian text.

It does not of course follow directly from these observations, as it is sometimes supposed to follow, that grammatical analysis, or prosody, must at once be excluded from our schools. But they have to be justified in their own right, as specialist capacities, not as an auxiliary to the teaching of more general capacities.

There have been two distinct reactions to the discovery that the teaching of grammar, in its systematic, traditional form, is neither necessary nor sufficient to improve the quality of English composition. The first reaction was to substitute for systematic grammar a piecemeal correction of the most common faults in the writing of English, as determined by a statistical analysis of the written work of children. So the child was no longer expected to learn that, let us say, 'quickly' is an adverb of manner; the object, rather, was to teach him to write 'quickly' instead of 'quick' in such sentences as 'She came quick enough when I called her'. Where he had once been asked to 'parse and analyse the following sentence', he was now expected to be able to 'correct the following sentences' or 'rewrite the following sentences, making any changes that meaning or grammar seem to require'. He was taught general rules only when, according to some sort of experimental evidence, learning the rule helped him in the task of correcting his literary habits. But this had the effect that the child was exposed to a great many, quite independent, corrections in what could seem to him to be a wholly arbitrary manner.

A second possible reaction is to abandon all claims that the systematic teaching of grammar automatically results in improving the child's capacity to speak or write, and to insist, rather, on the importance of language as a social phenomenon, well worthy of study in its own right. The traditional systematic English grammar, so it is now often argued, stands to modern linguistics much as Aristotelian physics stood to modern physics; to continue to teach it in the schools would certainly be preposterous, but it no more follows that grammar teaching should be reduced to a mere hotch-potch, unsystematic and unscientific, of practical advice on usage than it follows that physics should be reduced to advice on how to operate one's mechanical devices more effectively.

At this point, too, there are a number of different possibilities: there are several, distinct, ways of studying language systematically. One way takes as its point of departure Wittgenstein's distinction between 'language games'. It asks: 'In what different ways is language used? How are these differences reflected in the structure and vocabulary of English?' So the student of English will learn to distinguish between, for example, that kind of language which is used to describe experiments and that kind of language which is used to express emotions. As a practical auxiliary to this approach to language, he may learn the techniques of propaganda analysis, be taught simple logic, and introduced to the elements of semantics.[10] Or else the child may be introduced to one or the other varieties of contemporary linguistics, 'structural' or 'transformational'. This is one of the growing points of human knowledge; as matters stand, the teacher will have to take his pick among a variety of possible approaches, even at the secondary-school level.

Two problems then arise. The first is that the English teacher may not be at all prepared to teach general linguistics, in any of these forms. To do so successfully, he will need to know a great deal about language, not merely about English usage. The second problem is whether the study of linguistics really helps the child to communicate in English. If it does not, then there seems to be no good reason why it should fall to the lot of the English teacher to take the responsibility for teaching it. What is needed, rather, is a special linguistics teacher. Or perhaps, as Bruner has suggested, we should look rather to a course on man generally, in which man's language-making would form a part. These are problems to which we can only point. The controversies still rage, and will no doubt continue to do so.[11]

To turn now to the establishment and improvement of the child's capacity to read, listen, speak, write, it has first to be observed that each of these is in fact a complex of capacities. Take the capacity to read. There one has first to distinguish between the capacity to transpose marks on paper into spoken words and the capacity to understand what the words mean. These may be quite dissociated from one another. I may teach myself to look at a sentence of Greek and pronounce it aloud without having any idea what it means; I may be able to read Latin fluently – as, say, the Renaissance humanists could – and yet be quite mistaken, as they were, about how to pronounce it. Nor is that the whole story. A scholar may be able to demonstrate that he has a thorough knowledge of Greek and of Greek pronunciation and yet may not be good at reading Homer

aloud; he may lack skill in rhythmic emphasis and stress. A schoolboy may be able to read his science textbook with ease and accuracy
and yet be unable to make head-or-tail of *Hamlet*; or he may read
accurately, but very slowly; or so fast that he skims over passages
that demand close study.

The demands, in respect to reading, which an English teacher
makes upon his pupils are likely to be different from the demands
which are made by, say, a science master. The English teacher, since
he hopes that his pupils will come to appreciate poetry, may
emphasise reading aloud; competence in this respect is of no interest
to the science teacher. The English teacher is not content to have his
pupils skilled in the art of rapid reading, expert in extracting
information, which is all the science master demands. For the science
teacher reading is essentially a technique: an article or a book is a
tool. If some other more efficient method of acquiring information
can be discovered, he will be the better pleased. For the English
teacher, in contrast, it is an art; no mechanical device for information
retrieval could replace reading. To read with appreciation a
Shakespearian sonnet is to have developed an appreciation of subtle
nuances, of deliberate ambiguities, which is certainly not required in
everyday reading for information.

Similar considerations apply to writing. To be able to write is, in
the first place, to be able by means of a series of marks on paper to
perform an act which we could alternatively perform by speaking,
e.g. to enter into a contract, to make an assertion, to utter a
complaint, to ask a question, to register a protest. Any form of
writing involves some degree of capacity to spell and to punctuate. In
one sense of 'learning to write', a person has 'learnt to write' when he
is capable of writing down sentences in a properly spelt and properly
punctuated form. 'Learning to write' is, in this sense of the phrase, a
closed capacity. But what such a person writes may be dull,
platitudinous, intellectually vacuous; he may, as he does in his
speech, move ponderously from one cliché to another.

Most English teachers, however, would not be satisfied with a
situation of this kind. They hope to encourage not merely writing
which is 'good' in this limited sense, but writing which has virtues of
a different kind, which is 'creative' or 'imaginative'. Being creative,
being imaginative – these are not closed capacities, in the sense in
which punctuation, paragraphing, syntactic organisation are closed
capacities. Any intelligent person can be taught to acquire these
latter capacities with a fair degree of proficiency; and they can be
completely mastered. They can be taught in the way in which people
are usually taught to be skilful, by demonstration, instruction,

warning, correction. I do not mean that it is easy to teach people to write grammatical and well-punctuated prose. It is seldom easy to teach people to be skilful. But at least the teacher knows what he is doing and in general terms how to do it. His difficulties are more likely to arise out of such facts as that he has insufficient time available for correction than out of an uncertainty about how to proceed. (He may also, nowadays, have to meet a resistance from his class, based on the feeling that writing is 'out of date' in a television age.)

There is a similar ambiguity in relation to 'speaking well', an aspect of communication which is sometimes ridiculously neglected.[12] A person may be said to 'speak well', simply on such grounds as that his enunciation is clear, it conforms to an established pattern of 'good speech', his sentences are grammatically constructed, and his speech is reasonably fluent. 'To "speak well" or to write "good English",' according to Sybil Marshall, 'has come to mean to speak or to write within certain well-defined limits which are set by snobbery.'[13] We have argued that this need not be so, that there is no 'snobbery' involved in speaking clearly, grammatically and fluently. But there is another sense of 'good speech' in which to be a good speaker one must be lively, witty, full of fresh ideas. The teacher of rhetoric often toils to produce a simulacrum of these virtues – he instructs speakers to begin with a joke, and he teaches them how to produce an impression of liveliness and freshness by the use of certain rhetorical devices. But the results are appalling; the forced gaiety of the salesman's spiel may temporarily deceive the lonely housewife, but this is certainly not the sort of 'good speech' the teacher hopes to encourage. Genuine wit, liveliness, freshness are not the sorts of things one can learn as routines.

Let us then distinguish two kinds of oral communication: 'the closed capacity' level, to proficiency in which every intelligent student can hope to attain, and the 'open' or 'creative' level, where, on the face of it, at least, intelligence is not enough – at least the sort of intelligence measured by intelligence tests.

The difference between these two kinds of writing and reading sets before the English teacher a certain dilemma. For it is not as if 'creative' speaking and writing existed as a higher level of communicative capacities, so that one first learns how to write and speak in accordance with established conventions, and then in exceptional cases passes on to creative writing. There can be, from a fairly early stage, a certain degree of conflict between these objectives. No doubt the antithesis is anything but absolute. Creativity implies some degree of mastery over closed capacities; if a person cannot read, speak, or write at all, then he cannot do so creatively. But if the teacher's emphasis is on ensuring a high degree of communication-skill he may at the same time curb the creative impulses, which tend, in the early stages at least, to operate with a certain degree of inaccuracy and wildness. To take a simple example, the child who is emotionally involved in a story which has occurred to him and writes it down excitedly in the form of a composition for a teacher may well be careless about his writing, his punctuation, his spelling, his grammatical forms – to say nothing of blots and crossings out. Language is to him primarily a method of reacting to the world around him, coping with it, mastering it, not of communicating. He has by nature, in some degree, that freshness and liveliness characteristic, in adult life, only of the best writers.

What, in this situation, is the English teacher to do? At this point, English teachers tend to fall apart into two schools: the disciplinarians, who emphasise the importance of the capacity to communicate clearly and exactly, who think of language as a tool, and the Romantics, who emphasise the importance of freely exercising the imagination, even when the imagination is an impoverished one.

In his *The Secret Places*,[14] David Holbrook describes a child of eight who, he says, wrote long marvellous stories. 'After a year with a teacher,' he continues, 'who wrote "Please be more tidy", "Your spelling is awful", "Sloppy" and never a good word, she stopped altogether.' For Holbrook himself, the situation is perfectly clear. It is the English teacher's task to encourage children to write freely, spontaneously, creatively, to help them to see their emotions and the world around them as they really are, and in that way to fight against the falsifications of, for example, the popular novelette or commercial television. Indeed in his *English for the Rejected*, Holbrook writes as if the task of the English teacher were primarily therapeutic; to help troubled, 'rejected', children come to terms with themselves and their fellows. That, certainly, is not a task most English teachers have been trained to undertake; it is one thing to teach children to write, quite another to use what they write, as the psychiatrist does, as a clue to their inner conflicts and a stage in the task of recognising and overcoming their conflicts. The English teacher is not a therapist, even if it be true that the reading and writing of literature can have, of itself, a therapeutic effect.

The contrast at this point between two different conceptions of the task of the English teacher, the disciplinary and the creative, runs very deeply. For Holbrook, as he emphatically says, the child has a 'natural impulse to seek the good'; it is the teacher's task to help that impulse to mature and to fight against the influences which corrupt it. The disciplinarian, in contrast, is often afraid, as Holbrook suggests, of the natural impulses of the child; he thinks of it as being his task to inculcate in the child orderly habits and to assist him to develop techniques of control. So, in *The Future of our Educational Institutions*, Nietzsche complains of 'creative' school compositions that they 'prepare the road for outrageous and irresponsible scribbling'; he exalts, in contrast, 'a purely practical method of instruction by which the teacher accustoms his pupils to severe self-discipline in their own language'. His ground for objecting to the 'creative' approach is that it encourages 'self-complacency' and 'vanity', the presumption that 'everybody without exception is ... gifted for literature', as opposed to what Nietzsche advocates: 'the suppression of all ridiculous claims to independent judgment.'[15]

The ordinary English teacher, if I may judge from my limited experience, has often tried to steer an uneasy way between these two extremes. He thinks of the child neither, in a Rousseau-like manner, as naturally good, nor in the stern Calvinist fashion, as naturally corrupt, neither as a potential Shakespeare nor as being devoid of any right to independent judgment. He welcomes, where he finds them, suggestions of creative imagination and tries to foster them. But no one is going to blame him if he fails to turn out poets or novelists. On the other hand, the pressure is strong upon him to inculcate clerkly habits and to develop in his pupils a capacity to communicate precisely. If his pupils cannot spell, do not write grammatically correct sentences, make mistakes about paragraphing or the use of capitals, do not know how to compose a formal letter, then he will certainly be publicly criticised. That no potential poets or novelists pass unscathed out of his hands will not excite comment. Who is to tell what Miltons he rendered mute and inglorious?

This attitude is not wholly unreasonable. The capacity clearly to communicate is so vitally necessary in every area of life that it is both natural and desirable for the English teacher to lay great stress on it. The English teacher's life would, of course, be greatly eased if the old slogan: 'Every teacher is a teacher of English' could in fact be realised – although it should rather be put in the form: 'Every teacher should help his pupils to communicate.' If every teacher insisted on a high level of communicative skill, and insisted to the degree of being prepared to participate in the arduous task of correction and explanation, then the English teacher could lay correspondingly great stress on encouraging his children to 'write well' in the more literary sense of that phrase. He could think of their written works as contributions, however elementary, to literature, not as formal exercises in communication.

Another way of dealing with this situation is to separate out the two types of English teacher and give to the disciplinarian – under some such title as Teacher of Rhetoric – the responsibility for training in communication, leaving the English teacher free to be a teacher of literature. This device has indeed been adopted in some American schools but not, as one might expect, with entirely satisfactory results.[16] The major difficulty is that the capacity to communicate cannot be taught in a vacuum; the pupil has to communicate about *something*. And no one teacher is likely to be sufficiently a polymath to be able to teach him effectively to communicate in – or effectively to read – the wide variety of subjects taught at school. It is a much better situation if he writes, reads and discusses for the science teacher, the mathematician, the modern language teacher, the social science teacher, and so learns to communicate about a range of topics concerning which he is expected to have a certain amount of knowledge, and in some of which, at least, he can be expected to have some interest. These 'writings' need not be essays in the literary sense of the word, but accurate descriptions of chemical experiments, accurate translations, accurate expository paragraphs.

Similar considerations apply to reading. Reading literature is one thing, reading mathematics is quite another.[17] The capacities involved in reading mathematics are not only different from but may be antithetical to the capacities involved in reading a play, a drama or a short story. History, geography and science are different again. To read mathematics effectively one must at the same time work with what is being read: applying it to examples, making sure that the steps follow from one another, looking carefully for concealed presumptions. A misprint has an importance in mathematics which it only rarely has in a novel; only rarely in a novel, unless it be an intricately-plotted detective story, is the reader forced to look back to early pages with the realisation that he could not have understood what he previously read. In reading mathematics, as in reading philosophy, this is a very common situation. Only a mathematician can teach a child how to read mathematics, just as only a teacher who cares about poetry can teach him to read a sonnet. Yet it is comparatively rare for the mathematician, the scientist, the historian, the philosopher directly to instruct their classes on the reading-problems relevant to their particular subject. But that is their responsibility, not the English teacher's, just as it is their responsibility, not the English teacher's, to teach their pupils how to write, and how to discuss, the subjects they teach. It is quite absurd to presume, as it is often presumed, that once a child has learnt to read, in the primary school sense of 'read', he needs no further instruction.

As matters stand, the child may be expected to write essays on such jejune topics as 'What I did in my holidays' or alternatively, at the higher levels, he is expected to write essays about literature – about, let us say, the virtues of *Hamlet*. Now, literature is extremely difficult to write about; literary criticism requires a degree of penetration and understanding rarely to be found among children and, where it is found, not always conjoined with clerkly habits or the capacity to write clearly. Many famous literary critics, indeed, write in a manner one would certainly not wish to be imitated in everyday writing. It is much easier to teach children communicative skills by way of setting them written work in history, science, geography or some other branch of relatively firm and stable knowledge than by asking them to undertake the extremely difficult task of writing clearly, confidently and exactly about works of literature.

The suggestion that English teaching should be in any degree 'farmed out' is, however, sometimes greeted with distaste. 'The science teacher,' it has been objected, 'cannot relate what he has to say about the language of scientific experiment to the English language as a whole, or to the child's experience of it. He cannot, in fact, except to the extent that he has deliberately made himself a linguist, teach "scientific English", even in isolation from the rest of the language, in any systematic or structured way. He knows what is acceptable to him and what is not; but that is no more a qualification for teaching the pupils about the English language than the fact that I know what dishes are acceptable to me and what are not qualifies me to teach cookery.'[18]

Two things have, however, to be carefully distinguished: the teaching of scientific English 'in a systematic or structured way', and helping the child to write English in the manner in which scientists write it. There is a parallel here to the situation which arises in relation to the philosophy of science. A scientist is not, *qua* scientist, equipped to teach the philosophy of science in a systematic and structured way; adequately to do this, he must be trained in philosophy, he must look beyond science to compare and contrast science with other forms of human activity. But at the same time he is the best person to check the methodological rashness of the budding scientist, to persuade him that a hypothesis has been inadequately tested, that an experimental design is faulty, that a particular procedure will lead to inconclusive results. This he can do effectively, because he has absorbed the traditions of science, the traditions which the philosopher of science describes and codifies. Quite similarly, he may have thoroughly absorbed the traditions of scientific writing; he may be skilled in teaching his pupils to write scientific English more effectively, even if he would be quite unable to give a formal description of the structure and systematic character of scientific English – a kind of English which, again, exists as a tradition *before* the linguist sets to work to describe it, and has up to that point been handed on from scientist to scientist without the assistance of professional linguists. It is for the English teacher, as part of his teaching of linguistics, to describe to a class the difference between kinds of writing. But it is not his task to teach them how to write effectively in each of these manners.

In any case, even if it is true – and this is a question on which it would be unwise to dogmatise – that a teacher who is professionally trained as a linguist is bound to be better than a practising scientist at teaching students to write scientific English, as distinct from teaching them *about* scientific English, it would be quite absurd to expect the English teacher to take over the task of correcting the written work of all teachers in all subjects. Nothing but the careful correction of scientific writing by scientists will persuade the child that careful writing is something expected of him in every social situation, as distinct from being a mere foible of the English teacher.[19]

It is now customary to distinguish between different 'registers' in the writing of English. Scientific articles are written in a different register from works on literary criticism, business letters in a different register from love letters, journalistic articles on contemporary affairs from learned historical articles. These differences relate not merely to vocabulary but also to stylistic and even to syntactical detail. Of particular importance is the distinction between the personal and the impersonal register – each of these permitting of a variety of sub-registers.

Compare the two sentences: 'I had a wonderful time at Mary's party last night', and 'On 4 August 1914, Great Britain declared war on Germany'. The first sentence contains the word 'I', but that is not what makes it personal. The policeman's 'I then proceeded, acting on information received, to 73 Whooping Crescent, Craneville' is in the impersonal register, for all that it begins with the word 'I'. The reference to 'Mary's party' is more significant; the policeman would turn that 'Mary' into 'at the household of a Mrs Mary Brown', and, most likely, would prefer some circumlocution to 'party'. But the crucial phrase is 'wonderful time'; the function of that phrase is to bring out the speaker's *personal attitude* to the party, and this is carefully avoided in the impersonal mode. In the impersonal mode it might become: 'On 3 June 1967, I attended a party given by Mrs Mary Brown; I laughed several times during the night, danced six dances, was complimented by three boys' – a report which might as well be written by a Puritan, repenting at leisure, as by a person who had enjoyed the party.

Not long ago, the tendency of English teachers was to emphasise the impersonal mode. Furthermore they wrongly identified the personal mode with the use of 'I'; the child was carefully instructed not, in his written work, to use the word 'I' and, above all, not to begin with it. The use of the personal mode was identified with egoism; to replace it by an impersonal construction – 'One enjoyed oneself at the party last evening' or 'It was an enjoyable party last evening' – was, it was supposed, to subdue oneself, to communicate as distinct from merely expressing oneself. (In fact, the use of 'one' can be *extremely* egoistic; it then suggests that what I do is what 'one' does – as if I were a sort of universal arbiter. The manner in which it is used by a certain type of Englishman is for that reason infuriating in the extreme to other English-speakers.)

The pendulum has swung. The cult of impersonal constructions is by no means dead. But, in English teaching at least, the cult of 'self-expression' has largely swept it away. The more sensible view, however, recognises the importance of having at one's disposal a repertoire of 'registers.' In his writing as an adult, certainly, the pupil will be called upon to operate in the impersonal mode; not to be able to write to a business organisation, to prepare a summary of a course of events, to state a case, is likely to be a distinct disadvantage to him. This is still true, even in these telephoning days, although the contrary is sometimes maintained.

In part, no doubt, these differences in register are conventional, and the conventions change. The business letter which begins: 'In reply to yours of the 14th inst., we beg to inform you'; the sociology text which writes 'fractionisation' for 'division' or 'positive and negative affectional relationships' for 'like and dislike' does not necessarily have to be imitated. But the child does have to learn, and this is a very hard lesson for him to learn, to write as one who is communicating not with a teacher, a friend or a parent, who already knows the context, but with a remote stranger; he has to learn to look at a situation, an issue, a point in dispute, as if he were not himself engaged in it. Learning to write, even at this formal level, is, indeed, an exercise of the imagination.

All language involves such a capacity to some degree. The child finds this hard to recognise; at first he works on the assumption that what he wants to say *must* be understood; any failure to understand, on the part of his parents, is greeted with anger or with fear. He comes gradually to learn that he has to 'set the scene' for his remarks if he is to have any chance of being understood; that it is no use saying to a stranger 'Mary gave me this' or to a parent 'Today, teacher told us how to do it'. The 'Mary' and the 'it' have to be further particularised if he is to convey what he hopes to convey. (Children with particularly sympathetic, understanding parents are sometimes at a disadvantage in this respect; the parent anticipates their demands so that they do not have to formulate them.) He gradually learns that he has to give reasons, as distinct from being content with 'I want to'; he learns to excuse his actions, to exculpate himself, to explain, to justify. In doing all these things he is to some degree learning to look at a situation objectively, from someone else's point of view. But the 'someone else', most often, is a person he already knows quite well and who knows him; an encounter with an official, a policeman, a stranger brings home to him the need for a more extensive, a more thoroughgoing, objectivity.

Learning the impersonal mode can involve a loss, a drying up of the personal. This point was particularly emphasised by the existentialists; a person becomes a functionary, he no longer speaks with his own voice but in the manner which he takes to be appropriate to *any* father, *any* teacher, *any* official. He comes to think of language primarily as a means of concealing rather than revealing his feelings. As a lover, as a friend, in a situation which calls for the striking image, he is inarticulate – he falls back on the *cliché*, on what 'is said' because he has lost the power of thinking out afresh what to say, of responding immediately to the situation with a freshly-forged phrase. His language is no longer a mode of personal expression, any more than are his clothes.

Not surprisingly, the English teacher observes this change, from the imaginative personal writing of childhood to the stiff, cliché-ridden writing of so many adolescents, with a deep sense of regret. Literature, more often than not, is the English teacher's first love, and literature is above all the home of the personal mode.

The full complexity of the English teacher's task now begins to emerge. He has to develop in the child the ability to use the English tongue as effectively as possible, in an all-round way, in listening, speaking, reading, writing, and drama; for practical purposes of day-to-day living and also imaginatively and creatively; for communication with others and also as a means of coping with his own experience of living.[20] Nothing less will do; and yet to achieve these ends, to achieve impersonality without discouraging spontaneity, both accuracy and vividness, immediacy and clarity, is to attempt a task of dismaying proportions.

Yet this is not the whole story. It also falls to the English teacher's lot to teach the child to appreciate literature, and even to create it. Literary appreciation and creation are notoriously difficult to teach; one may be tempted to doubt, even, whether they are teachable at all. Such doubt, however, depends upon too narrow a conception of teachability – an identification of teaching with *instruction*. Instruction plays a relatively small part in teaching a person how to write creatively, imaginatively, just because, as I have already said, to write in this manner is not a closed capacity. This is so even though it depends upon the prior possession of closed capacities, and their exercise and development.

But the skilful teacher, confronted by a potential writer, can help him in various ways, by encouragement, by suggesting themes to him, by talking to him about writers who might seize and develop his imagination. This sort of encouragement and help is just as much *teaching* as is direct instruction. Indeed, even the teacher's exercise of self-restraint, his not demanding too much polish and refinement, not prematurely insisting on formal perfection, forms part of his skill as a teacher.

Potential literary artists, of course, form a very small percentage of the English teacher's class – just as potential historians form a very small percentage of the history teacher's class or potential contributors to science of the science teacher's class. On the other hand, the capacity to appreciate literature, at least at a certain level, is much more widespread in the community; the English teacher certainly has it as part of his responsibility to develop that appreciation in his pupils.

The conception of 'appreciation', however, needs a certain amount of analysis. The *Shorter Oxford Dictionary* suggests two meanings: the first, 'to form an estimate of the value of' and the second, 'to value highly'. And these two are, if naturally connected, none the less distinguishable. The first meaning suggests a rational, critical, attempt to compare what confronts us with other things of the same sort and to say in what its superiority consists; the second, a caring for, a liking, which does not necessarily imply a capacity to *grade* what we value, or formally to characterise in what its value consists. Liking good poetry is one thing; being able to explain in a precise, exact and illuminating way in what its superiority consists is quite another. Which of these does the teacher hope to produce in his class? Both, it might not unnaturally be replied; the teacher hopes that his pupils will value good literature highly and will be able to say in what the value of a particular literary work consists. But suppose there is some degree of conflict between these two objectives? Which ought then to be preferred?

The preference, if a choice had to be made, ought obviously to go to the second; if his pupils go out into the world caring about good literature, wanting to read it, this is far more important than that they should be competent literary critics. But in fact the two forms of activity cannot be sharply sundered. It is certainly part of the English teacher's responsibility to get his children to see through the shoddiness, the pretentiousness, the sentimentality of the standardised novel or the television play. (If he cannot do this himself, as is too often the case, that simply means that he ought not to be teaching English.) And he can do so only by making articulate or, at least, exemplifying, principles of criticism – perhaps most effectively in free and informal class discussion. But this is not to say that he hopes to form his pupils into fully fledged literary critics.[21]

There is no virtue in literature-reading as such; if the effect of the English teacher's work is that the pupils are raised to the level of being able to read sentimental and pretentious novels, or to watch with a degree of comprehension the latest instalment in some television family-saga, then he has certainly done nothing to educate his pupils; they would be better off without such teaching. For various social reasons literacy is essential in the modern community. But a total distaste for literature may well be preferable to a taste only for bad literature.

How can the teacher assist his children to recognise the kind of difference upon which I have just been insisting – such differences as that between the analysis of sentiment and mere sentimentality? This is an extremely difficult task, and the temptation is to substitute for it something quite different: teaching the child something *about* literature, whether it be information about literature in general or about a particular work of literature. For example, it is relatively easy to get a child to see the difference between a sonnet and an ode, between an iambic pentameter and a hexameter, between metaphor and metonymy. I do not mean that this is *very* easy: it is sufficiently difficult to enable the English teacher to feel that he is earning his keep if he succeeds in teaching these distinctions. But it is ever so much easier than getting pupils to see the difference between the good and the pretentious – a distinction which the English teacher himself may not be at all confident about. Similarly, it is relatively easy to give children information about the Romantic Revival, to tell them what a soliloquy is, or to explain to them what a passage in *Macbeth* means in modern English. It is relatively easy to dictate character-sketches of the main characters in *Macbeth* and to teach children to reproduce them in examinations.

Here, for example, is an 'appreciation' question from an examination paper. Students were asked to answer the following questions about a poem:

(a) What name is given to the figure of speech used in the first line?

(b) Explain in your own words what is meant by the third line of the poem.

(c) What comment would you make on the suitability of the title of the poem?

(d) The poem is written to a certain form. What type of form is it? What are the features of the poem which enable you to identify its type?

(e) Do you think the author is successful in conveying his feelings about his subject?

It is interesting to observe that these questions, with the possible exception of (e), could be answered quite successfully by candidates who hated poetry, or who hated this particular poem. Only in attempting to answer the last question is the candidate called upon to exercise any degree of literary judgment, and then in a manner not altogether easy to justify, since it seems to call for a comparison between the author's *actual* feelings – and how is the schoolboy, or anybody else, to know what they were? – and what is conveyed by the poem. The poem in question was in fact rather a poor one, or at least it contained some rather poor lines, but the student was not asked to make careful discriminations within it, a task which would test his literary judgment.

This approach to literature is perfectly natural, given the actual conditions of our schoolrooms, with their emphasis on drill, on instruction, on the conveying of information. It is accentuated, however, in school-systems which lay it down that children of a great variety of ability and experience must all study, let us say, a particular play by Shakespeare. This affects the teacher: he may not like, or may well be profoundly bored by, the play which is set in a particular year. And a teacher who does not greatly care for the literature he is teaching is unlikely to arouse any enthusiasm in his pupils. It affects his methods: if he has to teach a Shakespearian play to a class of children who can barely follow a comic strip he may quite legitimately feel that instruction is his only hope. It affects the teacher's conception of his task; getting the children through the appropriate examination naturally comes to represent the summit of his achievement.

Here, as so often, the whole fabric of the school system – the degree of emphasis it places upon the provision of libraries, the character of its examinations, the provisions it makes for the supply of textbooks, the degree of fluidity of its syllabus – affects the possibility of the teacher's being a teacher rather than a crammer.[22] The appreciation of literature is of all subjects ordinarily taught in the schools the least susceptible to purely instructional methods, least adapted to a rigid syllabus and a uniform examination. In few cases, furthermore, is the teacher so much cutting against the grain: for the English teacher's students are constantly exposed to shoddy literature, as the mathematics teacher's students are not constantly exposed to shoddy mathematics.

He is living in a period in which literature has been revolutionised, not merely in form but in sexual frankness. The pressure upon the teacher to concentrate, for obvious reasons, upon the 'safe' Romantic poets, the safe nineteenth-century novelists, bowdlerised versions of Shakespeare, has diminished but has by no means vanished. He may well leave his pupils with the impression that 'good' literature is devitalised, concerned only with an unreal world, devoid of violent passion – the world of Wordsworth's *Lucy* or Shakespeare's *Twelfth Night* or George Eliot's *Silas Marner*. Alternatively, he may, in a desperate concern to be 'up-to-date', wholly ignore the literature of the past and concentrate his attention upon the contemporary. And the effect of this – like the emphasis on 'current affairs' as contrasted with history – is to contain the child within the world into which he happens to be born, with its presumptions, its morals, its habits, its attitudes.

It seems to be not uncommonly presumed that there is no loss in doing this, because the present in some sense incorporates the past, includes whatever is of value and interest in it. But this is not the way human history works: paradoxically as this may sound, a child who only knows the present is totally unprepared for the future. He may be left to read contemporary literature for himself, although encouraged to talk about it and to make his own comparisons. In contrast, unless he studies Milton at school he is unlikely ever to study him.

The total consequence, whatever the causes, is that in regard to literary appreciation English teaching conspicuously fails to do what it sets out to do. One might reasonably expect, for example, that as a result of the teaching of Shakespeare throughout the schools, the theatres would not be able to cope with audiences for Shakespeare. This is by no means the actual situation. That simple fact alone is sufficient to show that something has gone terribly wrong.

On top of all his other responsibilities, the English teacher may be expected, in the words of *Half Our Future*, to take as his 'over-riding aim the personal development and social competence of the pupil'.[23] 'Personal development' and 'social competence' are phrases of a sort which have done great damage in the discussion of educational issues. In a sense, everybody can agree that the teaching of English, as indeed the teaching of anything else, has as its aim the development of the child's 'personality' and 'social competence'. But these phrases are often invoked in support of an education which is purely sophistical in character – in which 'personal development' and 'social competence' turn out to mean nothing more than the capacity to 'make friends and influence people'. One's instinct is, in Hamlet's phrase, to 'cry stinking fish' whenever one hears them employed.

Yet there is some point in what *Half Our Future* is saying. A child who is unable to express himself clearly and forcibly is, as we have already emphasised, to that degree crippled, not merely in the sense that he will find it very hard 'to get on in the world' – in some circumstances the right sort of accent will more than compensate for defects in clarity and forcibleness – but in the sense that he cannot fully participate in the life of the world around him. In a democratic society this is especially so.

The English teacher, then, has a terrible responsibility, a responsibility he only sometimes fulfills, and even then, only in part. It is not my task to suggest a solution to his problems. My object has been, simply, to disentangle the various threads which commonly make up the teaching of English. Let me recapitulate. The English teacher is commonly expected to inculcate certain habits of a formal kind, which I characterised as 'clerkly habits', as well as certain intellectual habits, e.g. the habit of consulting books for information; he is expected to train certain capacities – generalised capacities in the form of the capacity to communicate and professional skill in scholarly or linguistic analysis; he is expected to encourage such of his pupils as exhibit an inclination to be writers; he is expected to cultivate in his pupils a particular form of critical attitude, a capacity to distinguish the good from the pretentious in literature; he is expected to arouse in them a particular form of enthusiasm, enthusiasm for literature. He is held responsible for their personal development and social competence. Not surprisingly, he is often overwhelmed by the magnitude of his task, and the extreme difficulty of carrying it out under classroom conditions.

The result not uncommonly is failure, a failure manifest in our public life and popular culture. It cannot be said that our schools are sending out into the community large groups of pupils who speak and write clearly, concisely and critically; who greatly care for literature or contribute to it; who are capable of seeing through the inanities of the worst kinds of popular literature, that kind which is at once shoddy, sentimental and pretentious; who through their reading of literature, become more sympathetic, more tolerant, more humane. Only too often, what children take away from their English classes are rapidly forgotten snippets of miscellaneous information, a profound distaste for literature, and the barest elements of literacy in reading and writing.

It is not my concern to allocate blame for this state of affairs and least of all to load it on the shoulders of the English teacher. Part of the trouble is that the deficiencies of our mass system of education are at their most striking and most obvious in such fields of the teaching of English. Nowhere is the need for individual tuition, fluidity in curriculum to suit the varying degrees of preparedness of different classes of children, the maintenance of freshness and enthusiasm amongst teachers, at once more necessary and more difficult to attain. Yet the English teacher often finds himself with an impossible burden of correction, with unusually large classes, and is at the same time called upon to undertake more than his fair share of extra-curricular activity. It is a not unreasonable view that the English teacher and the history teacher should have a lighter burden of formal responsibility than other teachers; the reverse is too often the case. In some education systems English teaching is thought of as something which anyone, however ill-prepared, can do. Nothing could be further from the truth. But, excuses and explanations apart, there is no use pretending that the teaching of English is, at present, even broadly successful. Perhaps greater clarity about what is precisely the English teacher's function may throw a little light on the reasons for that failure – even if, by itself, it does little or nothing to relieve it.

NOTES

[1] *Freedom and Discipline in English: Report of the Commission on English* (New York 1965), p. 55.

[2] See the review by R. O'Malley of D.A. Beacock, 'Play way English for today', in B. Jackson and D. Thompson (eds), *English in Education* (London 1962), pp. 167-72. The question O'Malley raises is whether Caldwell Cook, for all the enthusiasm he aroused in his pupils, succeeded in laying the foundation for an *adult* appreciation of English.

[3] R. Ridout, *English Today*, book 3 (my reference is to the 13th impression, London 1958).

[4] (New York 1956), pp. 145-6.

[5] John Dewey, *The School and Society* (Chicago 1900), quoted from the Phoenix Book edition, 1956, p. 155 (Chicago University Press edition, 1949, p. 160).

⁶ Graham Hough, 'Crisis in literary education' in J.H. Plumb (ed.), *Crisis in the Humanities*, London 1964, p. 107.

⁷ The same thing happened to the teaching of German in Germany. So Nietzsche complains that 'people deal with it as if it were a dead language' and that 'the historical method has become so universal in our time, that even the living body of the language is sacrificed for the sake of anatomical study', *The Future of our Educational Institutions*, trans. J.M. Kennedy (London 1909), in O. Levy (ed.), *Works*, p. 50. The German example, indeed, profoundly influenced English teaching.

⁸ Quoted in F. Whitehead, *The Disappearing Dais* (London 1966), p. 219.

⁹ The claims which have traditionally been made for grammar are quite startling. Thus in his *Education of the Clergy*, written in the seventh century A.D., Hrabanus Maurus asks rhetorically: 'How could one understand the sense of the spoken word or the meanings of letters and syllables, if one had not learnt this before from grammar?' Grammar, that is, is treated as if it were a propaedeutic to spoken and written speech, whereas, obviously, it is an analytical study of what was spoken and written without benefit of grammar. For a summary of the experimental evidence see A.M. Wilkinson, 'Research on formal grammar', *National Association of Teachers of English Bulletin*, vol. 1, pp. 24-6. (An American Professor of Rhetoric once expressed great astonishment when I told him that rhetoric was not taught as a subject in English schools. 'But how,' he said, 'could Winston Churchill have otherwise acquired such a mastery over rhetoric?')

¹⁰ For a text-book designed along these lines, see R.W. Young, *Lines of Thought: Exercises in Reasoned Thinking* (Oxford 1958). On grammar-teaching generally, see *Freedom and Discipline in English*, pp. 21-41.

¹¹ See, for example, P. Doughty et al.: *Exploring Language* (London 1973).

¹² How many English teachers have fully accepted the judgment of *Half Our Future* (Her Majesty's Stationery Office, London, p. 153) that 'inability to speak fluently is a far worse hardship than inability to read or write'? There are a number of reasons why speech is often neglected. The schools do not teach children to speak *ab initio*, as they do teach them to read and write. Children go to school *already speaking a language*; the schools are likely to concentrate on teaching the child to develop new capacities rather than to improve already established capacities – particularly when that involves the difficult task of eradicating established habits. A second reason is that public examinations are written, not oral, examinations. A third is that speech training can be hard to handle in a formal classroom. What the teacher needs to develop is not, of course, the capacity to deliver set speeches, which few pupils, fortunately, will ever need, but the capacity to *contribute to a discussion*. This implies a capacity to listen as well as to talk, and the capacity to listen is often poorly developed even in pupils who speak fluently. One's general impression (cf. *Children and Their Primary Schools* – 'The Plowden Report' – Her Majesty's Stationery Office, London 1967, vol. 3, p. 211) is that American schools are in respect to encouraging fluent speech considerably in advance of English, and certainly of Australian, schools. But that is not always matched by a capacity to *listen* – the emphasis, in many cases, is on 'self-expression' rather than on the meeting of minds in a genuine discussion. In Australia, as in some parts of England, 'there is often a deep-seated corporate resistance to the very notion of "talking posh", (*Half Our Future*, p. 153), and, more than that, to any sort of fluency or, as it is commonly put, 'the gift of the gab'.

¹³ Sybil Marshall: 'English and idiom in the Primary School', in B. Jackson and D. Thompson (eds), *English in Education* (London 1962), pp. 26-7.

¹⁴ David Holbrook, *The Secret Places* (London 1964), p. 69. Compare *Half Our Future*,

p. 155. 'Teachers whose sole standard is correctness can dry up the flow of language and shackle creative and imaginative writing before it is under way.' But the appended comment that 'balance is needed', that spelling and punctuation must be taken seriously, but not with such ferocity that (as often happens) the pupil 'gives up trying' is rather irritatingly bland. Of course, one is tempted to reply, but what, in this context, does 'balance' consist in? How, given the condition of class-teaching can one be just ferocious enough not to discourage?

[15] *Second Lecture*, trans. O. Levy, pp. 53-5, p. 49.

[16] Compare National Institute of Adult Education, *Liberal Education in a Technical Age*. (London, 1955).

[17] See M.E. Bell, 'Developing competence in reading in mathematics', in H.A. Robinson (ed.), *Recent Developments in Reading*, Supplementary Educational Monographs, no. 95, 1965, pp. 155-8.

[18] M.A.K. Halliday, 'Linguistics and the teaching of English', in J. Britton (ed.), *Talking and Writing* (London 1967), p. 81.

[19] When a teacher of my acquaintance laid considerable stress on the quality of writing in history essays, she was rebuked by a member of her class: 'This isn't English, it is History!'

[20] Secondary Schools Examination Council, *The Examining of English Language*, H.M.S.O. 1964.

[21] On the more general relation between the teaching of literature and critical thinking, see Chapter nine. The absurdity of the questions sometimes set in university English papers – e.g. 'Consider the verdict that Byron is the most uneven of all great poets' – indicates a profound uncertainty about what the undergraduate in English can properly be expected to do or know. Often enough, questions which look as if they might demand literary judgment require, only, that the student be capable of repeating, with whatever degree of sincerity or insincerity, a fashionable set of critical judgments – 'standardised opinions'. Compare F.H. Langman, 'Examinations in English: a plea for variety' in *The Australian University*, vol. 2, no. 3, 1964, pp. 224-40.

[22] Even purely commercial considerations have their effect. The compiler of school texts may avoid recent literature not so much because it is difficult or 'dangerous' as because he will have to pay copyright fees.

[23] *Half Our Future*, p. 153.

Chapter Thirteen

Sex Education

The fundamental question I propose to discuss can be put thus: what is the *point* of sex education? No doubt, even after that question has been answered, a multitude of problems still has to be solved: who should teach it, at what ages it should take place, what should be its content at this or that age. But until we are clear about the *point* of sex education, none of these important and difficult questions – which it may be possible to answer only after empirical research – can sensibly be discussed.

Let us begin from the most aseptic concept of sex education. The sex educator, on this view, is to teach as a biologist; he is to inform his pupils about the anatomy and physiology of the sexual organs, maturation, coition, reproduction, in exactly the same spirit in which he might inform them about the workings of the heart, the circulation of the blood, the digestion of food. One can easily understand why this biological approach at first looked so attractive to educational authorities. It fitted into the classical conception of the school as an institution whose primary concern is the transmission of knowledge. Yet at the same time it was designed to bring enlightenment, to rescue sex education from the obscurity, the dark hints and darker threats, which had traditionally surrounded it. With enlightenment as its purpose and science as its method, who could possibly object? But in practice the situation was far from being so simple and straightforward.

In Western society the facts about sexual reproduction have been in a unique position, never to a greater degree than in the century which ended in the 1950s.* At least I can think of no other case –

* The dating is awkward, and in a way which throws light on the present situation of sex education. As Joyce's *Ulysses* will serve to illustrate, as early as the 1920s serious artists began to write much more frankly than their predecessors. However, to write was one thing, to be read quite another. Official censorship was exceptionally tight in the pre-war years. There was for a time an enormous gap between the sexual frankness of books read mainly – and often covertly – by intellectuals and the novels available to, and read by, the bulk of the population, whose principal sources of entertainment, the film, and later television, were even more severely censored.

except perhaps, but then to a lesser degree, excretion – where although the facts are undisputed, it has been widely believed that they ought not to be explicitly referred to or, this even more strongly, illustrated. No one is going to protest at an examination question which asks what changes take place in the heart as it expands and contracts and instructs the examinee to illustrate his answers with line drawings. A parallel question about the expansion and contraction of the sexual organs will be accused of corrupting the youth.

The effect is that biologically-centred courses on sex education have commonly been limited and confined in ways which make it impossible for them to achieve their officially-defined objective. I can illustrate the sort of inconsistency and incoherence which results by quoting from *The Handbook on Sex Instruction in Swedish Schools* – in many respects a pioneering document – published by the Royal Board of Education in Sweden in 1956. The Handbook lays it down that 'sex instruction ... should proceed in a completely everyday manner and be free from anything suggesting the sensational;'[1] it recommends, for that reason, a biological approach. But the *Handbook* nevertheless instructs teachers not to allow their pupils to copy down blackboard sketches or drawings since, it somewhat coyly says, experience shows that such copies can be used in an 'unsuitable manner'.[2] So children are at once to be persuaded that sex education is perfectly ordinary, in no way sensational, and at the same time they are to be prevented from making use of precisely the learning techniques which, were the heart or the lungs being studied, they would be praised for adopting. Sexuality is at once to be treated, and not to be treated, as an ordinary part of an ordinary scientific course. These confusions of aim are not accidental. The fact is that sex in our society – indeed, in any society – *is* sensational. And a school course which tries to pretend, in a supposedly scientific spirit, that it is not sensational will soon be forced into inconsistencies and hypocrisies.

An 'unsensational' biological approach, furthermore, can do more harm than good. Sex education classes, even of the most limited, biological kind, do not simply impart information to a passive, receptive mind. They attempt to counteract myths. No doubt, they are not unique in this respect; history and science can also be myth-destructive. But sexual myths are exceptionally powerful; they reflect the child's deepest fears, most secret desires. Children may well, for example, have interpreted what they have seen or heard of the sexual act as a form of violence. (Observe the way in which, in discussions of censorship, sex and violence are so often, and so strangely, paired.) A purely biological account of the sexual act, in the language of engineering, can easily reinforce rather than destroy that scarifying and at the same time deeply satisfying myth.[3] Only if the biological approach is broad enough to permit the teacher to talk about pleasure and passion can it avoid that danger. But talking about pleasure and passion is precisely what is meant by 'sensationalising' sex.

Let us suppose, however, that the biological approach is a broad one, not restricted, as it so commonly has been, to elementary anatomy and physiology – illustrated with unenticing diagrams, intelligible only to a trained anatomist. There are nowadays a good many textbooks, especially in Europe, which adopt this broader approach. They do not conceal the fact that sexual relationships can be pleasurable; they set that fact in a biological context. They are as interested in mating as in procreation. There is at least nothing in such a course to reinforce the child's myths. Neither will children be left with the feeling, which they so often got from earlier sex education courses, that they were obviously being cheated, enlightened about what they did not particularly want to know – usually the stages in the development of the foetus – but left as puzzled as ever about what really troubled them.

Does such a course suffice? At the end of it, our hypothesis is, the pupils are able to answer, in a way which displays comprehension, questions about the basic biology of maturation, coition, reproduction. They understand how and – biologically speaking – why sexual acts are pleasurable. Has the point of sex education then been secured?

There is growing agreement that much would still remain to be done, that even though precise biological information has a part to play in any sexual education programme, it is by no means sufficient. Biology is not enough, for two related but distinct reasons. The first reason is that human sexuality – although, of course, its roots are biological – is not a purely biological phenomenon. The second, more disputable, reason is that the sex educator has not merely to impart information, not merely to destroy myths, but should attempt to modify the sexual attitudes and the sexual behaviour of his pupils. To be content with biology, on this view, would be like, in a course on car-driving, doing no more than describe the workings of an internal combustion engine, the brakes, the steering-wheel and the gear-box – while adding only, perhaps, that driving can be a pleasurable experience.

Expanding the first objection, there is little or nothing in biology as such to help pupils to understand marriage, illegitimacy, prostitution, pornography, homosexuality, sexual myths, to mention only a few of the phenomena they are certain to encounter in person or in conversation. Their ignorance on such matters, the reply might come, could be dispelled by adding aseptic social science to aseptic biology. So children might leave school not only knowing how human reproduction occurs but also what percentage of the population are homosexuals, what are the principal grounds of divorce, what forms pornography takes, how prostitution is organised. Certainly, this would give them a much more realistic picture of human sexual life. (They would know the traffic rules, as it were, as well as how the engine works.) But if, when a teacher had endowed his pupils with all this information, they used it to set themselves up as pimps, to embark upon careers as call-girls or to modernise the pornography industry, few sexual educators would feel that their course of instruction had been wholly successful. They may be wrong: perhaps it is no more an objection to a course in sex education that a pupil can use it to become a more successful pimp or a more efficient rapist than it is an objection to a course on metal work that a pupil can use it to become a more successful safe-breaker. Certainly the position of the schools – while still difficult enough – would be much easier if they could presume that their task, purely and simply, is to impart information, that the use which is made of this information has nothing to do with them.

But few sex educators would be willing thus to wash their hands of responsibility. For, as I have already suggested, it is a widely prevalent doctrine that sex education is in essence a form of moral education. Even the Swedish Handbook, for all its biological emphasis, begins by pronouncing that sexual education must have a 'pronounced ethical bias', thus making it yet more difficult for unfortunate biology teachers to live up to the instruction that they were to teach sex in a quite unsensational, scientific manner.

To suggest that sex education is a variety of moral education, however, by no means puts an end to our troubles, by no means unambiguously determines the point of sex education. For unless we are one of those who believe that we can settle by definition what moral education 'really is', we shall still find ourselves having to choose between bitterly-contested alternatives.

At one extreme lies the Puritanical-Christian view that a moralised sex education should persuade children that sexual relations, even at their most licit, within matrimony and with procreative intention, are shameful, a 'deed of darkness'. ('Who does not know,' asked Innocent III, 'that conjugal intercourse is never committed without itching of the flesh and heat and foul concupiscence?') Or when hostility to sexuality is not carried quite so far, that at least all sexual relations are sinful unless they are blessed by the church, are to a minimal degree sensual, and are procreative in intent. In this tradition, ignorance is commonly regarded as a blessing; sexual education is to be not at all elucidatory, except insofar as a measure of elucidation is inherent in its being minatory. Granting the inevitability of some form of sex education, a distinguished ecclesiastic was recently reported as asserting that he much preferred it to take place furtively, as a whispered communication, in an atmosphere of guilt and shame appropriate to the topic. The upholders of this view sometimes describe themselves, or are described, as *opponents* of sex education. But at least in one sense of the phrase, they are quite certainly 'sex educators': they are communicating very powerful sexual traditions. What they are opposed to is sexual enlightenment.

The education they have in mind need not be entirely negative. Its objective may be not merely to make it less likely that pupils will engage in sexual behaviour but to encourage in them positive attitudes of mind – including, for example, a love and respect for virginity, not simply as a form of property which it is socially prudent to preserve but as a moral ideal. Sex education, thus understood, has formed the central core of moral education in a great many conventual schools, where it was made more effective by the existence of a certain consonance between the vows of chastity taken by the teachers and what they were teaching, a kind of consonance much more difficult to secure in pluralistic institutions. It was unashamedly negative, however, in relation to knowledge. Even the word 'virgin' was taboo except in its purely theological contexts. (This was so, indeed, until very recently; in some American States the film of D.H. Lawrence's *The Virgin and the Gipsy* could not be advertised under that title, and a little earlier the play *The Moon is Blue* caused deep offence by using the word.) It was only necessary to prohibit, as inconsistent with virginity, all bodily contact between pupils; it was not necessary to explain precisely in what virginity consists.

This attitude to sex education has now, quite suddenly, few articulate defenders, even within the Christian churches. Its influence, of course, is by no means dead; many parents were brought up in its shadow. Sex was unmentionable, especially in the family circle. That is one major reason why it is quite unrealistic, in our society, to leave sex education in the hands of parents. But its advocates, except for a few recalcitrant ecclesiastics of the sort I have just quoted, are generally silent.

Why so? Sometimes only because they realise that the world outside the school makes the ideal of innocent ignorance impracticable; the need for sexual enlightenment is then admitted with a sigh, as yet another indication of the corruption of our times. Sex education, for such reluctant converts, is still to be a prophylactic. Just in virtue of its being inexplicit, the argument then runs, the traditional moral education provided its pupils with little or no protection against unwanted pregnancies or venereal disease or those other contingencies against which, it is commonly presumed, an effective sex education should guard its pupils.

But if this were all that were involved, it is far from apparent that the fear of practical consequences is more successful than the fear of hell-fire as a prophylactic, that young men and girls who know how to use contraceptives are less likely to have illegitimate children, that knowing about venereal disease they are less likely to contract it or more willing to seek medical assistance when they do contract it. These are matters about which we know very little, but the little we do know is not very encouraging.[4] We certainly do know – for in this case smoking, alcoholism, drug-taking and fast driving are analogies – that quite rational arguments directed against practices which their peer-group values are often totally ineffective in altering the conduct of the young.

To an ever greater degree, too, 'prophylactic' sex education encounters problems in establishing a syllabus. Against precisely what sexual practices is it to be directed? As late as 1957, the *Swedish Handbook* could refer to homosexuality only as the enticement of young children: 'There are homosexual men, especially in big cities, who try to entice young boys by promising them money and the like.'[5] Public attitudes to homosexuality have changed very rapidly; many teachers, while condemning such enticement, would not be prepared to regard their course as prophylactically directed against, to quote the *Handbook* again, 'people who do not feel a natural attraction toward the opposite sex'. And what about pre-marital sexual relationships? Or promiscuity? The older certainties, if by no means gone, are considerably weakened.

At the opposite extreme from the prophylactic approach to sex lies what it will be convenient to call the hedonistic approach. The main objective of sex education, as the hedonist sees it, is entirely to remove the sense of guilt from sex, to make it clear that sex, in all its forms, is a pleasurable activity, valuable as such, to be engaged in with no more inhibitions than eating or drinking, to which it is, indeed, strictly comparable. *Does Sex Make you Feel Guilty?*, asks the title of a book by G.L. Simons. The policy it goes on to advocate is, as we might expect, unambiguous: 'We must get rid of sexual guilt – for our sake and that of our children.'[6]

We have recently witnessed, indeed, what one can only call an extensive adult education programme which has sought to persuade us, mainly through the medium of books and films, that sexual relationships should be a source of joy, of uninhibited pleasure, completely free from shame. Although such instruction is not intended for classroom use, it would be absurd to refuse to it the name of 'education', at least in the broad sense of that word. Many books – and many films – with such titles as 'sex education' are no doubt pornography in a transparent disguise. But this is far from being universally true. By no means all such works are either, to draw a necessary distinction, 'novelette' pornography, with its ever-amorous women and endlessly virile men, or 'horror-comic', crypto-Puritanical, pornography with its brutality, deliberate coarseness, devastating crudity, scarcely-concealed hostility to women. Often enough, indeed, they have the unmistakable tone of missionary tracts or political pamphlets: promising sexual bliss, demanding sexual rights.

To condemn such fervour *en bloc* would be a mistake; given the earlier situation, one can understand and even applaud it. Yet, as I have argued elsewhere,[7] there is something very unsatisfactory about most of the hand-books to sexual practice. They bear every sign of having been written in a technological age, in a consumer's society. In a characteristically technological manner, they threaten to replace anxiety about the moral character of one's actions by anxiety about one's competence in performing them. They do nothing to bring out the horrors and terrors of sexuality, the way in which sexual relationships can drive men and women to desperation. Or they suggest – falsely, I should say – that such desperation is solely a product of ignorance and prudishness.

We should remember, too, that one of the first to try to release men from sexual guilt was the Marquis de Sade. No doubt there is still controversy, bitter controversy, about the limits beyond which men should be ashamed of their sexual acts. But most of us would agree, I imagine, that where sexuality takes the form of violence, or involves the witting transference of venereal disease, or the selling of girls and boys as sexual merchandise, or the enticement of children, or reckless procreation, it has passed beyond the boundaries of permissibility. There are times, that is, when we can properly be called to account for our sexual acts.

We might agree, too, that sexual relationships, while they can properly be a source of pleasure, are greatly underestimated if they are thought of simply in these terms. So for all that it would be foolish, in discussing the more particular question how far, and to what degree, sexual education should form part of our school courses, to forget the existence of this large hedonistic literature, it would also be wrong to conclude, with a sigh of relief, that all the teacher need now do is to teach his pupils to read. This is quite apart from the fact that such handbooks are not designed either for the very young or for the semi-literate, both of whom may stand in special need of sex education.

Another way of looking at the matter is now much more widely canvassed. It is neither puritanical nor hedonistic. The object of moral education, and therefore of sex education, is to help the pupil, so it is argued, to learn to make 'a responsible and informed choice between possible courses of behaviour.'[8] This, one might say, is the current orthodoxy in circles where contemporary philosophy of education has penetrated.

The pupil's choice, then, is to be 'informed'. That justifies the giving of information, biological and social. But it is also to be 'responsible'. That is a more obscure concept. Responsible to whom or what? When one looks further, however, a definition usually emerges by implication. A course of action is responsibly chosen when the agent takes account of other people, of *their* 'right to choose', of their feelings, and of the broader social consequences of what he is doing. As James Hemming and Zena Maxwell sum up in their *Sex and Love* – a book for schools designed in the spirit of this moral outlook – 'everyone has a right to strive for sexual fulfilment, but not at the cost of others, by deceiving or exploiting them in any way'. And again, 'mutual consideration is the basis of sexual relations'.[9]

Certainly such a conception of sex education fits into what is now a popular conception of the role of the school, at least in democratic countries: that it is its task to teach the child to learn to 'think for himself', but in a way that takes account of the interests of other people. Only when this is their emphasis, so the argument would run, do sex education courses deserve the name of 'education', now in the eulogistic sense of that word, as distinct from mere instruction or outright indoctrination. It is entirely out of accord with the spirit of schools for a teacher to think of himself as attempting to persuade his pupils to act in one specific way rather than another; it puts his relationship with them on quite the wrong foot. If sexual education is merely aversive in intent, it has no place in the schools. But to teach children to act responsibly, to think about what they are doing, is very different.

And yet is there not more than a touch of hypocrisy in this conception of sex education, just as there is in the conception of an 'unsensational' sex-biology course? Or if not hypocrisy, then at least a limited sense of reality. I do not deny, of course, that there are choices to be made within a person's sexual life. A young couple may have to decide whether to live together or to marry, or a pregnant girl to decide whether to have an abortion or to bear a child, to take only what are relatively dramatic cases. Young people – and not only young people – are often ignorant of, or prefer not to think about, the wider implications of such decisions. There is value in encouraging them to do so. But sexual life styles are not, in general, *chosen*. We do not choose with whom to fall in love. It is hypocritical to pretend otherwise, to ignore the power of sexual passion, to pretend that all of us, if only we try, can live our sexual lives in a spirit of sweet reasonableness.

Here I reach a very difficult turning-point in my argument. Is it proper to think of sex education not only as a training in the making of deliberate decisions, insofar as they play a part in sexual life, but beyond that, as a preparation for love? Implicit in the notion of 'responsibility', I have suggested, is the concept of caring about, considering, other people. Here we make an assumption – that other people, or some other people, are proper objects of care – an assumption which our pupils may wish to question. To assume this, it is often replied, is to do no more than to assume that there are such things as moral considerations, i.e. that the idea of moral education as distinct from moral indoctrination makes sense. (To which the reply might come that it *doesn't* make sense.) However, I am going further still; I am suggesting that sex education might be a preparation for love, love thought of as a relationship which goes beyond consideration, conjoining consideration with enjoyment, which is directed towards particular persons and not towards people as such. (The proper attitude to our neighbour as such is not love but consideration and, in emergencies, concern.) I am taking it, that is, that just as, on my view, a teacher is perfectly justified in trying to arouse in his pupils a love for literature, so he is perfectly justified in trying to stimulate in them the capacity for loving people.

Notice, however, the phrase 'preparation for love'. I am not suggesting that a school can or should offer lessons in love, that it can teach love in the same sense in which it can teach arithmetic. Neither do I wish to deny that in this respect the role of the family is of central importance – we learn to love by being loved – even if the attitude of the teacher to his pupils and to their relations with one another can strengthen or weaken their capacity for loving. But direct teaching has a more limited aim – to remove obstacles to, rather than to create, the capacity to love. (Bosanquet's favourite phrase 'the hindering of hindrances' brings out what I have in mind.)

How can this be done? I have already suggested that ignorance can affect the child's capacity to love, ignorance in the form of sexual myths. But biological ignorance, in the narrow sense of the phrase, ignorance about the anatomy and physiology of sex, is not in itself of any considerable importance. Men and women loved, long before anybody knew anything whatsoever about the anatomy of the *vas deferens*. What is really important, so I have suggested, is that the child should learn that the sex act is not inevitably an act of violence, that it can be tender, affectionate. If biology is more broadly conceived, transformed in the direction of ethology, emphasising love as a bond of union as distinct from the traditional biological emphasis upon reproduction, then its role in this respect can be much more important.

So can the direct discussion of love be important, in the context of a broadly conceived consideration of institutions like marriage. In discussion, teachers can help their pupils to see through the sentimentalising of love which is characteristic of cheap literature and commercial advertising, can explore the difficulties and anxieties which are inherent in love.

The older sex manuals were very reticent on this point. But the newer ones are better. 'Any loving,' write Hemming and Maxwell, 'puts us under risk of pain. The love may not last and one, or both, be subjected to intense suffering. But nothing worth having in life can be got without risk.'[10] I do not think they fairly face the fact, however, that love can also be a source of suffering to third parties, that it is not always easy to reconcile love with consideration for others. (Did Romeo and Juliet consider the feelings of their parents? Was Gibbon a better model when he sighed as a lover but obeyed as a son?) Teachers, too, can recommend their pupils to read the kind of manual to which I have already referred, while drawing attention to its limitations.*

I am not at all suggesting that they should propagandise for love; even if they were desperately anxious to encourage their pupils to love, this would be a quite ineffective way of doing so, as ineffective as propagandising for literature. They can, and ought to, discuss the way in which Utopias – Plato's *Republic* is a case in point, but there are other examples, most notably the Oneida community in the

---

* When I say he *can* do these things, of course, I am speaking in terms of general principles. His school may prohibit him from doing so; his own upbringing, or his own sexual proclivities, may make the situation an extremely difficult one. The Swedish education system has a passion for uniformity, identified with equality. But it reluctantly has had to confess that from school to school, from region to region, from teacher to teacher, sex education is anything but uniform.

United States – have suggested that in an ideal society there is no room for the sort of particularised affection which I have characterised as love. They can talk, in an historical spirit, about the relationships between love and marriage in the ancient, the mediaeval or the modern world, making it clear that 'falling in love' has not been, in general, either a necessary or a sufficient preliminary to marriage. All this, certainly, counts as sex education. It helps children to make responsible choices, prepares them for love – or to renounce love, if that is their final decision.

But art and literature, I believe, are more important in this respect than either biology or social-science type discussion. In literature and art the delights and agonies of love are vividly and concretely depicted, in a way that can enlarge imagination, tolerance, emotional sympathy.

Once more, of course, there are practical problems. For a century or so, literature for school use was bowdlerised. Love poetry, so far as it was discussed at all, was at an etherealised level; narrative verse was accounted safer. The links between love and sexuality, on the one side, and love and terror on the other were carefully concealed. Nor was the child confronted with sensual painting, sensual sculpture. Many teachers are still embarrassed, indeed, by an art or literature with sexual overtones. But the fact is that the complication and the significance of sexual relations are nowhere better brought out than in literature, literature varying in range and style from simple songs and poetry – not so different in type from, although sometimes superior in quality to, contemporary 'pop' songs – to the tragic complexities of Tolstoy and Shakespeare. Every sex educator, at least, should know this literature, should read Euripides' *Bacchae* annually to remind him of the sheer explosiveness of sexuality, should know Catullus, Burns, should understand the feelings which lie behind *The Waste Land*. There are textbooks, especially in France and Denmark, which try to discuss sexual relationships in their full cultural extent; etchings by Picasso rather than clinical diagrams serve as their illustrations. And this, I believe, is the right direction in which to move. To leave sex to the biologists is quite to misunderstand its place in human life.

If I am right, then, the refusal of many young people to read even the simplest novels, their allegiance to television programmes which, often enough, falsify and oversimplify sexual relationships, is a serious obstacle to any serious sort of sexual education. So are the vagaries of a censorship or grading system which expose them to violence, cruelty and sexual triviality but forbid them attendance at films which conjoin sensuality and affection. At this point, as always, the sex educator who takes his task seriously goes against the grain of society; the myth he hopes to destroy, that society will everywhere reinforce.

One can readily understand objections to sex education, objections which come not merely from extreme conservatives – under which head I include, of course, large segments of what is conventionally known as 'the left' – but from men of undoubted sensibility, troubled by its insensitivity, its pretence to, but actual lack of, realism; its attempt, in the words of Ian Robinson, to make sex 'safe, clean, hygienic and the proper activity for a playground'.[11] Life would be much easier for the schools if they were to leave it completely alone. But to do this would be to cut themselves off from phenomena of central importance in the understanding of human life, human society, literature and art. Nor can they in fact leave it alone: to ignore sex, to refer to it only euphemistically, to censor children's literature, is in itself to engage in a form of sex education.

The point of sex education, I have suggested, is a triple one: first, to destroy sexual myths; secondly, to help pupils to make sexual decisions; thirdly, to prepare them for love, with its cares, its joys, its responsibilities. To say this, as I began by pointing out, is not to determine how, where, by whom it should be taught, or how far it should be carried. But it has implications in all these respects. As so often, those who need it most may be the hardest to reach; in this respect, as in every case, the illiterate or the semi-literate are at an enormous disadvantage. And so are those whose life has contained no love. Here, too, there is the serious risk that schools will first exaggerate what they can do, and then, failing in their ambition, lapse into cynicism, continuing in their courses out of habit rather than conviction. At most, I have tried to make it a little clearer what schools might, in principle, attempt; that the task they have before them is, as usual, of overwhelming dimensions, I am far from denying.

NOTES

[1] *The Handbook*, along with other official documents from Scandinavia, can conveniently be read in Theodore Reik (introd.), *What shall I Tell my child?* (London 1970). The quotation is on p. 101.

[2] ibid., p. 113.

[3] For examples of the kind of thing I have in mind see Maurice Hill and Michael Lloyd-Jones, *Sex Education, The Erroneous Zone*, National Secular Society (London 1970).

[4] The research reported in R.S. Rogers (ed.): *Sex Education* (Cambridge, 1974) mainly makes it clear just how little serious research has been undertaken.

[5] ibid., p. 123.

[6] G.L. Simons, *Does Sex Make you Feel Guilty?* (London 1972), p. 116.

[7] John Passmore, *The Perfectibility of Man*, p. 308.

[8] See, for example, Alan Harris, 'What does "sex education" mean?', in Rogers, op. cit.

[9] James Hemming and Zena Maxwell, *Sex and Love* (London 1972), p. 104.

[10] op. cit., p. 89.

[11] Ian Robinson, *The Survival of English* (Cambridge 1973), p. 172. I should perhaps add that Mr Robinson goes further in the opposite direction than I should be prepared to do; he positively seems to enjoy sexual agonising. Much of what troubles him in the contemporary scene does not disturb me; my recollections of its Australian antithesis in the nineteen-thirties are anything but nostalgic. But I must confess that a great many contemporary film makers and novelists are alarmingly successful in making sex boring and mechanical, even if others succeed in bringing out both its beauty and its terrors.

Index

Index

activity, 46, 48, 58, 60-1, 63, 67-8, 89, 108, 112-13, 133; and information, 108-16
Adams, Sir J., 22
Adamson, J.E., 29, 33n.
Agassi, J., 104n.
Ahlfors, L.V., 118n.
Aldrich, H., 95-6
analytic philosophy, 7-8, 10, 11, 15, 19
Anderson, J., 141, 144n.
appreciation, 16, 231-2
Aristotle, 16, 66
Arnauld, A., 136, 143n.
Arnold, M., 115, 116
art, teaching of, 159, 163
attitudes, 59
Ausubel, D., 82n.
authoritarianism, 6, 30, 88, 140, 164, 169-70, 171-2, 173, 176, 177, 186, 224-5, 226

Bacon, F., 81n., 114
Bajema, C., 106nn., 181n.
Ballard, P.B., 219
Barnard, H.C., 143nn.
Bauhaus, 163
Bayer, H., 165n.
Beacock, D.A., 236n.
Beatley, R., 144n.
belief, 153
Bell, M.E., 238n.
Bellarmine, St. R. (Cardinal), 113
Bentham, J., 160-1
Bereday, G.Z.F., 181n.
Berkeley, G., 113, 199
Bigge, M.L., 55n.
Black, Max, 9n., 11, 37, 55, 108, 118n., 167-8
Blanshard, B., 106n., 107nn.
Bloom, B.S., 104n.
Böll, H., 159, 165n.
book learning, 57, 59, 68, 90
Bosanquet, B., 247
'Bourbaki', 148
bourgeois values, 53, 54, 183-4, 186
Broad, C.D., 7
Broeck, J.O.M., 106n.

Bruner, J.S., 68, 82n., 94-8, 100, 103, 105nn., 106n., 117, 221

carefulness, ch. 10 *passim*: extrinsic, 184-5, 190; intrinsic, 184-5, 190
capacities, 16, ch.3 *passim*, 60, ch.6 *passim*, 188, 211, 221, 222-3, 226, 229f., 235, 237n.: broad, 52, 53; closed, 40-3, 42n., 44-5, 46-7, 50-2, 117, 209, 223; didactic, 111, 112; inferential, 111, 112; general, 219f.; narrow, 52; open, 40-3, 43n., 44-52, 55, 117, 162, 177-8, 208-9, 223; professional, 219f.
character traits, 86-7, 88, 121, 168-9
child-centred teaching, 23-4
Chomsky, N., 144n., 212
class, size of, 30-1
classroom, 16, 19, 30-1, 59, 123, 134, 235
Cohen, S.W., 82n
Coleridge, S.T., 150, 152, 153, 164n., 165n.
Collingwood, R.G., 59, 60, 81n., 152, 161, 165n.
Collinson, H., 165n.
Comenius, 81n., 143n.
communications, 38, 54, 97, 111, 135, 187-8, 198-9, 218-19, 223, 225-6, 227, 230f.
competencies, 41-4, 121-2
concepts, 32, 97, 104, 107n., 201, 202
conditioning, 130, 132
controversial issues, 179
Cottrell, T.L., 83n.
crammer, 215, 234
creativity, 120, 141, 158, 186, 222, 223-5, 237n.
Creber, J.L.P., 165n.
critical thinking, 32, 238n.
convergent and divergent thinking, 158, 186
Cook, C., 236n.
Corvinus, A., 143n.
Crossman, R.H., 20, 21, 33n.
current affairs, 92, 234
curriculum (*see also* School, role of), 31-3, 40, 51-5, 85-6, 100-1, 102-3, 117-18